Food *and* Drink *Service*

Levels 1 and 2

Roy Hayter

Hospitality Training Foundation

HtF

MACMILLAN

About this book

First published 1993
Reprinted 1993
Revised edition 1996

MACMILLAN PRESS LTD
Houndmills, Basingstoke,
Hampshire RG21 6XS
and London
Companies and representatives
throughout the world

in association with

HOSPITALITY TRAINING
FOUNDATION
International House, High Street,
Ealing, London W5 5DB

ISBN 0–333–65116–2

A catalogue record for this book is available from the British Library

Designed and typeset by the author

Printed in Great Britain by
Scotprint Ltd, Musselburgh

Your route to a qualification

To gain an NVQ/SVQ in Serving Food and Drink at Levels 1 or 2 you need between five and seven units, depending on your chosen qualification route (see matrix at foot of contents page, opposite).

This book begins with the three core units that are required for each of the qualification routes, those that deal with customer care (Section 1), hygiene, safety and security (Section 2) and working relationships (Section 3).

The other units have been clustered into seven sections, beginning with taking payment (Section 4), moving on through table and silver service (Section 5), carvery and buffet service (Section 6), drink and wine service (Section 7), counter and take-away service (Section 8), vending (Section 9), and concluding with tray and trolley service (Section 10).

To help you find your way through the book, the NVQ/SVQ unit and element numbers are given above the main headings used within each section. These are printed in purple.

How to use this book

This book can be used in any way which suits your needs:

- dip into it at the pages which catch your interest – perhaps because of an illustration, photograph or industry procedure

- to find information on a particular subject, skill or technique – use the index at the end of the book to find the page numbers

- concentrate on the topics you are preparing to be assessed in – the section titles closely match the titles of the NVQ/SVQ units.

This book and your assessment

The main text in each section helps with the three aspects which relate to your NVQ/SVQ assessment:

- what you need to do – as defined in the *performance criteria* for each element

- the situations, styles of service, equipment, etc. which apply – as set out in the *range list*

- what you need to know – as given in the *underpinning knowledge* statements.

Headings within sections use words similar to the element titles, performance criteria and range lists, or you will find range words printed in *italics* in the text.

Skills checks

To help you find out what stage you are already at, to monitor progress as you work towards a unit, and to prepare for assessment, each section ends with skills checks.

These summarise the performance criteria for each element of the unit, and the range list. Use the tick box by each statement as you wish.

Activity questions

These help you check what you have learned. Your assessor will ask similar questions to test your underpinning knowledge.

The illustrations on the activity pages give prompts and clues to what your assessor will be looking for. You may prefer to answer the question for yourself before you study the illustration.

Industry examples

Throughout the book examples are given of procedures, checklists and test yourself questions from employers in restaurants, hotels, licensed retailing and leisure. These show how the details of serving food and drink vary according to customer needs and workplace practices.

Qualification matrix

Level 1 Serving Food & Drink (Table)

all these units required for a qualification
NG1 Maintain a safe and secure working environment
1NG3 Maintain customer care
1NG4 Develop effective working relationships
NG2 Maintain and deal with payments
1NC1 Prepare and clear areas for table/tray service
1NC2 Provide a table or tray service
free-standing units
1NC10 Prepare and serve bottled wines
1NC11 Assemble meals for distribution

Level 1 Serving Food & Drink (Counter/ Take-Away)

units NG1, 1NG3, 1NG4 and NG2 plus
1NC3 Prepare and clear areas for counter/take-away service
1NC4 Provide a counter/take-away service
free-standing units
1NC9 Maintain a vending machine
1NC11 Assemble meals for distribution
1NC12 Provide a trolley service

Level 1 Serving Food & Drink (Vending)

units NG1, 1NG3 and 1NG4 plus
1NC8 Requisition, handle and transport vending stock and supplies
1NC9 Maintain a vending machine
free-standing unit
1NC13 Prepare & clear areas for vending service

Level 2 Serving Food & Drink (Table)

unit NG1 plus
2NG3 Develop and maintain positive working relationships with customers
2NG4 Create and maintain effective working relationships
NG2 Maintain and deal with payments
2NC1 Prepare and clear areas for table service
2NC2 Provide a table service
2NC3 Prepare and serve bottled wines
free-standing units
2NC4 Provide a carvery/buffet service
2NC5 Provide a silver service

Level 2 Serving Food & Drink (Function)

units NG1, 2NG3, 2NG4, 2NC1, 2NC4, 2NC5 and 1NC10

Acknowledgements

Industry liaison and research
Pam Frediani

Advice with text
Clive Finch, Visiting Professor, Thames Valley University

Reviewers
Dawn Blee, Copthorne Hotels
Hamish Cobban, Edinburgh's Telford College
Gaynor Curtis, Tom Cobleigh plc
Chris Gooch, Sankey Vending
David Graham, TGI Friday's
Jane Lane, Baxter & Platts
Alan Makinson, De Vere Hotels
Annie McLeish, The Gleneagles Hotel
Ingrid Newbould, Pizza Hut UK
Lorraine Ragosa and Roger Loiselle, Corporate Catering Company
Pam Rotherforth, Gardner Merchant
Garry Tapping, South Devon College
Janine Whittaker, Sutcliffe Catering Group

Graphics
Tom Lines

Cover photographs
Tom Stockill

Text photographs
Martin Brown, Simon Green, Simon Hawkins, Christine Osborne, Tom Stockill, Keith Turnbull

Photographic locations
The Bellhouse, Beaconsfield, De Vere Hotels
Butlin's South Coast World, Bognor Regis
Café Rouge, Putney
Clementine Churchill Hospital, Harrow
Conrad Hotel, London
Ealing Hospital, London
GEM Vending Ltd, Derby
The Grand, Brighton, De Vere Hotels
La Mancha, Putney
McDonald's, Wandsworth
Pizza Express, Clapham
St John's College, Cambridge
Shenley Church Inn, Milton Keynes, Toby Restaurants
Thames Valley University, Slough

Also: Barclays Bank, City of London; Cranks Wholefoods, London; Gatwick Hilton International; Matt's Café, Chelsea Harbour; Maxwell's Fish Restaurant, Ealing; St Faith's School, Wandsworth; Safeway Naturally, Safeway, Wood Green

Contributing industry procedures and other material
Association of Payment Clearances
Baxter & Platts Ltd, Jane Lane
Butlin's South Coast World, Mike Combes
Castle View Services Limited, Barbara Copland
Catering & Allied (London) Services, Sarah Banner
Caterveg, Mary Scott Morgan
Chase Restaurants Limited, Robert Wingate
Clementine Churchill Hospital, Michael Morrison
The Committee of Scottish Clearing Bankers and Clydesdale Bank plc
Compass Retail Catering Division, Nikki Cartwright
Coppid Beech Hotel, Michael Phipps
Copthorne Hotels Ltd, Dawn Blee
Corporate Catering Company Ltd, Lorraine Ragosa
De Vere Hotels Ltd, Alan Makinson
European Air Catering Services Ltd, Eddie Edwards
Forte UK Hotels, Jackie Abrahams
Gardner Merchant, Pam Rotherforth
GEM Vending Ltd, Steve Gallagher
The Gleneagles Hotel, Annie McLeish
Greenalls Inns, Stephen Holosig
Groupe Chez Gérard Restaurants Ltd, Debbie Jelph
Haven Leisure Limited, Tim Sims
Holiday Care, Brian Seaman
Hotel & Catering International Management Association, Rosemary Morrison and Kalpana Amin
Hudson's Coffee House, Tim Penrose
Inflight Catering Services Ltd, Richard Heavie, Michael House
ISS Mediclean, Phil Ruddock
Kentucky Chicken Great Britain Ltd, Fiona Newstead
LSG-Sky Chefs, David Letherman
Morland & Co plc, Marcus Harborne
National Restaurant Association, Washington DC
National Westminster Bank plc, Streamline Section
Nestlé UK Ltd, Multisnack, David Llewellyn
Pizza Hut UK Ltd, Ingrid Newbould
The Portman Group, John McGovern
Rank Leisure, Mark Lindsell
Royal Naval Stewards Training School, Warrant Officer S R Morris
St John's College, Cambridge, Nigel Bruce
Sankey Vending, Chris Gooch
Scottish & Newcastle Retail (including Old Orleans), Kim Paris
Sutcliffe Catering Group, Janine Whittaker
TGI Friday's, David Graham, Jane Moger
Toby Restaurants, Debbie Phillips
Tom Cobleigh plc, Gaynor Curtis
Vaux Inns Ltd, Diana Wilkinson
Visa® Napery Fabrics
J D Wetherspoon plc, Jane Biss
Whitbread Inns, Mike Cowan, Barbara Murray
Wittenborg UK Ltd, Jan Podsiadly

Customer care
in food and drink service

Dealing with customers

How much customers enjoy what they eat and drink in your workplace depends partly on your people skills:

- how well you understand customers' needs and requirements

- what you say to them and how you say it

- your reaction to their questions and requests.

Even if you are naturally good at dealing with people, there are new skills you can learn and others you can improve on. This is no different from the more practical aspects of serving food and drink. With experience you become more efficient at those and can devote even further effort to better customer care.

Understanding customers' needs and requirements

Customers come to your place because they want food, a drink or both. But these are not the only reasons – think for a moment why customers choose your restaurant not another one.

Are they attracted by the menu? Are they passing by? Are they meeting friends? Have they heard that it's a good place to eat? Is your restaurant part of a nationally-known chain? Is it a facility provided to employees of the company? Are they students at the school, college or university, patients in the hospital, or residents in the home?

There are many more questions you can ask and a wide range of answers. Even the same customer is likely to give different answers according to the circumstances at the time.

The success of customers' visits to your workplace – their satisfaction – depends on how well their needs are met. When you understand what customers require, you are in a stronger position to give the quality of service that means:

- new customers come because they have been told how good it is

- new customers return

- regulars stay loyal

- all customers enjoy their visits, and spend more.

Local knowledge

You are very likely to be asked questions on local knowledge. People may be new to the area and may wish to find out where they can go after leaving our restaurant.

An important part of your job is giving an answer to everything and being a valuable source of information. But if you are asked something you don't know, ask the guest to wait a moment and find somebody who has the answer.

Below are the main items you have to find an answer for. Complete the table and keep it as a permanent reference.

CLOAKROOM/TOILETS ....

PUBLIC TELEPHONE ....

LOCAL TAXI TELEPHONE NUMBER ....

NEAREST TOBY HOTEL ....

LOCAL BANKS ....

LOCAL POST OFFICE ....

LOCAL GARAGE ....

LOCAL NEWSAGENT ....

NEAREST CAR PARK ....

NEAREST CINEMA ....

NEAREST THEATRE ....

NEAREST NIGHT CLUB ....

NEAREST SHOPPING CENTRE ....

NEAREST CHEMIST ....

NEAREST BUS STOP ....

Quality service standards

You can often tell what customers think of the quality of service from their behaviour and what they say. They may make a direct remark to you or your manager, or keep their views to themselves.

Service standards may be set out in company documents and even used in advertising. A decision is made about what attracts customers and gives them satisfaction. This leads to guidelines like:

- every new customer should be acknowledged within 30 seconds of entering the restaurant

- no customer should wait more than two minutes before receiving a menu.

The emphasis will reflect the type of restaurant:

- *fast food* – times queuing and waiting for food once ordered

- *hospital* – choice of dishes, and how long in advance choice must be made.

Answering customers' enquiries

It gives a good impression and customers appreciate it when you reply helpfully to questions about:

- the range of food and drinks available
- what can be provided to meet special needs, e.g. dishes without dairy products, high chair for a child, wheelchair access, no-smoking area
- how long special dishes take to prepare
- other facilities of your workplace – where the toilets are, areas available for private parties, etc.
- other restaurants, pubs, hotels, etc. belonging to the company you work for
- the local area and what's going on – theatres, taxi and public transport services, opening times of the local museum, places to stay, where to visit, etc.
- services they would like – fill the car with fuel, reserve a table or overnight accommodation, leave a message for another customer, etc.

Providing information and help

You should have no problem providing information about your restaurant and the local area. When you don't know something, you can point the person towards help. So you could direct them to the tourist information centre, or give the telephone number of a motoring organisation for reports on driving conditions to their next destination.

How much you can help

Some questions require decisions you shouldn't take.

For example, to reply that it's no problem to accept an IOU would go against the policy of most restaurants. Taking a booking for a special party in a private room would be wrong if this is done by someone else who has the reservations book and up-to-date information about the availability of rooms.

Scope of your authority

Questions like this go beyond the scope of your authority. Explain to the customer that you will get the manager or someone with the authority to help.

When you can't give the help the customer has asked for, say 'no' nicely, and suggest other ways the request can be met.

Information that is not disclosable

There are some questions which require a careful answer, so as to avoid giving confidential information:

- about the personal affairs of customers or staff – besides the embarrassment and difficulties you might cause for the people involved, it would harm the reputation of your restaurant if it is seen as a source of gossip
- about security or business-related matters – you could be helping the plans for a robbery or terrorist action, or useful facts going to a business competitor.

It's easy to recognise direct questions, e.g. 'Has Mark left his wife?', or 'Where's the money kept?', and to give vague answers, 'No idea, I'm afraid'. Indirect questions are harder to spot, e.g. 'I hear you're rushed off your feet on Fridays. You must serve 200 meals. Is that a good guess, would you say?' Clever people collect little pieces of information, which when put together provide a valuable picture.

Customer comments

It is difficult when you work behind the scenes (in the dispense bar or kitchen) to get feedback from customers. What you may hear are the complaints.

You can avoid this if the people who receive customer comments share the good and the not-so-good news. In larger workplaces, or those which are part of a chain, there may be a system for recording and passing on customer comments. Otherwise, it's down to individual thoughtfulness. Remember to tell your colleagues and managers what customers have said.

Everyone likes compliments and positive feedback. The nice things customers say to you about the atmosphere, service, food, flower displays, etc. will be appreciated by everyone who made these things possible.

You should also pass on comments which will be helpful to those in a decision-making role: food and beverage manager, head chef, restaurant manager, etc. Some indicate a change in the pattern of customer demand, for example:

- 'Oh, don't you have any organic wines?'
- 'Menu's OK, but the choice is very limited for someone who doesn't like beef.'

Overheard customer remarks can draw attention to facilities or services which should be improved:

- 'The toilets are through that door and down the stairs, but they're not well signed.'
- 'I always have trouble finding the entrance to the car park.'

Comments like these also provide warning that the customer is not satisfied.

When comments become complaints

Lack of satisfaction can easily turn into a complaint. Another customer, perhaps in a bad mood, or unhappy with other aspects of the service, could express the same views more forcibly, for example:

- 'We'll never come back here. Parking is terrible. My wife has difficulty with stairs. The service is slow, no one smiles ...'

Try to notice – and report to your manager – other signs that may indicate dissatisfaction. For example:

- customers who move to a different table – is it because they found the first too draughty, or the room very smoky?

- a lot of food left on plates – is it because the portions were too large, or the food was not properly cooked, or it doesn't taste nice?

- customers leave abruptly, ignoring your good-bye – is it because they were unhappy with the service, food, drinks, etc?

Incidents of this sort may mean they are customers who are very difficult to please, or have already eaten, or are of the unfriendly type. But it is still worth telling your manager, because he or she may see a pattern emerging.

Customer complaints

When you are face-to-face with a dissatisfied customer, try to put aside any feeling of anger, or hurt, or embarrassment. Deal with the situation calmly and professionally. Don't wait for the customer to actually use the word 'complain' or 'complaint' before acting. You can recognise dissatisfaction from the general behaviour of customers, the words they use, the expressions on their face and their body language (e.g. tapping the table impatiently).

Dealt with well, unhappy customers can become your best customers. Instead of remembering the worst, staying away and telling others of their bad experiences – the main dangers if the complaint is not properly acted upon – they return.

Listen to the complaint without interruption. Show that you are concerned and want to help.

Many workplaces have a complaints procedure and rules limiting the action you can take, e.g.:

- offer a replacement dish
- deductions from the bill must be authorised by the manager.

A complaint is an opportunity to turn customer dissatisfaction into satisfaction.

When dealing with a complaint, we are looking to control the conversation with the customer and to empathise, not sympathise. By presenting you with a complaint, a customer wants you to know they are upset, what has upset them, and what is to be done. Given this, we should always:

- pay attention
- make no assumptions
- listen for free information
- acknowledge, respond and inform
- never defend, make excuses or ignore the customer's point of view.

Guidelines on dealing with complaints

1 Listen to the complaint fully. Do not interrupt, even when you know you will be asking someone else to handle the situation.

2 Apologise properly and sincerely, but do not admit that you or the restaurant/company is at fault.

3 Do not make excuses or blame anyone else.

4 Never argue or disagree. React as if the customers are right, even when you believe otherwise.

5 Keep calm and remain polite.

6 If appropriate, and it is the procedure in your workplace, offer a replacement (e.g. if the complaint was about an undercooked steak), or an alternative drink/dish.

7 Where you do provide a replacement or alternative, do so quickly, with another apology for the inconvenience. Check later that the new dish/drink is satisfactory. Complete the special order or form to avoid problems with stock or cash control.

8 Never offer something you cannot provide – consider what would happen if the customer accepts your suggestion of another fish dish, but you find the kitchen have run out.

9 Thank the customer for bringing the matter to your attention – said with feeling, this will show the customer that you are genuine in your efforts to put things right.

Health and safety issues

As claims for compensation may be made, and because of the possibility of prosecution, complaints to do with health and safety must be dealt with carefully:

- never say or agree whose fault it was or whose responsibility it is

- if an accident has occurred, e.g. a cut lip from drinking out of a chipped glass, follow your workplace accident/emergency procedure

- if it is a complaint or information about a safety hazard, e.g. slippery steps at the main entrance, thank the person and inform your manager urgently.

Dealing with customer incidents

From time to time, things go wrong and customers are directly involved. Perhaps they have seen what has happened, or they caused the problem, or it involves their property. This is what is meant by 'customer incidents' and there are four main types:

- *spillages* – a drink or food is spilled by a customer, by you or by one of your colleagues, e.g. at the self-service counter, at the customer's table, or when carrying food or drink on a tray through a customer area

- *breakages* – from a dropped plate, cup, glass, bottle, etc., or an accident near a window or in the toilets

- *lost property* – a customer claims to have left behind a bag, briefcase, coat, umbrella, etc.

- *equipment faults* – equipment provided for the customers' use or comfort does not work properly, e.g. a vending machine takes the money but fails to deliver the paid-for items, or the hand drier in a toilet is not working.

Establishing priorities

You may find yourself in the centre of a mini-drama, especially if people are upset. What do you do first? Wipe up the spill or breakage, call your manager, move the customers, or get another meal?

These decisions have to be made quickly. Give priority to:

- safety – remove or clear away broken glass, china etc. which might cause a cut, wipe up liquid spills which might cause people to slip and fall, turn off and isolate equipment which might injure people (e.g. a faulty heater causing an electric shock)

- the comfort and convenience of your customers – tidy up the area affected by the breakage or spill, offer paper towelling so spills on customer's clothes can be dried, move the customers to another table, get the details of lost property and ask the customer to be seated while you check (see page 26)

- getting things back to normal – bringing another plate of food or drink.

What you can do to help

No set rules cover all types of incident and the many circumstances which can happen.

Remain calm, polite and helpful. Although you may feel nervous, flustered or even angry, try to hide these feelings behind a calm exterior. This will help the other people involved to overcome their fear, anger or shock.

Getting help elsewhere

Often an extra pair of hands gets things back to normal more quickly. One person can concentrate on the clearing up, while the other helps the customers.

When someone asks about lost property, but it has not been handed in, check with your colleagues. Did they notice anything unusual at the time the loss occurred?

Some incidents are set up, to distract staff and management while money or valuables are stolen. To avoid this, one person must keep an eye on what else is going on.

Limits of your authority

Others may have seen what has happened and come to your assistance. If not, let your manager know as soon as you have dealt with the immediate priorities. Usually your manager makes such decisions as:

- offering the customers free food or drinks, or making an allowance on their bill – because the incident was not their fault, or if it was, as a gesture of goodwill

- genuineness of the claim regarding property left behind, or money lost in the vending machine

- paying for dry cleaning of a customer's clothes.

Other customer incidents

Of course, other things can go wrong, e.g. a reserved table is not free because earlier customers have lingered over their meal.

Apologise, explain the problem as soon as possible, and offer alternatives – e.g. somewhere to sit comfortably, study the menu and have a drink until a table is ready.

You may not know a dish has run out until you have taken the order to the kitchen. This can be very irritating to customers. Apologise immediately, explain and suggest alternatives – but do make sure these are available and check details, e.g. no extra charge in spite of a price difference.

Reporting customer incidents

You may be asked to make a record of what happened:

- the date and time, names of people involved

- description of the incident

- what action was taken, and by whom

- any follow-up action required, e.g. to arrange repair of faulty equipment.

A system for recording incidents helps deal with claims for compensation and investigations into the cause of accidents or injury. Sometimes people exaggerate the circumstances to get increased compensation, or make claims for incidents which never occurred.

Presenting a positive image to customers

The atmosphere in your restaurant is one of the main reasons people visit. It's made up of many different things, but mostly by people – all the people who serve, and the other customers.

What you contribute makes a real difference. Being well presented and cheerful helps everyone. Sometimes it is hard to have a positive influence, especially if you are tired, worried, or in a bad mood. Try not to let problems and negative feelings affect how you deal with customers or work colleagues.

Being courteous and helpful – always

If you were a robot, you might program yourself to give customers a smile, and use words like 'good evening', 'what can I get you', 'certainly', 'please' and 'thank you'.

One reason restaurants are not staffed by robots is that customers like someone with personality! The expressions and words you use should show:

- your personality – the positive aspects, that is, not any bad moods or feelings

- the style of your workplace and the customers it attracts – friendly, formal, business, tourists, local community, trendy, young, elderly, exclusive, etc.

Handling stressful situations

In moments of stress, e.g. when the restaurant is packed and customers are impatient, you have to keep your cool – somehow. No one finds it easy.

Try to keep an even-handed approach. Remain polite. Often people's bad temper can be overcome by an apology, 'I'm really sorry to keep you waiting'.

Try to ignore rudeness or bad temper which has nothing to do with the quality of service. Unlike you, customers are allowed to bring their problems with them! Do not take such behaviour personally. Many people develop a sort of professional shield to protect themselves, keeping up the smiles, 'pleases' and 'thank you's', even though they are not returned.

Keeping up standards

Take trouble over your appearance. Customers judge the standards of the restaurant and company by how you look and behave. It gives a good impression of:

- hygiene standards – when they see clean hands and neatly trimmed fingernails as you serve the food

- customer care – when you remain alert and attentive, during quiet as well as busy moments.

The way you look

Your appearance should give the impression that you are:
FRIENDLY – CLEAN – SMART – ORDERLY – ORGANISED

If you are immaculate, your customers will be convinced that everything else is equally clean and fresh.

Take pride in your appearance. Our customers expect it! You'll feel better for it!

First impressions really do count

A nice big smile will win over your customer right from the start. Without saying a word, a smile puts your customer at ease.

Try to remember the difference between a forced, formal smile and a smile that you would use if you were greeting a friend, sincere and full of warmth.

A smile has the added advantage of being infectious! Nine times out of ten they will smile back. Try it, it works!

Your clothes or uniform should be clean and look fresh. You should also be clean and fresh. Use a deodorant to help keep you sweat-free when it's hot or you're working hard.

Follow your workplace rules on the wearing of jewellery and make-up, and hair styles. These reflect the atmosphere or style which is being offered, and the practicalities of hygiene and safety.

Customer care back-up

When customers ask if your restaurant does special parties, or which tourist attractions to visit, you can help by giving them leaflets on these facilities. If your workplace belongs to a chain or franchise, or is part of a hotel, leisure or licensed retailing organisation, there will be a range of promotional material to tell potential customers what is offered.

Customer care supplies

These are examples of customer care supplies. They encourage sales, provide information, and support your role in providing quality customer service. The range, with examples, might include:

- *literature* – brochures, price lists and posters

- *stationery* – order pads, till rolls, bills, business cards, postcards, compliment slips and letterheads

- *forms* – to take bookings and reservations, to record details of lost property, complaints, customer incidents and to enter competitions

- *consumables* – give-away pens, drink mats and napkins with the name of the restaurant/company.

Find out where these items are kept. It may also be part of your responsibility to order supplies, arrange and keep tidy displays of brochures and similar items.

Customer care equipment

Every time you take payment for a meal, you (or perhaps the cashier or a manager) use the till to record the details (the procedures are described in Section 4). Most tills are *electronic*, some with pre-set keys so that you don't have to remember the price of individual items.

Some restaurants have *mechanical* tills – the force you use to press each key works the price display, and perhaps prints the amount on the till roll.

Working to improve customer relations

You serve customers with the food and drinks they require. You also help create the atmosphere that they come to your restaurant to enjoy. One of the differences between your restaurant and others in the area is the relationships you and your colleagues build up with the customers.

Building and maintaining constructive working relationships with customers

Customers form a positive impression of your restaurant when you treat them well. As customers are individuals, the same approaches do not work for everyone. With experience you'll get expert at suiting what you say and do to the circumstances and the person, so that most customers are pleased most of the time. Here are some starting points.

1 Show you are genuinely pleased to see customers, and to serve them.

2 Greet customers as they arrive. If you're busy at that moment, give a smile or say a few words to reassure the new arrivals that they have been noticed.

3 Take an interest in what customers order. Make suggestions where appropriate. Tell them about the special dishes and drinks.

4 Apologise if customers have been kept waiting. Warn them when there will be delays, e.g. a dish that takes a while to prepare.

5 Remember what regular customers like to eat and drink, and any favourites. Even if they always have the same, confirm the order. Customers are allowed to change their mind!

6 Offer to move chairs or carry drinks when you can see customers are having difficulty.

7 Find out and use customers' names. Look in the reservations book. See what is printed on the credit card or cheque. Ask colleagues to tell you the names of regulars.

8 When the restaurant style is informal and friendly, you may be encouraged to talk to customers. Do not interrupt or try to take over customers' conversations.

Balancing needs of customer and organisation

What customers ask for or expect can require a special effort. Sometimes, it is just not possible to meet their wishes. You have to keep a balance between customers' needs and what your restaurant can provide.

Being persistent

The first stage is to try. If a customer asks for:

- the chocolate gâteau to be served in a bowl, don't say 'We only serve gâteau on flat plates'

- a table by the window, don't say 'Sorry those tables are only for parties of fours and sixes'.

The first time you get an unusual request, your immediate reaction might be to think of the reasons why you can't do it. But stop for a moment before you say 'No'. If you need more time, say 'I'll see what we can do and get right back to you'.

Involving colleagues and other departments

Colleagues can help you get a wider perspective, review the options, and check the knock-on effects of each one. If they feel involved, your colleagues are more likely to cooperate in meeting unusual or special requirements.

Consider the gâteau request:

- wider perspective – very young customers, those who are blind or partially sighted or suffering from conditions which affect the use of their hands, find it is easier to manage gâteau when it's in a bowl

- the options – use a breakfast cereal or soup bowl, or some other dish with deep sides that looks attractive

- knock-on effects – none in this example. There are no hard and fast rules for serving gâteau.

Now take the request for a window table:

- wider perspective – reserving popular window tables for parties of customers can ensure that the greatest number of people are satisfied. On the other hand, people in a group get enjoyment from each other's company, so the position of their table is less significant. Single diners prefer tables around the edge of the room so they can see what is going on, but do not have the feeling that everyone is looking at them

- the options – if a window table is free, the extra settings could be removed

- knock-on effects – if all the best tables are claimed by single diners or small parties, big-spending and regular customers might be disappointed.

Organisational limitations

When you balance customers' needs with what it is practical to offer, you are taking account of 'organisational limitations'. There are three:

- *time* – how long it takes to collect a bowl and transfer the gâteau to it, to remove the extra place settings from a window table – and whether this would delay serving other customers

- *resources* – availability of suitable bowls and window tables

- *cost* – the cost of washing the flat plate on which the gâteau was first served is negligible. If a party of customers arrived after the last window table had been given to a single diner, refused any other table and went elsewhere to eat, there would be the cost of lost sales.

The prices charged at your workplace for food, drinks and the other facilities reflect the time, resources and cost which go into their preparation and service. When a customer asks for a proper glass and plate, not plastic or paper ones, at the refreshment tent at a busy outdoor event, that is an unreasonable request. It isn't unreasonable in the VIP enclosure, where much higher prices are charged, and glasses and china can be more easily collected up.

Explaining to the customer

It's best to leave your manager to tell customers that their request is unreasonable. To avoid reaching this stage:

- be flexible and creative – offer alternatives within the limits of your authority

- involve your colleagues – get their ideas and cooperation, benefit from their experience

- present your proposals convincingly – so that customers accept your ideas as better or equivalent to what they originally wanted. Or, if a compromise is necessary, they accept it because you have explained the circumstances.

Sometimes meeting a special request can create problems for the future. This might mean you have to say 'No, sorry' to the customer, or to make the conditions clear, for example:

- 'Usually the latest time for serving food is 9 p.m., but I've had a word with the chef. Room service could bring you a meal at 9.30. Will that suit you? Only, if we serve you in the restaurant or bar, other customers might wonder why they are expected to eat before 9.'

Knowing what your workplace offers

It gets easier to respond helpfully to customers' special needs as you learn more about the range of food and drinks available.

Take an interest also in the other products and services offered by your workplace. Serving at the counter or table puts you in line for all sorts of questions, especially when you have proved yourself helpful over the customers' food and drink order:

- 'We're getting married soon. Do you know anywhere for the reception?'

- 'We're looking for a B&B for tonight.'

- 'It's our 7 year old's birthday in a few weeks. She wants a party with her school friends ...'

Promoting your workplace

Questions like these give you an opportunity to bring extra business to your workplace, or to other places in the same group. So you could:

- mention the attractive function room, ideal for private parties, anything from snacks to a sit-down dinner can be provided

- show on the map locations of roadside lodges and give the freephone number for reservations

- present a copy of the menu and brochure advertising children's parties.

Also you can promote your workplace by being alert to what customers say in your hearing, e.g.:

- while you clear their plates, the customers are discussing where to hold their wedding reception

- as you say goodbye to a couple, one says 'Come along dear, we've still got to find somewhere to stay tonight'

- you are thanked for the nice meal you have served, and the child says she's been promised a party in a restaurant for her birthday.

Service standards and codes of practice

In some restaurants – more so in the larger ones and those that are part of big companies – two types of formal document, statement or guidance are produced by top management:

- *service standards* – describe, in specific terms where possible, the level of service customers should expect. They give staff and management a common goal to work towards, and a means of measuring their achievement
- *codes of practice* – provide step-by-step instructions on how to handle certain situations, e.g. foreign objects found in the food. Because everyone is following the same detailed guidance put together by experts, there is less risk of things going wrong.

If you have not already done so, find out what service standards and codes of practice apply to your work, and make sure you are familiar with them.

Giving accurate information to customers

There is a danger of misleading the customers you are trying to help. This might happen because you have:

- remembered something wrongly – check information first or warn customers that you are not sure
- guessed information – resist the pressure some customers put you under, in their anxiety for details
- left out a crucial fact – when you are describing other services available, or promoting a special event, be clear what the customers have to do.

Say you have had a discussion with a couple about food and places to eat. They are staying at a nearby caravan site. Taking the opportunity to promote your workplace, you tell them of the gourmet evenings every Friday. Next Friday the couple turn up to celebrate a birthday – but you hadn't said that early booking was essential, and the couple are turned away.

Information that you should not disclose

In your enthusiasm to help customers, or promote your workplace, there is a danger of saying too much. This can happen quite easily, when the information you have given leads to an in-depth conversation.

Suppose you have been describing how the menu will be changed. As the conversation develops, you mention that the kitchen is being refitted, which is why the new menu is being brought in. The customer comments that standards for restaurant kitchens must be very high – you agree, and add that the work had cost over £50,000, which the proprietor has had to borrow. When the customer comments that the proprietor must be confident the new menu will be popular, you are once more indiscreet: 'No choice, the environmental health officer said it was that or get closed down.'

WHITBREAD INNS

Quality service

- The customers are being entertained – treat them with consideration – make them feel welcome.
- Answer questions from customers fully but briefly.
- Some customers want to be left alone, others want to be entertained – be aware of customer moods.
- Guide customers in their choice if they appear doubtful.
- If customers ask for a product that is not available, suggest an alternative.
- Keep your appearance neat, tidy and clean – tidy hair, hands and clean fingernails.
- If there is a grievance about your work, raise the matter after the session, not in front of customers.
- Handle difficult customers discreetly, so that any trouble is not visible to other customers.
- If offered a tip, it is courtesy to appear pleased.

When to seek assistance, when to use your own initiative

Another danger area, is when you have not been able to provide what a customer wants because it is against company policy or the law (e.g. serving alcohol to someone under age). If the customer tries to draw you into a discussion about the rights and wrongs of the policy, or different interpretations of the law, it is time to seek assistance.

Try to recognise when you are out of your depth in a situation, or have run out of suggestions and offers. It is wise to be over-cautious. Not calling on the help of a senior colleague or your manager can cause worse difficulties.

CATERING & ALLIED

Your role

We're in the theatrical business. We put on a 'performance' whereby the food is beautifully cooked 'backstage' and attractively presented 'front of house'. Staff are pleasant and helpful and everywhere is spotlessly clean.

But, like any show, there has to be more. There has to be a touch of magic, of style and imagination. We must create an aura of well-being around our customers from the moment they step into our restaurant.

This means bringing something special to the job over and above the basic courtesies of listening to clients, advising them and giving them the benefits of our experience.

This is where you come in – the reason we are successful is because we are different. And this is because we encourage you to add your own touch of individuality to the performance.

How can you achieve this?

Through training, through being part of a dynamic team, through developing your particular skills, by taking opportunities to move into other areas or other restaurants and by recognising that it is your unique talents that make us special.

Serving the guest

To find out what guests' needs and wants are, begin by asking yourself questions:

- *why have the guests come?* – an entertaining celebration, on business, or a relaxing evening
- *what are the guests' time and money limitations?* – e.g. secretaries back at their desk within the hour, executives more time as business is conducted over lunch
- *what are the guests' food preferences and how hungry are they?* – our portions are large, first-time guests may not know this.

Then ask the guests appropriate questions:

- How are you fixed for time today?
- Would you like a leisurely meal, or would you like to keep things rolling along?
- Do you have time to look through the menu or would you like some suggestions?

Memorise a repertoire of your personal favourites from each menu category and suggest them to your guests. Find out which items are quickly prepared and suggest those to guests with time constraints.

Recording what you have done

In some workplaces, there are systems for recording customers' special or unusual needs. You will be asked to make a note of the time, place, people involved, etc., what was requested, what you proposed and the outcome. There may be a form for doing this.

Records are a requirement in systems for monitoring customer service standards. They also help deal with complaints made some time after the event, or perhaps to head office direct.

Informal communication routes

It is always helpful to tell your manager if an incident has happened, especially if there is no formal system for recording the details. Then if the matter leads to a complaint, your manager is forewarned. And should the customer give a rather different description of events, your manager will be able to see both points of view, and support the action you took, knowing that you did the best you could.

Your manager is also in a position to make or propose changes which would avoid similar problems in the future, e.g. introducing new dishes or drinks.

Legal aspects

There are four areas of possible conflict between the law and what customers ask for:

- *safe working practices* – you should not agree to or propose anything which would put at risk the safety of others in your workplace, e.g. blocking open fire doors to make the room cooler on a hot day
- *trade descriptions* – when you suggest dishes or drinks which are not exactly what the customer asked for, say what is different, e.g. that the plaice fillets are frozen, the coke brand X
- *weights and measures* – a customer asking for a glass of wine should be offered 125 ml or 175 ml (the legal measures, see page 77), steaks and burgers should be the advertised weight before cooking
- *licensing law* – a person you believe is under the legal age for buying alcohol should not be allowed to bully you into acceptance: ask for proof of age and, if this is not produced, get your manager.

Unit 2NG3, Element 3

Responding to customers' feelings

Restaurant work gives you the chance to respond to customers' feelings, helping them to enjoy their visit more. Customers who are cheerful, satisfied, content or good-humoured are likely to appreciate friendly, good-natured, good-humoured responses from you. There is usually no difficulty in responding to positive feelings like these.

Presenting more of a challenge are feelings of the opposite sort. These include:

- *anger* – customers who are very annoyed or antagonistic. The customers may arrive angry (e.g. after an argument at work or a bad car journey), become angry because of what another customer has said or done, and get angry with you or a colleague. This may be because of something you have said or done, or not said or done. Your action may just be the trigger for their anger
- *distress* – customers who are worried or upset. This may be because of a work or personal problem, worry, illness, side-effects of medicine, drugs, alcohol, etc.
- *vulnerability* – customers who are easily hurt or upset. This may be because they are worried, ill, etc. or because they are very shy, nervous, or feel ill at ease for some reason
- *frustration* – customers who feel dissatisfied. This may be because something has happened or not happened, or a more general feeling that things are against them.

By learning to judge or gauge anger, distress, vulnerability or frustration – 'negative feelings' – and respond in an appropriate way, you can reduce the risk of complaints, awkward situations and other difficulties.

You can get clues to customers' feelings from their body language.

Judging or gauging negative feelings

With someone you know well, you may be able to detect changes in their mood from small signs – not talking as much as usual, not listening to what you are saying, staring into the distance, etc. Perhaps you are naturally sensitive. Many people have to make an effort to pick up the signs. You may know people who never take notice until you have reached the stage of shouting or crying and then ask in a surprised tone of voice if you have a problem!

Anger

Some customers when angry shout, swear, thump the counter or table, and gesture with their fists. Perhaps they cannot control their temper, or they want their anger to be obvious to those around them.

Signs of more controlled forms of anger include: red face, unhappy expression, fidgeting, abrupt demands and sarcastic tone.

Distress

As with anger, the signs of distress vary from person to person. They may include: crying or sobbing, shaking of the body, higher pitch to the voice, fidgeting, wringing of the hands, covering the face with hands, wild expression in the eyes, and constantly going to the toilet.

Vulnerability

With customers you know, you may notice changes to their usual behaviour, worried expressions and nervousness. With people you don't know, signs you might notice include: keeping as far away as possible from everyone else, anxiety not to attract attention, apologetic attitude when waiting to be served.

Frustration

This is quite difficult to pick up from people's behaviour. You might notice restlessness (e.g. moving from one seat to another), lack of enjoyment of food or drink (e.g. pushing it aside, leaving some), look of distraction (e.g. not involved in conversation), or difficulty to please (e.g. long discussion about order, rejecting most suggestions with a shake of the head).

Terms used to describe the outward signs

As these examples show, you can tell that all is not well by taking notice of – in other words, *observing* – customers' behaviour. The other two terms are:

- *body language* – the information you get on the customers' feelings from their gestures, facial expressions, how close or far away they are standing from other people, where they are looking, etc.

- *tone of voice* – the sound of the customer's voice, how loud or soft it is, the pitch (high, low, deep, shrill), the quality (warm, cold, hostile, aggressive), and the pace or speed of talking (fast, slow).

Using sensitive questioning to confirm outward signs

Sometimes you know from customers' behaviour that things are wrong, but you need to find out more about the cause (frustration, anger, etc.) to deal with the situation. Here carefully worded questions can play a useful role.

What you don't want is to make matters worse. What you do want is to help the person help himself or herself. Often just one or two very general questions give the opportunity to talk, and that is sufficient for the problem to blow over. The danger is to be seen to be prying, or appearing to cause aggravation.

Consider, for example, a regular who has been drinking much more than usual with his meal. Jim has reached the stage when you should refuse him any more alcohol, but you would rather persuade him not to have another drink and to go home, than risk a row by refusing:

- a general comment might be sufficient to get him to talk, e.g. 'Jim, you seem rather low this evening ...'

- if you know from previous conversations that he has a problem, your question could be more specific, e.g. 'Have things at work been getting you down?'

- if you think it unwise to make any reference to his mood (because recognising that you and others have noticed it might depress him further), you can try the mutual sympathy line, e.g. 'I'm having a terrible time with my car at the moment, one expense after the other which I just can't afford'.

Responding to customers' feelings

Angry or distressed customers spoil the atmosphere in the restaurant, and create unpleasantness for everyone. Similar difficulties are caused by customers who feel frustrated or vulnerable, especially if this turns into anger or distress.

When you become aware of any negative feelings, or see the warning signs, your priorities are:

- keep calm
- remain polite
- act in as normal a manner as possible
- don't put yourself in danger.

Acknowledging customers' feelings

Usually it is sufficient to be with the customer, talking, listening to their problems or complaint, taking care not to make the situation worse. Through your action you show that you realise the customer is angry, distressed, etc. This is usually more effective than trying to identify the mood. Saying 'I can tell you're frustrated' is unlikely to help, especially if you are wrong about the nature of the problem.

Adapting your behaviour accordingly

You do this by not returning anger with anger, or getting distressed because a customer is distressed.

You may also have to control some of your natural characteristics. For example, being bubbly and humorous might cause a person feeling vulnerable to be even more worried and nervous.

Checking perception of customers' feelings

You have to be watchful that the anger or distress is not getting worse, or feelings of frustration or vulnerability are turning into anger or distress. When this happens, or at any time you feel the situation getting out of control, ask your manager to take over.

Hopefully, through your calm approach and awareness of difficulties, most situations will get easier. Normal relations can be restored, but take care not to cause a relapse, perhaps by making a joke in poor taste.

All complaints received in the restaurant have to be recorded on the investigation forms.
This will enable us to produce some kind of pattern.

Within reason, complaints should always be accommodated as in most cases it will create goodwill.

Obnoxious customers will have to be treated with even more care and tact.

Any little remarks from the customers to a chef de rang or commis have to be reported to the manager immediately.

Complaint handling

1 Listen and respond with empathy.
2 Apologise sincerely.
3 Get all details of the complaint.
4 Respond by showing you understand.
5 Agree on specific action to be taken.
6 Thank the customer.

Angry customers

- remember it is not personal – avoid showing emotion
- empathise with the problem by showing concern – think about your reaction if you were the customer
- listen to the complaint – if you can't agree and can't manage the problem, involve the support of the manager
- always follow up on what you have agreed.

Complaints from customers with negative feelings

When customers complain to you about the service or some other subject to do with your workplace, they are quite likely to be frustrated. Some will be angry, some distressed, some feeling vulnerable.

Recognising these feelings helps you adapt the way you deal with the complaints (see page 3 for guidelines). For example:

- keeping a careful distance from someone who is very angry, and avoiding prolonged eye contact (this makes the person feel uncomfortable)

- persuading a very upset customer to move, so you can discuss matters away from other customers – 'Let's sit over there, so you're more comfortable'

- offering a distressed customer a cup of tea or coffee when you think this will calm the person down

- not leaving a distressed customer alone – if you have to go away, ask a colleague to remain with the customer.

Rank Leisure

Complaints procedure

Always listen and respond positively.
All complaints must be resolved to the customer's satisfaction.
All complaints should be reported to a manager.

Benefit

You have transformed dissatisfaction into satisfaction. A customer will remember this and tell others.

Complaints create a hostile atmosphere. When they are resolved, a fun and friendly atmosphere is resumed.

Guide

1 Give the person your full attention. If necessary invite them to a quieter location.
2 Ask them to tell you what the problem is – use a warm and encouraging tone.
3 Listen carefully to what they say.
4 Maintain eye contact and positive body language.
5 Take action to resolve the complaint and inform the customer what you are going to do.
6 If you are unable to satisfy the customer, contact a manager.

Adopting methods of communication

It is not always straightforward getting information across to customers, or understanding what they are trying to communicate to you. Think of the times when the room is very noisy, or you've not understood a strong accent.

Types of communication

In food and drink service, most of your communications with customers are spoken, talking to them *face-to-face*. You may also:

- use *written* communication to record the food and drink order, take down the details of a complaint or incident, and messages for colleagues or customers

- deal with customers on the *telephone*, e.g. when they call to book a table or order room service.

Using suitable language

Customers find it easy to understand what you are saying (or have written down) when you use everyday language. The restaurant is not the place to impress people with long or unusual words, or your command of English grammar. Nor is it the place to offend or shock (or try to impress) by using swear words or foul language.

With so few restrictions, you have plenty of scope for putting feeling and a sense of your personality into what you say. Customers prefer to be served by a person rather than a robot-like object who uses a few standard phrases said without thought or meaning.

Be sensitive to the customer's viewpoint and feelings:

- avoid words, remarks or jokes which might give offence because of their connection with religion, politics, race, skin colour, disabilities, sexual orientation, etc.

- try to match your language to the style of the people you are talking to – a chatty, casual response is unlikely to be appreciated by those who say something rather formal to you, e.g. 'Good day, my name is Colonel Jones and you have a table reserved for Mrs Jones and me.'

If in doubt, use the conventional greetings – 'please', 'thank you', 'sir', 'madam', 'good afternoon', etc., and avoid any remarks or topics of conversation which might be controversial.

What information to communicate and when

You want customers to feel welcome and enjoy their visit. They appreciate a pleasant greeting when they arrive, when you come to take their order, the usual 'pleases' and 'thank you's' when you take and serve their order, and 'good-bye's' when they leave.

Customers also appreciate accurate, helpful information when they ask about the food and drinks available, or put more general questions to you (e.g. about taxi services).

The information is inappropriate if you:

- give too much so as to bore them – if the subject is a wide one (e.g. wines, and you have a lengthy wine list), ask some questions to establish their likely interest (e.g. white to go with their fish, Australian or French)

- give too little – saying that all cocktails are half price, but not that 'happy hour' ends in one minute's time

- time it poorly – after delivering food to customers, saying that they could have eaten in a non-smoking area if only they had mentioned it earlier

- give information they cannot use – describing the house wine to a couple who have asked about non-alcoholic drinks

- are insensitive to their needs – customers will be irritated or embarrassed when you have heard them tell their children to have a glass of milk because the other drinks are too expensive, and you answer their question on beers by starting with the top-price imported lagers

- pass on business or personal information which is not disclosable (i.e. confidential – discussed earlier in this section – see page 2).

Customers with special communication needs

All customers like special treatment, and it is one of the main reasons they enjoy their visits to your restaurant. But there are some customers who have special communication needs. Not recognising these, could turn their visit into a humiliating experience.

Offer to assist, but don't feel snubbed if your offer is rejected.

Acknowledging communication difficulties

If you do not have much experience of handling communication difficulties with customers, call on a more experienced colleague or your manager to help. Don't pretend to have experience and skills you don't have. This will only make things more difficult for the customer.

Special mobility needs

WHITBREAD INNS

If you know a visitor is due who has special mobility needs, you may be able to make special arrangements in advance. Consider their needs from the moment of arrival, in particular:

- car parking
- access to the building
- ease of movement round the building
- access to facilities, such as toilets.

Guest experience

The American Restaurant & Bar

Elderly people like to sit in the quieter areas and usually require your expert assistance with the menu. Housewives with children or families appreciate quick service to get the young ones fed so that the parents can enjoy a leisurely meal if they wish.

When escorting guests to their table, pace yourself to match the guests' pace. Elderly people and mothers with children to cope with have a tendency to walk more slowly. Never leave guests at the door, always *ask* them to follow you.

Always return to a party with children to give them balloons and high/booster chairs if required.

Speech impairment

When someone has difficulty talking or is unable to speak at all, you may have to take the lead in finding out what they would like. Show them the menu and drinks list, so they can point to their choice. Alternatively, talk them slowly through the range available and with each choice, wait for a sign, e.g. nod for yes, shake of the head for no. Before you get too far, check that you understand the sign as some people have difficulty controlling certain body movements.

Begin with the general, e.g. 'Would you like a starter?', then gradually home in on the choice, e.g.: 'Soup ... pâté ... salad ... fish ... fruit cocktail?'

When customers can speak a little, but it is very difficult to understand what they are saying, avoid correcting, interrupting or trying to finish what you think is being said. Wait before asking short questions that can be quickly answered (e.g. with a gesture) to clarify what is required.

Hearing impairment

The first step is to realise that the customer is having trouble hearing what you are saying. Those able to lip read might not give any clues until you say something with your face turned away.

1 Look directly at the person as you are talking. Seeing the expressions on your face and lip movement helps the person to follow what you are saying. Stand so the light is on your face (i.e. with your back to the room, not a window).

2 Keep your hands well away from your mouth. When this will help, use them to gesture and point.

3 Speak as clearly as you can, slowly, using short sentences and short words.

4 Raise the volume of your voice a little. Do not shout as this creates more noise and the words are no clearer.

5 Make use of printed menus and drinks lists. Point to items that the customer might like, e.g. on the buffet table or counter display, the ice and lemon for a drink, the milk or cream and sugar for coffee.

Sight impairment

Touch is the way that blind people see and that is the key to communication. If you just call out: 'Can I help you?' the blind person doesn't know who is being spoken to.

1 Talk naturally to the customer. Do not conduct the conversation through a third party unless this is obviously preferred.

2 Describe the layout of the restaurant/dining room. Knowing why particular sounds or smells are coming from different parts of the room will help the customer to relax and enjoy the meal.

3 If a braille menu is not available, offer to go through the menu. But don't confuse the person with too much detail, and do give the price for each item.

4 Touch to ask the order, then touch again to hand the drink or food over. Having taken the glass the blind person will remember where it is on the table.

5 Tell the chefs you have a customer who cannot see the food. If it is a set menu, ask if the fish or meat can be boned, another vegetable offered in place of peas, and the lettuce leaves for the salad cut smaller.

6 Once you have put the plate down in front of the guest, touch to indicate the guest is being spoken to, and then describe what is on the plate using the hands of a clock: e.g. fish at 12 o'clock, potatoes at 3 o'clock, vegetables at 6 o'clock.

7 When you present the bill, tell the customer the amount, and ask if you can itemise the different charges. When you return with the change, identify the value of each note so the blind person can fold it in a particular way.

Don't:

- grab your customer and take him or her to the table. Ask or wait for the person to tell you how he/she would like to be guided

- fill cups or glasses to the brim. If you are serving a slice of gâteau, put it in a bowl rather than a flat plate, and provide a spoon and fork to eat it with

- play with or pet guide dogs in the restaurant.

Never make assumptions. People with disabilities also have abilities.

Physical disability

Customers who arrive in a wheelchair may need help to get to a place where they can be comfortable: by opening doors, moving chairs or tables aside, etc.

- if possible, encourage the customer to sit at a table which has plenty of space around it. A wheelchair user could feel uncomfortable if other customers are clearly inconvenienced by his or her presence

- ensure that menus and other information are within easy reach of a wheelchair user.

Don't:

- make decisions on behalf of a wheelchair user unless he/she asks. A wheelchair is merely a form of transport

- move the wheelchair without first consulting the occupant

- discuss the needs or requirements of the wheelchair user with a third party – always direct any questions or comments directly to the wheelchair user.

Be ready to help customers with disabilities that affect control of their hands or head – e.g. offering to pour the drink into an over-sized glass, putting the food on an extra-large dish, cutting the food for them and providing a spoon.

Language differences

Working in a restaurant where many of the customers are from outside the area means that you will meet and have to try to understand a range of:

- *accents* – words said in a distinctive way, indicating the region, country or social class of the speaker, e.g. Cornish accent, Australian accent, 'English public school' accent

- *dialects* – form of the language (with different words, grammar and way of saying) spoken by a particular group of people, especially those living in one area, e.g. farm workers in Lincolnshire

- *other languages* – from any part of the world if you are near a top tourist attraction or major airport.

Some customers, especially those with regional accents, will expect you to know what they are saying – not out of any arrogance, but because they are used to being understood. One of your colleagues may be able to help interpret. Often you can persuade the customer (in a light-hearted way) to modify the accent. If all else fails, you can point to the menu items or drinks people seem to want. Fingers come in useful for finding out how many servings of food they want.

Customers who don't speak English greatly appreciate the effort you make to learn the most important words and phrases of their language: 'hullo', 'good morning/afternoon', 'please', 'thank you', 'meat', 'wine', etc.

Learning difficulties

Learning difficulties may explain why a customer asks you to read the menu, or write the cheque, or explain something again. Of course, these are matters you can easily help with. There is no reason to enquire what might be the problem.

Checking understanding of communication

Whoever the customers are, communication can easily go wrong and often does. This happens when people:

- hear what they want or expect to – e.g. that they can have a light snack, but the 'minimum charge' you mentioned is taken to mean only that they must have some food, not at least one of the main courses

- are distracted by their own thoughts or worries, or other activities in the room, so they miss some of what you have said

- take a different meaning from what you meant – usually because you have been ambiguous or not specific, e.g. 'Yes, smart casual wear is fine', when the customer considers designer jeans as smart casual, but the rules exclude anyone wearing jeans.

To reduce the risk of such misunderstandings, look the customer in the face while you are communicating. Watch for signs of inattention – blank expressions, the customer turning away while you are talking, looks being exchanged among the group.

When you are dealing with important factual information, e.g. making a table booking or taking the customer's address to send details of Christmas lunches, repeat the information back to the customer.

Procedures for dealing with customer incidents

Remind yourself of what these are (see page 4). Because of the nature of a customer's impairment or disability, things can go wrong no matter how carefully you try to help, for example:

- someone falls out of the wheelchair, or another customer trips over the chair

- there is an angry scene because no one seems to understand the customer's accent (or language)

- an adult with Down's syndrome becomes distressed.

Activities
Maintain customer care
Develop and maintain positive working relationships with customers

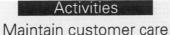

1 Give the rules on behaviour and what you wear at work.

2 Give examples of how you can help customers in your restaurant be safer.

3 What can go wrong if a spill or breakage is not cleared up quickly?

4 Give examples of questions from customers which you should not answer fully.

5 And examples of questions which must be answered accurately.

6 How do you deal with customers who are rude to you?

7 Give examples of customer comments you should pass on and to whom.

'Now my dear, you know the menu says this fish has been steamed, well...'

8 Why must complaints be dealt with quickly? Give the steps for dealing with a complaint.

9 You're handed an umbrella by a customer who found it. What information can you get to help find the owner?

Who? What? Where? When?

10 A customer phones asking if an umbrella has been found. What information should you ask for?

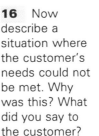
Where? Who? What? When?

11 Describe what you would do if a customer has just knocked a full glass of wine over the table.

12 Give four examples of how you can promote the products/ services of your restaurant and (if this applies) of the organisation it is part of.

THIS WEEK'S SPECIAL OFFER!

13 Give two examples of service standards in your restaurant. What is the reason for having service standards and codes of practice?

So much for their 2 minute service standard!

14 Give examples of information about a) your workplace and b) customers, which must be treated as confidential.

They always come here together!

15 Describe a situation when you used your initiative to meet a customer's needs, and another where you had to seek help.

16 Now describe a situation where the customer's needs could not be met. Why was this? What did you say to the customer?

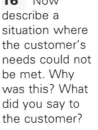

17 Describe how you can help a customer with a) hearing impairment, b) speech impairment, c) physical disability, d) learning difficulties, e) language differences.

I can't hear you... / I can't say what I mean... / I can't climb those stairs... / I can't read that... / I can't understand you...

Illustration (question 12) with thanks to Rank Leisure

15

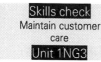
Use this to check your progress against the performance criteria.

NVQ SVQ

Skills check
Develop and maintain positive working relationships
with customers
Unit 2NG3

level 2

Use this to check your progress against the performance criteria.

Element 1

Deal with customers

Deal with customers in a polite and helpful manner ☐ PC1

▲ Customers: adults, children, those with mobility difficulties, those with communication difficulties

Act upon customers' needs and requirements without delay ☐ PC2

Answer customers' enquiries accurately, or refer to other help ☐ PC3

Give information in line with your authority ☐ PC4

Acknowledge customers' comments politely & pass on where appropriate ☐ PC5

Deal effectively with complaints ☐ PC6

Do your work in an organised, efficient and safe manner ☐ PC7

Element 2

Deal with customer incidents

Identify nature of incident quickly, and establish priorities ☐ PC1

▲ Incidents: spillage, breakage, lost property, equipment faults

Deal with customers politely and helpfully ☐ PC2

Assure customers that incident will receive immediate attention ☐ PC3

Resolve incidents within your authority calmly, as soon as possible ☐ PC4

Refer incidents outside your authority to appropriate person ☐ PC5

Report incidents according to procedures/the law ☐ PC6

Do your work in an organised, efficient and safe manner ☐ PC7

Element 1

Present positive personal image to customer

Treat customers helpfully and courteously ☐ PC1

Meet workplace standards of personal appearance and behaviour ☐ PC2

Equipment/supplies for dealing with customers up-to-date, in good order ☐ PC3

▲ Equipment and supplies: literature, stationery, forms, mechanical, electronic, consumables

Seek opportunities for improving customer relations ☐ PC4

Element 2

Balance needs of customer and organisation

Make persistent attempts to meet customer needs ☐ PC1

Explain organisational limitations to customer ☐ PC2

▲ Limitations: cost, time, resources

Minimise conflict between customer needs and organisational limitations ☐ PC3

Recognise organisational limitations and seek assistance from managers ☐ PC4

Make record of outcome of proposals put to customers ☐ PC5

Element 3

Respond to feelings expressed by the customer

Accurately gauge customers' feelings ☐ PC1

▲ Customers' feelings: anger, distress, vulnerability, frustration

Acknowledge customers' feelings and adapt your behaviour ☐ PC2

Regularly check perception of customers' feelings ☐ PC3

Operate relevant procedures to respond to customer complaints ☐ PC4

Element 4

Adapt methods of communication to the customer

Select type of communication to inform customers ☐ PC1

▲ Communication: face-to-face, telephone, written

Use written and spoken language suited to the customer ☐ PC2

Use method of communication suited to customers with individual needs ☐ PC3

▲ Individual needs: hearing impairment, speech impairment, physical disability, learning difficulties, language differences (includes dialects and accents)

Regularly check customers' understanding of communication ☐ PC4

Openly acknowledge communication difficulties and seek help to overcome ☐ PC5

Test yourself on customer service skills

1 What must you do if a customer orders 'Coke'?

2 At which units can a customer order alcohol?

3 How must a server be introduced?

4 What must all under 12's be given?

5 How many follow-ups should a customer receive?

6 Within what time should the bill be presented after a request?

7 Why is it important to repeat the order back to customers?

8 What parting remarks should we use when speaking on a telephone?

9 How many times is a phone allowed to ring before being answered?

Answers

1 Inform them politely that Pepsi is available. We cannot take an order for Coke and serve a different branded product. This is against the trade description laws.

2 Only at restaurants with a licence.

3 By name.

4 Goody bags and kids' menus.

5 Two or more if appropriate.

6 Within 3 minutes.

7 To ensure both the customer and the server have the same products in mind.

8 Always be polite, confirm details such as times, products, name, etc. Give a cheerful general final remark.

9 Always before the fourth ring.

Hygiene, safety and security in food
and drink service

Hygiene in food and drink service

The food and drinks you serve become harmful to health if they are contaminated by:

- bacteria found on raw food – usually destroyed in cooking or removed in the preparation (e.g. washing salad vegetables), but easily spread from raw to cooked food (e.g. using the same knife for the two types of food and not washing it thoroughly between use)

- bacteria carried by people – spread when someone sneezes over the food, hands are not washed (e.g. after using the toilet), glasses, china and cutlery inadequately washed between use

- bacteria found in dust and dirt – they live on, and get spread by, flies, ants, spiders, mice, rats, birds and other pests

- dirt, dust, pieces of broken glass or china or any other non-food object – spread to the food from dirty surfaces and equipment, or as a result of breakages

- cleaning substances or agents and other harmful chemicals – mistaken for food (e.g. because they have been kept in a food container or not clearly labelled) or come into contact with food (e.g. because instructions for use have not been followed).

Legal requirements relating to food safety

Under the Food Safety Act 1990, caterers, restaurateurs, hoteliers and other proprietors of food businesses commit an offence if they serve food (which includes drink) that is harmful to health. The scope of the Act is wide. It is an offence to make food harmful, offer for sale food that is contaminated, and describe food in a way that misleads the customer.

Regulations made under the Act deal with aspects of food safety. These include the Food Safety (General Food Hygiene) Regulations 1995 which require:

- your employer to ensure that the preparation, storage and handling of food is carried out in a hygienic way. The regulations set general standards for the design and cleanliness of food premises and equipment, personal hygiene and training of food handlers

- you to report to your employer or manager any illness, wound, infection or other medical condition which might contaminate food (see page 19)

Most people carry *Staphylococcus aureus* bacteria in their nose and mouth. Each time the nose or mouth is touched, or someone sneezes, bacteria are transferred to glasses, drinks, food, etc.

- your employer to identify steps in the preparation, storage, handling and service of food that are critical to food safety, and ensure adequate safety procedures. You may hear this referred to as HACCP (said as 'hassop').

These safety procedures require you to follow cleaning schedules, workplace rules, and to check date marks on bottles and packets. You may also have to record temperatures of refrigerators and freezers, etc.

The Food Safety (Temperature Control) Regulations 1995 require food which supports the growth of harmful bacteria to be kept at safe temperatures:

- at or above 63°C for food which is being kept hot

- otherwise at 8°C or below for businesses in England and Wales, in a refrigerator or refrigerating chamber or cool ventilated place for businesses in Scotland.

Foods which can be kept at ambient (i.e. room) temperature without risk to health include bread, tea leaves and tea bags, ground and instant coffee, biscuits and cakes (unless filled or decorated with fresh cream), fresh fruit (unless prepared as a salad or in a dessert).

Limited periods outside temperature control are acceptable while the food is being handled and prepared, in the event of equipment breakdowns, and similar situations.

Food which is served cold from a buffet table, counter, sweet trolley or cheese board may be kept outside temperature control for a single period of not more than four hours. Once food has been on display outside temperature control, no further exception is allowed.

The maximum time outside temperature control for cooked or reheated food kept for service or display is two hours. At the end of this period, the food must be rapidly cooled to 8°C or below and no further exception is allowed.

Element 1

Personal health and hygiene

When you are tired or unwell, your concentration is below its best. You are more likely to make mistakes and drop things, endangering yourself and the people around you. Work may seem more difficult, and it is harder to relax outside work.

These problems are less likely if you follow a healthy lifestyle. Try to have regular exercise. Get enough sleep and relaxation, and keep a balance in what you eat and drink.

But the following pages focus on another aspect of personal health: your responsibility to protect the safety of the food and drink you serve. This affects what you wear at work including any jewellery, perfume and cosmetics, your personal standards of hygiene, and what to do if you have a cut or graze, or feel ill.

What you wear at work

You spend long hours on your feet. Wash them every day, and keep your toe nails trimmed. Change socks daily. Wear comfortable shoes that will not slip, and which protect your feet from dropped objects.

If you change into a uniform at work, leave your outdoor clothing and footwear in the place provided for this purpose. Don't take it with you into the restaurant or any area where food is prepared or stored.

If you wear your own clothes at work, choose a combination that is comfortable, practical and safe. Avoid loose fitting clothes, accessories and jewellery which might get caught on things. What you wear should suit the style of your workplace, and give the right impression to customers.

How you look

Long flowing hair might get trapped in doors, furniture or machinery. Strands of hair are likely to fall into food and drinks. There is usually a rule that long hair must be tied back, and that anyone preparing food should keep their hair covered.

Hair, beards and moustaches absorb smoke and food smells. Wash your hair daily to keep it clean and free from smells.

Hairstyles should be neat and away from the face. Long hair should be tied back.

Appearance and personal hygiene checklist

1 Bathe at least once a day and use a good deodorant.
2 Never wear strong perfume or aftershave.
3 Keep hair and uniform tidy. Tie back long hair.
4 Report and cover any cuts or abrasions.
5 Wash hands frequently, before coming on duty and especially after using the toilet or smoking, handling waste or cleaning materials.
6 Keep nails short and free of varnish.
7 Keep make-up to a minimum.
8 Always demonstrate a high standard of personal hygiene, i.e. being clean shaven.
9 Do not display unpleasant habits, i.e. chewing gum.

Personal hygiene

The body excretes moisture constantly through sweat glands located all over it. When it's hot you perspire more. Working under pressure has a similar effect. Sweat itself is virtually odourless and normally evaporates quickly. The smell comes from bacteria which live on the perspiration, especially in areas such as the underarms where it cannot evaporate freely. A daily bath or shower and a good deodorant are the best protection.

You depend on your hands for most tasks. Customers are likely to notice the state of your hands. The sort of impression they get of the standards in your workplace depends on what they see.

Wash your hands thoroughly and often, and always before touching food. Use a wash hand basin, with plenty of hot water and soap. Then rinse your hands, and dry them well. Use the paper towels, roller towel or hot air drier provided – never a service or drying-up cloth. Do not wash food service equipment or food in wash hand basins.

Keep your fingernails clean and neatly trimmed. Nail varnish is best avoided, and must not be worn if you are preparing food.

If you feel a sneeze coming or the need to cough, turn away from any food or drinks. Hold a disposable paper tissue over your nose and mouth, and wash your hands afterwards. Control any impulse to lick your fingers, bite your nails, or touch your nose, mouth or hair.

Never smoke or spit in any room where food is prepared, stored or served.

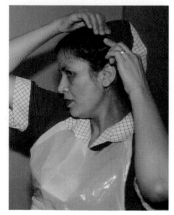

In some workplaces, a head covering forms part of the uniform.

Reporting illness and infection

Report *any* illness or infection as soon as possible. Your manager will make the judgement of whether it is safe for you to work with food. Don't break the law (see below) or put other people's health at risk, just because you don't want to admit to feeling ill.

Covering cuts, grazes and wounds

Cover cuts, grazes, open sores and wounds with a waterproof dressing. Usually dressings for food handling staff (from the first aid box) are coloured blue, so that if they do drop off they will be easily spotted.

If the wound or sore is infected, or you think it might be, report this to your manager.

Legal requirements

Under the Food Safety (General Food Hygiene) Regulations 1995 you must tell your manager if you:

- know or suspect you are suffering from, or may be a carrier, of any disease likely to be transmitted through food

- have an infected wound, a skin infection, sores, diarrhoea or any similar medical condition such as stomach upset or vomiting.

Until you have been cleared of the condition, you will not be permitted to handle food or drinks, or do tasks which might put at risk the safety of the food.

Your employer has a responsibility to ensure that every person handling or serving food:

- maintains a high degree of personal cleanliness

- wears suitable, clean and, where appropriate, protective clothing.

The regulations also require the provision of adequate hand washing and toilet facilities, and somewhere to change into uniform and store personal and work clothing.

Regular hand washing is one of the basic rules of good hygiene at work. Do not rely on gloves to provide protection.

Fire procedures

Restaurants and kitchens have a plentiful supply of the four things that lead to really serious fires, those that destroy businesses, injure people and sometimes cost lives. The first three are the basic ingredients that any fire requires: oxygen (in the air), fuel (anything which will burn) and heat. The fourth is opportunity.

Discarded matches and cigarette ends not cleared away at the end of service are a common source of fires in restaurants. Trapped in upholstered seats, or lying on a carpet, they have the opportunity to smoulder away unnoticed. Some time after everyone has gone, the fire starts in earnest. In the minutes it takes to trigger the fire detection system, and for someone to respond, the fire can cause great damage.

The other main causes of fires are cooking equipment, electrical faults (in wiring and equipment), arson (i.e. someone starts the fire deliberately), rubbish storage and room heating appliances (including open fires).

Raising the alarm

Speed is vital. The sooner people are warned, the better their chance of getting to safety. The alarm will bring help from those who have been trained to fight the fire and to rescue anyone trapped by it.

Make sure now that you know what to do if you discover a fire. Your employer has a legal duty to train you, and there will be fire notices and other reminders in staff and customer areas telling you what to do. Don't put people at risk by waiting for a real emergency before you learn what has to be done.

Using fire fighting equipment

Never fight a fire if this puts your own safety at risk. Don't play the hero. Concentrate on raising the alarm and helping evacuate the building.

In each of the customer and staff areas of the restaurant, there will be at least one fire extinguisher and possibly other appliances for fighting small fires. Get to know where they are, how they should be used and what fires they are suitable for:

- public areas – usually water extinguishers, possibly automatic fire sprinklers or a fire hose

- rooms where there is electrical equipment – carbon dioxide or powder extinguishers, sometimes foam extinguishers (if the suitable type)

- kitchen – fire blanket, foam or powder extinguisher.

Using the wrong extinguisher can make the fire worse. So can a few moments' delay, if you have to work out how to get the fire extinguisher to work.

Water extinguishers

Coloured red, these are suitable for fires involving wood, paper and cloth. To use:

- direct the jet at the base of the flames
- keep it moving across the area of the fire
- after the main fire is out, respray any remaining hot spot
- if the fire is spreading vertically, attack it at the lowest point, then follow upwards.

Do not use on live electrical equipment, burning fats or oils.

Extinguishers in use: water (above), *carbon dioxide* (top right), *foam* (lower right).

Carbon dioxide extinguishers

Coloured black, these are for fires involving flammable liquids or liquefiable solids, e.g. oil, fat, methylated spirits. They are safe on live electrical equipment. To use:

- direct the discharge horn at the base of the flames
- keep the jet moving across the area of the fire
- do not touch the discharge horn – this gets extremely cold.

The fumes can be harmful – ventilate the area as soon as the fire has been extinguished.

Carbon dioxide cuts off the oxygen supply to the fire, but whatever was on fire remains very hot. Watch that it does not re-ignite.

Foam extinguishers

Cream-coloured, these are used for fires involving paper, wood and cloth. AFFF (aqueous film-forming foam) extinguishers are suitable for fires involving flammable liquids. To use:

- stand well back and sweep jet from side to side
- for fires in a container, direct the jet at the inside edge.

Do not aim the foam directly into a burning liquid in case it splashes the fire further.

Some types of foam extinguisher are not suitable for live electrical equipment (check the instructions).

Powder extinguishers

Coloured blue, this type will put out fires involving flammable liquids or liquefiable solids, e.g. oil, fat or grease. It is safe for fires involving electrical equipment, but does not readily penetrate spaces inside equipment, so the fire may re-ignite. To use:

- direct the nozzle at the base of the flames
- with a rapid sweeping motion drive the flame towards the far edge of the fire until the flames are out
- repeat as necessary (some extinguishers can be shut off and used again if the fire re-starts).

For electrical equipment:

- disconnect the equipment from the mains
- direct the jet straight at the fire if possible, so that the powder can penetrate right inside the equipment.

Powder extinguishers have a limited cooling effect, so take care the fire does not re-ignite.

The powder makes a great mess. It can take several hours to clean up after even a small fire.

Fire blanket

Used for small fires involving burning liquids and burning clothing. You will find one by the deep fat fryer.

Hold the blanket in front of you using it as a shield to protect your body and hands from the fire, and place it over the flames. Take care not to waft the flames in your direction, or towards bystanders. You may need to put something across a large fryer, e.g. a metal tray, to stop the blanket falling into the oil.

For a fire involving clothing, wrap the blanket around the burning area, but not over the victim's nose and mouth. Roll the patient on the ground.

Fire do's

- Know your quickest and safest evacuation route.
- Assemble in orderly manner at the assembly point.
- Close all windows and fire exit doors.
- Turn off all appliances, e.g. hot plates, heaters.
- Take all fire drills seriously.

Fire hose

This is for fires involving wood, paper and cloth. To use:

- release the locking mechanism on the reel
- open the valve (to allow water into the hose)
- unreel the length of hose required to reach the fire
- aim the jet of water at the base of the flames and move across the area of the fire.

Safety and emergency signs and notices

These are there for a purpose. Respect this. Don't make your own rules, or persuade yourself that nothing can go wrong because it hasn't so far in your experience.

Too many fires start because people have disobeyed a no smoking sign, or not followed instructions for using electrical equipment. Many fires cause great damage because people have ignored a notice saying FIRE DOOR KEEP SHUT. Too many people have been injured or lost their lives in fires because emergency exits have not been kept clear, or the doors have been locked in spite of the instructions.

A lot of effort goes into the appearance of safety signs, the symbols and the words they use. There are detailed regulations designed to ensure their uniformity throughout Europe, and specific requirements that your business has to meet when deciding on their use and location.

Evacuation procedures and the assembly point

Become familiar with the fire notices around your workplace. They tell you:

- what to do if the fire alarm sounds, how to leave the building and where to assemble
- how to raise the alarm if you discover a fire.

They also tell you what not to do:

- do not stop to collect personal belongings
- do not run
- do not open a door if you suspect there is a fire on the other side
- do not re-enter the building until advised to do so by the manager/officer in charge.

From time to time there will be a chance to practise an evacuation. If you find problems during such a fire drill (e.g. a door which is hard to open, or uncertainty about your assembly point), tell your manager about them.

Be quite clear about any specific responsibilities you have been given, such as turning off the gas or electricity, or shutting windows.

Maintaining a safe environment

Everyone at work, no matter how junior or senior their position, whether they are full-time, part-time or casual, has a duty to protect the health and safety of those around them. This is a legal and moral responsibility.

The ultimate sanctions of the law – many thousands of pounds in fines and legal costs, possibly a prison sentence – are usually reserved for top management. But your employer can dismiss you without notice for serious breaches of health and safety procedures.

While you would be concerned about being in trouble with the law or losing your job, the fact is that most workplace accidents are caused by inattention, carelessness, forgetfulness, or gradually falling into bad habits. None of these may be serious in themselves. Until, that is, an unlucky chain of events and one or more errors combine with fatal results.

When you and your colleagues are under many other pressures, it is not easy to maintain the highest safety standards. Whatever the effort involved, safety has to be a top priority.

Identifying hazards

Your work exposes you and others in your workplace (including customers) to a range of hazards.

Some hazards are unavoidable. Strong cleaning agents have the potential to cause harm, the accepted meaning of the word 'hazard'. Electrical equipment can go wrong, no matter how well maintained it has been.

Some hazards occur during the normal, day-to-day life of a busy restaurant. Drinks or food get spilt. Glasses and bottles are knocked or fall over and break. Smokers drop smouldering cigarette ends or lighted matches. Customers put shopping bags in the way of other people.

Some hazards are avoidable:

- injury to your back from using the wrong method of lifting a heavy tray or moving furniture
- cutting yourself when handling knives or other sharp objects
- burns or poisoning when using cleaning agents.

Rectifying hazards

You can quickly deal with many of the everyday hazards. Close the fire door that was left propped open. Pick up things that have been dropped on to the floor. Move chairs back into place after customers have gone, so others can get by more easily.

Don't put safety at risk by doing nothing. You may be able to see your way down a corridor when the light bulb is not working, but someone less familiar with the route, or with poor eyesight, would be in danger.

Be prepared to put effort into keeping your workplace safe. For each hazard, consider how safety can get the priority it needs. For example, if you are rushing to serve some customers, and you spill a drink or food on the floor, do you:

- leave the spill while you get on with serving?

- ask a colleague to take over with the serving, while you attend to the spill?

- clear up the spill, explaining to the customers that you will be with them in a moment?

Warning others and reporting hazards

Do not assume that because you can see a hazard, other people will. Always:

- tell your manager when you find equipment not working properly

- label equipment which is out of order, so that no one else tries to use it

- unplug faulty electrical equipment or turn it off at the mains switch

- where practical, move faulty equipment to a secure place to await repair (this reduces the risk of someone using the equipment without realising it is faulty)

- report anything that is or might become a hazard, e.g. a broken leg on a chair or table, a shelf coming away from its fitting, or the smell of gas in the kitchen

- position a hazard warning sign, rope off the entrance or put a safety barrier in place to prevent access to dangerous areas.

It is not enough to tell colleagues that equipment is not working, or not to go into an area which might be dangerous. Nor can you assume that customers won't enter closed rooms or staff areas, nor that someone else will, who is unfamiliar with that part of the building. Safety notices must be put in place.

Learning safety

You will be trained or instructed on how to use and clean the various items of equipment you are expected to operate, and the safety precautions necessary. Don't be afraid to ask questions. Don't put yourself and others in danger and risk damaging equipment, by trying to use something you are not familiar with, or saying you have already had training when you haven't, or acting the expert when colleagues can't get equipment to work.

Dealing with an accident

If you are a trained first-aider you will know what to do to help the injured person. Otherwise, immediately tell the manager or other person who has been appointed to take charge if a serious injury or illness occurs. In larger restaurants and those which are part of a hotel, leisure centre, school, college, office, factory, etc., there will be one or more first-aiders with this responsibility.

Check that you know who to contact and the location of the first-aid box. A notice or poster should be on display in your work area to remind everyone of this information.

In the first-aid box are dressings and bandages for minor injuries and a card with general first-aid guidance. Tell your manager if you find items running low or missing.

CHECK **P**list
Preventing accidents

✔ walk, don't run. When carrying something hot or heavy, warn people as you approach them

✔ look after floor areas. Pick up items and clear up spillages and breakages quickly

✔ watch out for hazards such as customers' bags and feet. Don't put items where they can be tripped over or might fall

✔ keep power cables to equipment tidy, not trailing across floors or work surfaces. Use safety signs to close off the area you are vacuuming

✔ load trays carefully, so that items do not fall off or obstruct your view. Get help to carry heavy items

✔ take care when using matches, and with lighted candles on tables and buffet displays

✔ treat hotplates and gas or spirit lamps carefully – never carry when plugged in or lit

✔ use your service cloth to hold hot plates. Warn customers when plates are very hot

✔ take special care when handling or putting down anything with a sharp surface or which might break

Reporting accidents

There should be an accident book (or a suitable form) kept where you have ready access to it. By law you must tell your manager when you have had an accident. If you prefer, you can do this by writing about the accident in the accident book, or asking someone else to do this on your behalf.

So that you do not forget important details, or miss some information, make notes as soon as possible after the accident about:

* what happened, where and at what time
* action taken to deal with the accident
* names of any witnesses, and their addresses if they are not usually based at your workplace.

The requirement to record accidents applies even to minor ones. For more serious incidents arising out of, or in connection with work, there is an additional procedure for reporting them to the enforcing authority (usually the environmental health department). Normally your manager has to do this.

If you make a claim to the Department of Social Security for benefits in respect of personal injury, or work-related illness, your employer will have to provide detailed information on the accident. This includes where and what you were doing at the time, and whether you were authorised to be in that place and to do what you were doing.

Calling an ambulance, the fire brigade or police

999

1 Use the nearest telephone.
2 Dial 999. No money is required.
3 Ask for the necessary service: ambulance, fire brigade or police.
4 When you get through, give the number of the telephone you are calling from so that the operator can call you back if necessary. Speak clearly.
5 Give the location of the accident.
6 State the nature of the accident or illness, the number of casualties, and as much detail of the injuries as you know.
7 Remain on the phone until the emergency service operator rings off – to be sure that you have given sufficient information.

While help is on its way, stay calm.

If the accident has been caused by an electric shock, break the contact by switching off the current at the plug or mains. Do not touch the casualty until the current has been switched off, or you will become a second victim.

Reassure any casualty kindly and confidently. Keep the casualty protected from the cold, but do not cover major burns.

Do not move the casualty unless absolutely necessary.

Safety with electricity

* Always switch off and disconnect from the mains before moving portable electrical equipment.
* Keep electrical cables and plugs away from wet floors.
* Use only one appliance per plug. Do not use adaptors.
* Do not leave electrical cables where they might cause someone to trip or fall, get caught under a door, furniture or equipment, or damaged when moving goods about.
* Switch off all equipment except refrigerators, when not required, especially during non-trading hours. TV sets and amplifiers should be disconnected at night by removing the plug from the socket.

More on the legal requirements

The main piece of legislation covering health and safety at work is the Health and Safety at Work Act 1974. Your employer must:

* provide safe equipment and safe ways of carrying out tasks
* ensure that articles and substances are used, handled, stored and transported in a safe way and without health risks
* provide information, instruction, training and supervision to ensure health and safety
* maintain the workplace in a safe condition, and provide and maintain safe ways of getting into and out of the workplace
* provide a working environment which is safe, without risks to health and has adequate facilities and arrangements for the welfare of employees
* prepare, and keep up-to-date a written statement of general health and safety policy, which should also describe the organisation and arrangements for carrying out the policy, and bring this statement and any revisions of it to the notice of all employees.

Various regulations have been made under the Act. These include first-aid and the reporting of accidents (described above), the control of substances hazardous to health (including cleaning agents and the gas cylinders used in drink dispense systems– known as COSHH for short), gas and electrical equipment, noise and safety signs.

Regulations have also been made to bring the UK law into line with EC directives on equipment and workplace safety, the wearing of protective clothing, and manual handling.

You have a legal duty to follow workplace instructions for the safe use of materials and equipment.

Your legal responsibilities

You must follow the measures your employer has set up to reduce the risk of accident and injury. If the instructions are to use a trolley to move stacks of chairs, then you are at fault if you decide to carry the chairs. Similarly you must wear the gloves provided for cleaning tasks.

Under the Health and Safety at Work Act 1974 you must:

- not interfere or misuse anything provided in the interests of health, safety or welfare

- take reasonable care for the health and safety of yourself and of other persons who may be affected by what you do, or do not do, at work

- perform health and safety-related duties and comply with health and safety requirements set down by your employer or any other person with health and safety responsibilities.

Under the Management of Health and Safety at Work Regulations 1992, you have a duty to use correctly all work items provided by your employer, in accordance with the training and instructions you have received to enable you to use the items safely. You must inform, without delay, your employer (or the person with responsibility for health and safety matters) of any:

- work situation which might present a serious and immediate danger to health and safety

- shortcomings in the health and safety arrangements at your workplace.

Getting information on current health and safety legislation

A copy of the Health and Safety Executive (HSE) poster *Health and safety law: what you should know* should be on display in your workplace. In the space provided on the poster you will find contact details of those who enforce the legislation in your area.

Alternatively (or in addition), you may have been given a copy of the leaflet published by the HSE (code number HSC5), and a separate note of useful addresses near your workplace.

Many employers have their own health and safety material. Others provide their employees with leaflets or books published for general industry use, and to meet special needs, e.g. of those whose first language is not English.

Maintaining a secure environment

Restaurants are popular targets for the dishonest, for troublemakers, for the opportunist thief, and for terrorists. Large sums of cash are about. Even when this is not so, because the takings have just been banked, the expectation is that restaurants are cash-rich. Stocks of wines and spirits are very attractive to thieves because they are valuable, easily re-sold and difficult to track back to where they were stolen.

Restaurants and bars sometimes have to ban certain customers because they are troublemakers, or dealers in drugs, or prostitutes. Where restaurants are part of entertainment venues or clubs, people may try to get in without paying the entrance or membership fee, or to avoid rules about dress.

Identifying and reporting security risks

Your workplace will have physical security systems appropriate to its needs – from a safe to keep cash, etc., to remote control cameras. There will also be rules and procedures to reduce the risk of security problems – clearing cash tills regularly, using different routes to the bank, checking toilets and other places where people might hide before locking-up time, and never leaving the till unattended.

The effectiveness of these arrangements depends on you. You should:

- notice what goes on around the premises

- be alert to anything unusual or out-of-place

- promptly report the unusual or out-of-place

- recognise the warning signs of violent behaviour, drunkenness, drug use, prostitutes, etc.

- remember the faces of customers who have caused trouble, or who should not be served.

CCC
LEISURE

Security rules
- Alarms on during non-working hours.
- Toilets checked at least twice per session and at the end of the trading day before securing building.
- All supply or service visitors asked to produce identification.
- All rear entrances locked when adjoining areas are unoccupied (e.g. kitchen).
- Upstairs windows secure when accommodation is unoccupied during business hours.
- Outside area tours carried out at frequent but irregular times during trading day.
- Access not given to 'non-expected' visitors after securing building at end of day.
- Never jeopardise your safety to protect cash or property.

Preventing unauthorised access

There are parts of the premises where customers should not go, entrances (and exits) they should not use, and perhaps areas where you are not allowed, or only allowed at certain times or for particular reasons. This is to protect security and sometimes for safety.

Entrances and exits

Ideally, no one should be able to enter or leave the building without being seen by a manager or member of staff. Customers should not be able to go direct to the carpark from the toilets, for example. Otherwise there is a risk that people can leave unobserved not having paid the bill, or with stolen property.

Fire exits should never be locked or closed off in such a way that they cannot be used in an emergency.

If you do find a door open which should be locked, or see other signs that suggest people have been gaining unauthorised access, tell your manager at once.

Storage rooms

When you have access to the wine cellar, a storeroom or other area which is kept locked, you are responsible for leaving it locked. Even if you have to leave the room temporarily, relock it.

Do not let anyone else in while you are there, unless you are sure of the person's identity and reason for entering the room. Keep the key with you, not in the door or somewhere it might be removed without your noticing.

CHECK list
P rotecting property

- ✔ keep keys on you, never left in locks, or lying around in supposedly safe places such as the drawer of your service station

- ✔ never lend keys to others, sign them back first

- ✔ leave your personal valuables at home. If you have to bring some to work, keep them locked in your locker while you are on duty and the key with you

- ✔ put equipment and materials in the correct place after use. Storage areas must always be kept locked when unattended

- ✔ report anything of yours, colleagues, customers or your employer that is missing. Notice what is going on around you

- ✔ respect rules on taking bags and handbags, personal shopping, etc. into work areas. Employers may wish to check these for stolen property

Key control

Good key control is essential. You may be asked to sign keys in and out. If instead you pass keys on to a colleague and they go missing, it could be your responsibility, since the keys were signed out to you.

Missing keys are a great worry. Have they been taken deliberately, by someone planning a break-in? If the keys turn up later, has someone had copies made? If someone found the keys by chance, might they be used dishonestly?

Usually the only solution is to change the locks. This is expensive, especially as it has to be done quickly to limit the time when the old keys could be used.

Cash boxes

There may be a cash box in your workplace for small-value purchases in local shops, or emergency supplies. If you have use of this, you will be expected to produce receipts or some other record to account for what has been spent. Make quite sure you return the cash box to its proper place, and that it is locked.

Safes

Usually only the manager will have access to the safe. It will be in a part of the premises where customers and staff do not normally go. Great care will be taken to prevent anyone else from knowing the combination which opens the safe (or getting hold of the key).

If you do see anyone behaving suspiciously near the safe, tell your manager at once.

Suspicious items

If you work in a place where politicians, royalty, celebrities and leading business people are customers, or which is in a target area for terrorists, you will be used to strict security procedures.

These will probably include regular searches of the entire building and restrictions on when deliveries come from suppliers. You will be expected to report anything that looks suspicious, and trained to recognise anything that is out of the ordinary. You may be asked to help search your area of the workplace if a bomb threat has been received.

In these and similar situations, there are two general rules that you should follow:

- if you see a suspicious-looking item, do not touch it yourself or let colleagues or customers put themselves in possible danger

- get help, from management and security officers. Tell them calmly and accurately where the item is and why you think it is suspicious. They will get in touch with the emergency services.

Reporting lost property

When a customer's or colleague's property, such as a coat, bag or umbrella, is left behind, it should be handed in immediately to a manager. Attach a note to the lost property with details of the place, time and date it was found. This will help identify the true owner.

When a claim is made for lost property, ask for a description of the item and where and when it might have been lost. If there is any doubt that the claim is genuine, or the lost property is a valuable item, ask a manager to deal with the matter.

Dealing with suspicious individuals

The identity of contractors, sales representatives, tradespeople, local authority officials, meter readers and so on should be checked before they are allowed into the premises. In large places and those which are part of an office or factory complex, there will be a security officer who does this. All visitors and staff will be issued with an identity badge. In this case you should report anyone you see in the building who is not wearing a badge. Where appropriate, ask politely if you can help the person.

In a small restaurant, you will be very aware of the comings and goings, and perhaps have less reason to be suspicious. But there are people who take advantage of this, pretending to be an engineer calling to collect the till or a hand drier for repair, or a supplier to take back a case of wine delivered to the wrong address. They expect you not to check their story.

Dealing with bomb threats

Bombs vary in design and appearance. They can be disguised as briefcases, handbags, carrier bags, holdalls, radio cassettes, 'cigarette' packets, etc. or expertly hidden.

Receiving a bomb threat

Most threats are made by telephone because the caller:

- knows or believes an explosive device has been placed and wants to minimise injury
- wants to disrupt normal activities by creating anxiety and panic: this caller may simply be a disgruntled employee or customer.

If you take a telephone call which turns out to be a bomb threat, try to find out from the caller, and make note of:

- where the bomb is located
- what it looks like
- when it will go off
- what will make it go off
- why the bomb was planted.

Also note any details about the caller: accent, male/female, background noises, etc.

After taking the call, immediately tell a manager.

Customers who may leave without paying

Keep an eye on what customers are doing. Towards the end of the meal and before the bill is paid, be especially careful that everyone does not leave the table, either together or one by one. You or a colleague should always be nearby, ready to say good-bye and thank you. This would also be the opportunity to tactfully check that correct payment has been left on the table. If not, remind the customers before they go from the restaurant.

When customers refuse to pay all or some of the bill, get the manager. If you have asked if everything is satisfactory during the meal, and acted immediately on any complaints, the customer will have less reason for not paying.

Dealing with violent customers

Your manager will deal with the problem and call the police. Although you shouldn't get involved, you can do much to help prevent violence from occurring:

- *spot the warning signs* – observing, watching and listening for rowdy behaviour, arguments, aggressive gestures, etc.
- *prevent frustration from building up* – serve customers in their turn, avoid treating some customers differently from others, don't argue with customers, apply rules fairly, apologise if you have made a mistake or keep customers waiting
- *tell your manager before the situation becomes serious* – do this quietly and calmly. Don't threaten the customers that you will get the manager. If you need to explain your absence, or feel they will be calmer once they know the manager is to be fetched, say what you are doing in your normal tone of voice. Speak firmly, slowly and deliberately.

Legal requirements

You have a duty to protect the property of your employer, customers and others in your workplace. You also have a duty to protect the safety and welfare of customers, staff and visitors by preventing unauthorised access to the premises.

The law is also there to support your action. For example, someone destroying or damaging property which is not their own, stealing or attempting to steal, is committing a criminal offence.

You have a duty to protect the property and safety of others (and yourself).

1 Give three reasons why high standards of personal hygiene are required in restaurants.

2 What should you wear, and how should you look at work?

3 What should you wear (and not wear) if asked to prepare food?

4 If you are feeling unwell, who must you tell, when and why?

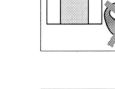

5 What must you do if you have a cut, graze or wound? Why?

6 Give the main rules for working hygienically in the restaurant.

7 What are the most likely causes of fire in your work area? How can you help reduce the risk?

8 Say what you should do if there is a fire. What must you do if you discover the fire?

9 When and how do you use each type of fire extinguisher: a) water, b) powder, c) foam, d) carbon dioxide, e) fire blanket, f) fire hose?

10 Give some ways you can help make your restaurant safe for everyone.

11 What accidents or injury could occur in your work area? How can the risk be minimised?

12 What do you do about reporting hazards? How can they be made safe in the meantime?

13 Where is the first-aid equipment? Who is responsible for taking charge in the event of an accident?

14 State your legal responsibilities for health and safety in the workplace.

15 What would make you treat an item or package as suspicious? What do you do in this situation?

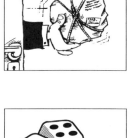

16 Give the main security risks in your restaurant, and what you can do to prevent them.

17 What do you do when a) you find something a customer has left, b) lost property is handed to you by a customer, c) a customer claims lost property?

18 Describe the security and safety checks made after the restaurant has closed.

Illustrations with thanks to De Vere Hotels (questions 7, 11, 12 and 15), Rank Leisure (questions 4 and 8)

NVQ SVQ

Skills check
Maintain a safe and secure
working environment
Unit NG1

levels
1+2

Test yourself on fire safety

1 Which three ingredients can result in fire?
2 What are the principal causes of fire?
3 What is the safest and most effective way to stop fire spreading in a building?
4 How can we a) cool a fire, b) smother a fire, c) starve a fire?
5 When is it unsafe to tackle a fire?
6 When should the fire brigade be called?
7 Should the fire brigade always be called, even if the fire is out?
8 When should people be allowed back into a building after the alarm has been raised?

Test yourself on health and safety

1 What does COSHH stand for and why is it important?
2 How must chemicals be stored?
3 How must broken glassware be disposed of?
4 How must fire extinguishers be stored?
5 What type of fire is the red fire extinguisher used on?
6 When mopping floors how must you warn people?
7 What must you do if you notice any fault in wiring, equipment or other hazard?
8 What must you do to report an accident?
9 What illnesses must you report to the manager?

Element 1
Maintain personal health and hygiene

Wear clean, smart and appropriate work clothing ☐ PC1

Keep your hair neat and tidy ☐ PC2

Comply with workplace rules on jewellery, perfume, cosmetics ☐ PC3

Have cuts, grazes and wounds treated by the appropriate person ☐ PC4

Correctly report illness and infections ☐ PC5

Follow good hygiene practices ☐ PC6

Carry out your work in an organised, efficient and safe manner ☐ PC7

Element 2
Carry out procedures in the event of fire

In the event of a fire, immediately raise the alarm ☐ PC1

Use fire fighting equipment correctly ☐ PC2

⚠ Fire hose, fire blanket, foam extinguisher, powder extinguisher, water extinguisher, carbon dioxide extinguisher

Conform to instructions on safety and emergency signs and notices ☐ PC3

Follow evacuation procedures in a calm and orderly manner ☐ PC4

Reach assembly point ☐ PC5

Carry out your work in an organised, efficient and safe manner ☐ PC6

Element 3
Maintain a safe environment for customers, staff and visitors

Identify and where possible rectify hazards and potential hazards ☐ PC1

Follow procedures for making people aware of hazards ☐ PC2

Follow procedures for giving warning of hazards ☐ PC3

Correctly report accidents, damage and hazards you cannot rectify ☐ PC4

Carry out your work in an organised, efficient and safe manner ☐ PC5

Element 4
Maintain a secure environment for customers, staff and visitors

Identify and report potential security risks ☐ PC1

⚠ Prohibited areas, suspicious items, unauthorised open entrances/exits, missing keys

Secure customer and staff areas against unauthorised access ☐ PC2

⚠ Public facilities, public/work/staff areas

Secure storage and security facilities against unauthorised access ☐ PC3

⚠ Storerooms, safes, cash boxes

Follow procedures for reporting lost property ☐ PC4

Challenge (politely) or report suspicious individuals ☐ PC5

Carry out your work in an organised, efficient and safe manner ☐ PC6

DE VERE HOTELS

Restaurant safety

1 Do not stack crockery or service dishes too high, or overload shelves.
2 Avoid over-filling service stations (dumb waiters). Pull cutlery drawer out slowly and carefully.
3 Do not stack chairs and tables above chest height. Check that the stack is secure before leaving it. Never stack furniture behind doors, in corridors or fire escape routes.

4 Take special care with flammable or potentially explosive materials, e.g. methylated spirits, gas cylinder aerosols. They should be kept away from heat and direct sunlight.
5 Follow instructions for using silver dip and other cleaning agents. Always wear gloves. Always rinse serviceware after cleaning and polish with a clean cloth.
6 Never carry anything over the head of a customer or colleague. Take extra care near boisterous customers.

7 Do not overfill soup tureens/ dishes, coffee or teapots.
8 Take care when using matches, and with lighted candles on tables and buffet displays.
9 Watch out for guests' handbags, briefcases, etc. They present a tripping hazard. It's also likely that the guest will move them during the course of the meal, so check each time you approach the table.

Working in food and drink service

Units 1NG4 and 2NG4, Element 1

Working relationships with other staff

You enjoy your time at work when you get on well with the people there. You do your job better.

Good working relationships require effort to develop. You have to respect the points of view of others, and be willing to sort out problems before they become serious. It helps to have a polite, good-tempered attitude to everyone, even when you're working under pressure.

Doing what's asked of you

You're in a team. The standards of service your customers get depend on the contribution of other people as well as you. Standards are highest when:

* everyone's efforts are coordinated – this is mainly the job of your managers, but they can't do it without your cooperation

* everyone knows their role and responsibilities – this depends on being given information, but also on taking notice of it.

When you start a new job, you are guided about your role and responsibilities. You have an up-to-date job description, and questions are encouraged as you settle into your job.

In a busy place, you may find yourself doing a wider range of tasks, especially when other members of the team change, or there are staff shortages. Some of these may involve more responsibility – this is a valuable way of developing your skills, getting experience and proving your readiness for promotion.

Fitting into the team

Good teamwork depends on people knowing how they contribute, and on thinking of the needs of others. Where does your work tie in with that of other people? How can you make your colleagues' jobs easier? Do you do what your manager asks of you? Do you meet your commitments to others within the agreed time?

Work as a team

All jobs in the restaurant are important and necessary for the efficient running of the business. Be friendly and respect each other's jobs.

House rules

Telephone calls – incoming personal calls will not be accepted unless of an emergency nature. You may make personal calls on the public phone during break times.

Smoking – you must not smoke except in the staff restroom.

Drinking – alcoholic drinks must not be consumed while on duty or before coming on duty.

Complimentary food and drink – you may not offer or supply complimentary drinks or food at any time.

Handbags and personal belongings – keep personal belongings in the lockers provided in the staff room. Please do not bring valuables to work. If you have to, for some reason, ask a manager to lock them in the safe.

Absence – should you fail to arrive for work you will not only burden your colleagues with extra work pressure, but the standard of service to our customers may suffer. If you are unable to attend due to sickness or other personal problems, contact your manager in person or by telephone urgently, so that alternative arrangements can be made.

Acceptable working practices

Get to know your workplace rules on timekeeping, accepting tips, dealing with complaints, etc. When you undertake a new task, check the right way to do it: by asking your manager or from workplace instructions.

Don't rely on your own sense of what is right and wrong. In a hygiene or health and safety prosecution, an employer's main defence is the procedures established to reduce risk and ensure good practice. If so, why have you not followed them? When you tell a complaining customer the drink or meal will be free, and this is against policy, you make the situation worse.

If you have a grievance

A grievance is an employment-related matter that troubles you, perhaps hours of work, overtime payments, training opportunities, promotion prospects, or holiday entitlement.

Even if you work in a very small business, your employer will have a procedure for handling grievances. This is usually set out in your employment contract or the staff handbook, stating who you should approach, and what you can do if the outcome is still not satisfactory.

3 Working in food and drink service

Your rights in a disciplinary situation

Doing or not doing something that gives your employer dissatisfaction may become a disciplinary matter when it is serious, e.g. deliberately ignoring an instruction that relates to licensing laws, health and safety or hygiene. Your action puts the business at risk, and puts in danger the well-being of all those in your workplace.

Similarly, being drunk on duty or under the influence of drugs, violent or abusive behaviour and theft are serious disciplinary matters. If your guilt is established beyond reasonable doubt, you can expect to be dismissed without notice. Your employer will have a procedure (set out in your contract of employment or the staff handbook) covering such matters.

There will also be a sequence of verbal and written warnings which follow timekeeping offences, poor standards of work, or other problems that do not justify immediate termination of your employment.

The disciplinary procedure protects your rights, and establishes what action your employer can take.

Passing on information

Your job is made easier if you know, before you take the customer's order, what the day's specials are, or if a wine is not available. In the same way, kitchen staff appreciate being told that a large party has just arrived, and asked for menus. They can warn you about any dishes that are running low.

Other examples of how you can help by passing on information are:

- telling a new colleague that a regular customer likes tea with lemon not milk

- mentioning to the manager that a variety of soft drinks is not selling, and its best-before date is near.

Handling compliments

WHITBREAD INNS

Compliments can be a great motivator and a valuable clue to improving the business.

1. If customers want to compliment you, listen to what they have to say.
2. Thank them for their support and show you are pleased to hear their comments.
3. Find out what else they feel about the operation and other areas for improvement.
4. Use the opportunity to promote other services or products. Take positive action, e.g. ask if you can book a table for them for next week.
5. Thank them for their custom.
6. Keep the compliment to yourself – but tell others!

It is not only your efforts that are being complimented. You will have had the support of many others in the team, some of whom never come into direct contact with the customers, so they rely on feedback from front line staff.

Requesting assistance

If in doubt, ask. You don't help yourself or anyone else by struggling on.

When everyone is under a lot of pressure, it may be difficult to find the opportunity to ask. But people know you are learning, and that they have a duty to help you.

Building better working relationships

There will be occasions when:

- you can help a colleague contribute more fully to the team, e.g. by being friendly and supportive

- your influence has to be directed to the whole team, e.g. saying things at staff meetings, in order to make the work easier for everyone

- you want to persuade your boss, for example, to let you try out some new napkin folds.

In deciding how to do this, do learn from the effects of other people's actions (at work and outside work) on you. In your mind, run through your friends, tutors, trainers, bosses, etc. How do they make you feel more significant, more confident, more positive – in other words, encouraged? Perhaps by:

- asking your opinion and taking your ideas seriously

- letting you take the lead

- trusting you to make decisions

- encouraging you to try new skills and ideas

- telling you what you have done well

- supporting you in front of other people.

Now try out these suggestions with colleagues.

Contributing ideas and making proposals for change

As you would like your idea listened to, think about the best occasion to explain it. Often the most effective time is during a quiet moment in the day, and your boss is in a relaxed mood.

In larger organisations, there is usually a mixture of informal and formal channels of communication. Staff meetings are a useful forum, free from pressures and distractions. Meal breaks can be a chance to share

ideas. Other opportunities may arise in a training session or during an appraisal interview. Written methods include responding to a questionnaire, putting a note in the suggestion box, or writing a memo.

Discussing ideas face-to-face may require courage. But it can provide better opportunities to explain your ideas, and to answer questions.

Prepare for the questions you might be asked. Plan your answers from the point of view of your audience. Your boss will like ideas that are going to increase sales, or reduce costs. Your colleagues may focus on the impact it will have on their jobs. Will it save them time? How will their customers benefit?

CHECK list
Handling disagreement or conflict with colleagues

✔ have the discussion when interruptions are less likely

✔ be courteous, polite, even-tempered and listen to the other person's point of view

✔ ask the other person to explain the objections, point by point

✔ go for points where you can get agreement, restate what these are, then move on to the other areas, one step at a time

✔ if your point has not been accepted, say you can understand the objection, but ... and proceed to explain your point of view

✔ make a joke, or introduce another subject to lighten the atmosphere, before returning to tackle the argument from a different angle

✔ suggest another person (who you think will see both points of view) is brought into the discussion

If your ideas and proposals are rejected

Rejection of your proposals can be a disappointment. Knowing the reasons helps, and a personal presentation will give you the chance to ask. If opinion is going against you, try to be detached. Present your responses calmly but firmly. Anger will not help. Nor will weakness, giving way without comment.

Your proposals may have to be taken to others in the company. If rejection follows, don't take this personally, or dwell on the set-back. Try to:

• understand the pressures management is under

• accept that management is paid to make decisions.

Dealing with difficulties

There are two aspects here: doing your best to play a positive and full role in the team, and doing what you can to help colleagues overcome difficulties.

Calm discussion may clear the air, and lets each person express points of view. Often the team leader or manager can provide the necessary authority.

Understanding how difficulties can arise, willingness to listen, and sensitivity are strong healing forces. It does no good to dwell on disagreements, or build up grudges.

Telling your manager about problems

Not all managers are easy to approach with a problem, and you might be afraid of wasting their time. But your manager is human. It is part of a manager's job to recognise the help that an outsider can give.

You also have to weigh up the consequences of keeping silent. Someone else may say things which are not true, or only part of the story. You don't want to lose the trust of your manager, nor leave the problem to develop to the stage where the manager can't do much to help.

When problems affect your timekeeping, concentration at work, or your relationship with your colleagues, your manager will soon notice. You need help. You are more likely to have this when your manager knows the reason is not laziness, or lack of interest in the job.

If you become aware of a work colleague's problem, think first what you can do to help as a friend or fellow team-member. Encourage the person concerned to find a solution and take action.

Using suitable methods of communication

Good teamwork and getting a clear understanding of your job role depend to a large extent on effective communications. In the sort of work you do, the spoken word will be the most used method of communication. But there may be forms and documents to complete (e.g. requisitions for new stock), food and drink orders which have to be written down and messages to leave for colleagues on duty at a different time from you.

Choosing the best methods

If you need to ask your manager for a day off to go to a friend's wedding, would you do so in the middle of a busy session, or interrupt a conversation? Almost certainly not. Instead, you might decide to write a note.

In this example, you would be choosing the timing and method of your communication to increase the prospect of a 'yes' answer. You want to avoid anything which distracts from your message. In deciding whether to speak or write to your manager, you will balance the advantages:

- speaking gives the chance to answer questions and explain further

- writing gives your manager more time to think about the reply

and the disadvantages:

- speaking carries the risk that your manager will tell you off for being late recently, an incident you do not intend to repeat and would prefer not to discuss

- a written message might not be dealt with soon enough.

Choosing the best way to communicate extends to all areas of your work. It is not helpful to mention that the fuse on the plug for the plate warmer has gone, as the manager rushes out to a meeting. A scruffy note for the person on the next shift 'Don't use the plate warmer' is not enough. Does the fuse need changing (the later shift might get maintenance to change it), or has it been overheating (which could be dangerous)?

Communicating to colleagues with special needs

Some colleagues – if not now, then in a future job – may have difficulties hearing, a speech impediment, sight problems or a combination of these. Similarly, colleagues whose first language is not the same as yours may find it hard to communicate with you. These situations require patience, and the use of some simple skills (see checklist on right and pages 12 to 14).

BMI *The Clementine Churchill Hospital*

How we care for each other
- work as a team dedicated to meet our customers' needs
- flexibility in work areas
- show respect to each other
- listen to each other
- share ideas and discuss constructive comments and ideas
- communicate at all times
- help each other where possible
- discuss internal matters with each other
- no recriminations
- compliment, when in order
- be polite, cheerful and helpful to all customers.

Respecting the confidentiality of information

Some of the information you get could cause problems if you talked about it outside work, or answered a customer's questions too helpfully. For example:

- to know the number of meals served, or the average spend, would help a competitor undermine your employer's business

- a journalist who overhears you telling friends in the pub about the environmental health officer's recent inspection (and exaggerating to make a more interesting story) could result in bad publicity.

Your legal responsibilities

The law makes it illegal to discriminate on the grounds of sex, race, marital status or disability in work-related matters. Behaviour towards a colleague could contribute towards a charge of discrimination, e.g. by unfairly picking on someone of a different ethnic group.

CHECK list
Communicating to those with special needs

✔ move away from loud noises

✔ look directly at the person

✔ speak slowly and clearly, using plain language

✔ let the person see your face – keep your hands away from your mouth and avoid standing with your back to a window or bright light

With speech difficulties

✔ avoid correcting or trying to take over what the person is saying

✔ ask questions that can be quickly answered or only require a nod of the head or other simple gesture

✔ be honest if you don't understand something

✔ repeat what you do understand, check from the person's reactions whether or not you are right

Greeting and assisting visitors

Besides customers, three main groups visit your restaurant:

- engineers to repair or service equipment and meter readers (gas and electric)

- representatives from a whole range of companies calling to sell their products and services

- officials from local authority and government departments and agencies.

If they suspect the law is being broken, the Police and Customs and Excise officers have the right to entry at any time. Environmental Health Officers, Trading Standards Officers and Fire Officers may do so at any reasonable time.

Safety, security and hygiene

When a stranger comes into the kitchen or any staff-only area, one of your first thoughts will be 'What's this person doing here?' There are:

- safety risks – e.g. the visitor gets in the way of a colleague carrying a heavy case and an accident results

- business risks – e.g. the visitor is a trickster, posing as a health inspector, with plans to blackmail your employer

- security risks – e.g. the visitor is a thief, watching for a chance to take something valuable – a bottle of spirits, a wallet left in a hanging jacket, even a valuable painting. Such things are regularly stolen because of lack of attention to security

- hygiene risks – e.g. the visitor carries bacteria into a food room on dirty outdoor clothing.

Greeting styles

You will often be the first person to greet a visitor, face-to-face or on the telephone:

- remember that you represent the restaurant, the company, etc.: the first contact with a member of staff can form a powerful impression on the visitor – when it's a good one, that helps everyone

- overcome any shyness you feel: don't hang back, hoping that someone else will help the visitor or answer the telephone

- follow any house rules

- politely greet the visitor – this has as much to do with your tone of voice and the look on your face (even if you are on the telephone) as it does with the words you use. A warm smile and 'hullo' are more effective than a long form of words said without feeling.

BMI *The Clementine Churchill Hospital*

Confidentiality of visitors

For royalty, politicians, dignataries and other VIPs, the level of security and anonymity they expect is established before admission. Where requested:

- an agreed pseudonym will be used at all times instead of the patient's real name

- no acknowledgement of the patient's presence will be made at any time unless specific authority has been given

- all visitors and telephone calls will be screened – only those which the patient has agreed to accept will be put through

- any press enquiries will be referred to the hospital director.

When answering the telephone, say who you are. You waste time if you let the caller assume you are the manager. Be accurate when giving names – know the correct pronunciation, spelling, style, etc. A lot of thought goes into the names of restaurants and businesses, because they give a message to customers.

Helping visitors (who are not customers)

The next step is to establish how you can help the visitor. Usually this means finding the right person to take the matter over. Obtain, politely, the information which will help you do this:

- name of the visitor

- company or organisation he or she represents

- reason for the visit and confirmation of who the visitor wants to see.

It helps when you are given a business card. Most representatives from suppliers will do this, while government or local authority officials, the police, engineering contractors, etc. will be happy to show their identity cards. This is a widely accepted security precaution.

Be wary when you answer questions. Do not give information which is no business of the visitor, or say things which might cause your employer difficulties. For example, someone anxious to get the contract for pest control on your premises might try to find out who currently does the work.

Knowing your workplace

If visitors don't know who can help them, or the person they want is unavailable, offer alternatives. Your manager may be the only person who can help. If he or she is absent, you might offer to take a message. But should you suggest another time for the visitor to call? Do you know when the manager will be back, and if so can you tell the visitor? These decisions, which have to be taken quite quickly, are much easier if you take an interest in what goes on around you at work, and have a good grasp of who does what.

Security systems

Some conference centres, hotels, leisure centres and other premises with restaurants have special security procedures. This is usual when catering is not your workplace's main activity (e.g. the armed forces, a commercial office such as a bank or insurance company, hospitals, schools and factories). Visitors will be required to sign in at the security officer's desk or reception, and to wear an identity badge. Your own responsibility will be clear, e.g. to call security immediately if you see someone not wearing a badge.

Security may require visitors to be met at reception by the person they are seeing, or escorted to the catering area by you or one of your colleagues. In other cases, you will have to choose a waiting area, where the visitor will be comfortable, not in the way of people who have work to do, and safe.

Some hotels and large catering firms have an office at or near a goods or staff entrance. Visitors for the catering department may have to report and sign in there, including anyone making a delivery, or engineers calling to repair or service equipment.

Routing procedures

There are usually places where visitors should not go – for safety and security reasons, or because it might give them a wrong impression. Find out where suppliers should be taken, e.g. to the office or the restaurant. Some visitors, like the environmental health officer, have a right to go to many areas, but usually they will do so with a manager or the proprietor.

Explaining delays

Visitors get a poor impression of your workplace if they are kept waiting for a long time without explanation or apology. Ask for an indication from your manager, or the person the visitor has come to see, of how long the delay might be. The visitor will appreciate being offered suitable refreshment (e.g. tea or coffee).

When, at the end of this time, the visitor is still waiting, ask for an update from your manager and pass the information on, with renewed apologies. The visitor may decide not to wait any longer, and you could find yourself acting as a go-between. Awkward situations like this, and a visitor who gets cross with a few minutes' wait, can usually be overcome by doing what you can to help.

Visitors appreciate courtesy and an explanation if they have to wait.

Dealing with aggressive visitors

Try to contain the situation while you get help from a manager or security officer:

1 Keep calm, or at least give that impression to the visitor – inwardly you might be very angry or very nervous. Becoming awkward or aggressive yourself only raises the temperature higher still. Try to control your body language so that you appear relaxed. Maintain a careful distance. Avoid prolonged eye contact.

2 Gently encourage the visitor to move away from any other people who might be disturbed or provide an audience, preferably to a room where he or she can be comfortable and from which you can phone for help. Stress that it's their comfort and convenience you are considering.

3 When the matter is related to security (e.g. a stranger you have accosted in the corridor, who probably shouldn't be in the building at all), try to get him or her to an area where other people can keep a watchful eye, or remain with the person yourself until help arrives. But don't put yourself in danger.

Dealing with emergencies

In an emergency, you have the advantage over visitors – you know what to do. Re-check your workplace procedures specifically on how you can help visitors, e.g. escorting them out of the building, helping to calm them, helping those with vision or hearing difficulties, or special mobility needs.

Special mobility needs

When a person depends on a wheelchair to get around, or uses crutches or walking sticks, what others take for granted can become obstacles. Stairs can be difficult or impossible to manage. Doors which are on a strong spring – as many fire doors are – can be very hard to deal with.

You can help by being aware of these difficulties. Some businesses which provide for those with special mobility needs get their staff to use a wheelchair and experience for themselves the journeys customers and visitors might make.

Don't make assumptions about the help the person needs: some wheelchair users do not want to be pushed. Ask if and how you can help (see page 14).

Communicating with visitors

On the occasions you found visitors difficult to deal with, what do you think went wrong? Did you misjudge some aspect of their visit, which caused problems?

Verbal and non-verbal communication

Communicating with visitors must have an element of uncertainty. You won't know the visitor as well as you know colleagues. This means you have to listen very carefully to what they say. But you can also pick up valuable clues from how they say it, their facial expressions and what they are doing with their arms and hands, or how they are standing. For example:

- someone bright red in the face might be angry – perhaps after a bad journey and thus not your fault, but you know this is not a person to keep waiting

- fidgeting with a briefcase – could indicate nervousness, in which case you can help put the person at ease.

These non-verbal forms of communication, which can be very powerful, are described as body language (see page 10).

Paging systems

Some people move around quite a lot during their job, e.g. the company's area manager. In these situations you may find yourself using a paging system:

- sending a signal to a bleep which the person carries (the unit to do this will be at reception or some other convenient place)

- broadcasting a message through the restaurant, other public and work areas over the loudspeaker system.

When using a public address (PA) system, don't shout. Keep your mouth at the right distance from the microphone and speak slowly and clearly. Ask the person concerned to contact security (or whatever), without giving more details than you need to. Some places have messages for particular situations, e.g. 'Duty manager call 9' means go to the main entrance urgently.

Special communication needs

Find out the best method of reaching an understanding with visitors who have special communication needs (see pages 12 to 14).

A combination of words and gestures may work: pointing to show a direction, nodding to indicate 'yes', shaking your head for 'no', shrugging for 'don't know', etc. If the visitor is non-English speaking, you may be able to call on a colleague who speaks the other language.

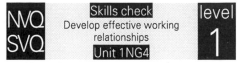

NVQ SVQ | Skills check — Develop effective working relationships — Unit 1NG4 | **level 1**

Use this to check your progress against the performance criteria.

Element 1

Create and maintain effective working relationships with other members of staff

Promptly and cooperatively action requests from colleagues	☐ PC1
Pass on information to colleagues promptly and accurately	☐ PC2
Politely request assistance when required	☐ PC3
Discuss or resolve difficulties, or report them to the appropriate person	☐ PC4
Use methods of communication and support suited to needs of colleagues	☐ PC5

Element 2

Greet and assist visitors

Promptly and courteously greet visitors and identify their needs	☐ PC1
Give visitors only disclosable information	☐ PC2
Direct or escort visitors to destinations as required	☐ PC3
Explain politely reasons for delay or unavailability of information	☐ PC4
Refer situations outside your responsibility to appropriate person	☐ PC5
Use methods of communication and support suited to needs of visitors	☐ PC6

SCOTTISH & NEWCASTLE RETAIL

QUIZ – workplace rules

1 What is the policy regarding the wearing of jewellery, cosmetics and perfume when on duty?
2 What clothing should you wear at work? Where should it be kept when you are off duty?
3 Where can you smoke on duty? What are the other rules regarding smoking?
4 What sickness must you report to your manager?
5 Why must sickness and infection be reported immediately?
6 What accidents must be reported? Where do you record these accidents?
7 What is the procedure for lost property?
8 What is the procedure for dealing with trouble?
9 Who is it an offence to serve alcohol to?

Extracts from Service for Sales, *a training package which helps the staff of Scottish & Newcastle Retail gain their NVQ/SVQ*

1 How can you help to build work relation-ships? Why should you?

TRY TO:

Thank
Explain
Apologise
Mention

BE:

Welcoming
Open
Respectful
Keen

2 How can you improve communications with a) your colleagues, b) managers, c) someone with special needs?

3 What can you do to persuade someone that an idea of yours is good?

Pros | Cons

4 How do you try to sort out a problem a) with a colleague, b) with your boss?

OK... AH-HA...

5 What can you do to help a new colleague at work? What helped you when you started this job?

They usually like...
This is how...
The Friendly Plaice Restaurant
We often get...
It's easier if...

6 List six rules you must follow at work.

Do's | Don'ts

7 Besides customers, who might visit your workplace? Who would they be coming to see?

Trading Standards
POWYS FIRE SERVICE
Herts Police HQ
MALDWYN COUNCIL
Environmental
Health Officer
Jean Vaughan

8 Say what you do when you are the first person to greet a visitor.

Smile!

9 When answering visitors' questions, what rules should you follow?

10 Describe some ways that visitors to your restaurant might be a security risk. What can you do to prevent such problems?

Charity For Us Reg.
SAFETY 'R' NOT US LTD.
No Crime Prevention Co.
The Bogus Food Guide
INSPECTOR
Vera Bogus

11 What do you do if the person the visitor has called to see is not available? If the visitor gets angry at this stage, how do you react?

I'll see what I can do ...

12 If you come across someone in a part of the restaurant where customers are not allowed, what do you do?

WINE CELLAR

NVQ SVQ
Skills check
Create and maintain effective
working relationships
Unit 2NG4
level 2

Use this to check your progress against the performance criteria.

Element 1

Establish and maintain working relationships with other members of staff

Take appropriate opportunities to discuss work-related matters with staff ☐ PC1

▲ Staff: line managers, immediate colleagues, other members of staff with related work activities

Promptly and accurately pass on essential information ☐ PC2

Maintain effective working relation-ships with individuals/teams ☐ PC3

Meet commitments to others within agreed time-scales ☐ PC4

Use methods of communication and support suited to needs of other staff ☐ PC5

Element 2

Receive and assist visitors

Greet visitors promptly and courteously ☐ PC1

Identify the nature of the visit and match visitors' needs to products, personnel or services ☐ PC2

Receive and direct visitors in accordance with procedures ☐ PC3

Describe and promote services, etc. to visitors ☐ PC4

Use suitable methods of communication and support ☐ PC5

Openly acknowledge communication difficulties and seek help ☐ PC6

Acknowledge difficulties in providing support to visitors and seek help ☐ PC7

Make complete, legible and accurate records ☐ PC8

Follow procedures for dealing with awkward/aggressive visitors ☐ PC9

Taking payment
for food and drinks

Maintaining a payment point

Where and when customers pay for their food and drinks varies. Typically the control point is a cash till:

- in self-service restaurants, customers go to the till with their selection of food and drinks

- in take-away restaurants, customers order, pay, and then collect their food from the same point at the counter. In a drive-thru' restaurant, there may be separate windows or points for ordering, paying and collecting

- in table service, the bill is presented at the end of the meal by serving staff, or the restaurant manager. The same person may use the till, or act as a sort of messenger between a cashier and the customer.

Cash tills make a record of every transaction. At its simplest this is a printout (on the till roll) of the price of food and drinks ordered by the customer, and the total the customer was asked to pay. By operating a special key, your manager can get a total for all the transactions during the session. This is used to check the amount of cash taken, and to provide information for the accounts of the business.

Security procedures

The money that customers pay belongs to the business. The amount they pay should be exactly the advertised selling price of what they have been served.

As in other aspects of security (see pages 24 to 26), you can do much to discourage dishonesty by:

- being alert to the unusual – the customer who is undecided on which credit card to offer, possibly a genuine reason, possibly because the card is stolen

- promptly reporting suspicions to your manager – the customer who, as you are handing over the change for a £20 note, says he or she meant to give you £10, could the £20 be given back, possibly a genuine muddle, possibly a ploy to confuse you

- promptly telling your manager of problems – the regular customer whose payment by credit card is not authorised, possibly a temporary problem, possibly a sign of serious financial difficulties

- reducing the opportunity for problems – keeping the cash drawer shut when not in use, locking your till when you have to leave it, following the checking procedures for accepting payment (see page 43).

Cash security

1 The contents of tills must be placed in the safe after each trading session. All safes are to be kept locked. The manager is responsible for the keys.

2 All tills must be checked at least once per day.

3 The manager is responsible for the cash in accordance with the till readings and the house float. Spot checks may be carried out at any time.

4 IOUs to customers are forbidden.

5 All personal money and/or valuables kept in the safe must be properly labelled. The company accepts no responsibility for such items.

Following workplace rules

The rules in your workplace for handling cash and taking payment are there to protect everyone. The emphasis depends on the sort of transactions you have to deal with. Typical rules include:

- when you give change for a £20 or £50 note, have a colleague watch the transaction

- for payments by card over the floor limit (e.g. £50), authorisation from the card issuing company must be obtained

- guests in a hotel restaurant who wish to put the bill on their accommodation account, must produce their room card and sign the bill.

From time to time there may be security alerts, e.g. forged notes circulating in the area, a stolen credit card being used to pay local restaurants, hotels and shops.

Some customers will tell you to ignore workplace rules. With others, you may feel you know them well enough to rely on their honesty. Don't! Customers should respect – and most will – that you have to carry out company procedures. If they insist that an exception should be made, call your manager to take over.

Tips procedure

All tips will go straight away to the supervisor's desk.

At the end of the week the money will be distributed to everybody in equal shares according to hours worked.

Do not put tips into your pocket. You could be misunderstood.

NEVER KEEP TIPS, even when given to you personally.

Pre-opening procedure

At the start of your shift, check you have sufficient change to give customers paying with £5, £10, £20 notes, etc. You need a reasonable quantity of each coin, and some £5 notes. A reserve of change, usually pre-counted in bags of particular values, e.g. £1 of 2p coins, may be kept by the manager.

You may be given a *float* (of change) which you hand back at the end of the session. Check the float is correct and, if requested, sign that you have done so.

Check that you have sufficient stocks of till rolls, credit card vouchers (for hand-operated machines), customer bills and pens (to loan to customers to write out cheques or sign credit card vouchers).

During operation

Keep an eye on the change. You should not have to ask customers for the exact amount because you've run out.

Too much cash in the till is a security risk. During busy sessions, your manager will periodically collect most of the notes, any cheques and credit card vouchers and put them in a bag with the till number or your name. The filled bags are kept in the safe and counted at the end of your shift.

Some places have a note safe bolted to the counter. A few £5, £10 and perhaps one £20 are kept in the till. All other notes are put straight into the note safe, which only the manager has the key to.

Keep coins and notes in their proper compartments in the till. This makes it easier to find the change you need, and reduces the risk of giving the wrong value coin or note by mistake. Notes and cheques should all be facing the same direction, and the same way up.

Close the cash drawer after each transaction.

Closing down

After taking out the float you started with, the total value of cash, cheques, etc. in the till, plus any that have been put in the safe during your shift, should agree with the till reading for total sales. You may be asked to count this with your manager, who will keep a record of any differences with the till reading.

Differences can arise because customers were given too much or too little change, or some orders were not rung up properly on the till. Occasional discrepancies may be accepted, repeated problems will not. If all the staff use the one cash drawer, everyone will be under suspicion.

Once emptied at the end of a session, the cash drawer is usually left open. Should someone break into the building after closing, it will be obvious that there is no cash in the till to steal.

Dealing with payments

No one likes mistakes over money. They arise from carelessness or a genuine misunderstanding. Unfortunately, customers, colleagues and your employer may suspect dishonesty.

Suspicions are less likely when each step of the transaction is clear and easy to follow.

How much customers are being asked to pay

When prices are clearly displayed (in menus, on promotion panels, on the counter), you can assume customers have the information. But if you are offering alternatives, something special (e.g. a double portion of chips), or selling a more expensive item, be careful to tell customers the price, or point to the specials board where the price is stated, or offer a menu or drinks list that gives descriptions and prices.

If you feel the customer has asked for something that will cost a lot more than he or she might expect, find some excuse to clarify what is being ordered. In doing so, you can mention the price, e.g. 'We have two very good cognacs, a VSOP which is excellent value at £3, or a 20 year old at £5'.

How the calculation was arrived at

Bills presented to customers at table are usually itemised, so that customers can check prices of individual items against what they were served, and any extras such as service charge. If customers query the service charge, perhaps because they feel the service was unsatisfactory, get your manager to take over. The customer does have the right to refuse, but it is not an easy situation to deal with.

In a take-away or self-service restaurant where receipts are not given (unless by special request), customers can watch you ring up the charge for each item on the till. If they query the total, go through the calculation for them. It may help to write down the prices and total on a piece of paper. As further reassurance, have a copy of the price list to hand.

These students use a special credit card issued by their college. A record is kept of every purchase and students are billed at the end of term. The card also doubles as an identification card for entrance to the library, etc.

What change is due

Confusion often arises (or is created) because of doubt about the value of the note handed over by the customer. To make it clear to the customer that you are not likely to be confused or mistaken:

- state the value of the note when the customer hands it to you, e.g. 'That's £20 you've given me, thank you', or 'Change for £20 coming up'

- stand the note above the cash drawer (in the clip if there is one) while you count the change

- count the change to the customer, working up from the cost of the order to the value of the note handed over, e.g. '£8.80 (the cost of the meal), £9 (as you hand over a 20p), £10 (as you hand over a £1 coin), your change for £10, thank you.'

Ideally, you should not put the customer's note in the cash drawer and close the till until you have given the change to the customer. If there is a query, the note is still in view, and the customer will find it difficult to argue that he or she gave you a higher value note.

But if you have to move away from and perhaps turn your back on the till to give change to the customer, it is unwise to leave the note out, or the cash drawer open.

Reporting errors and problems

The sooner you tell your manager of a problem or mistake involving money, the better:

- it is more difficult at the end of the day, or some days later, trying to explain why the cash in the till was short, or why a transaction went wrong. Delaying such explanations might suggest you were planning on the error going unnoticed

- if the customer complains before you have said anything to your manager, you put your manager in a difficult situation. Instead of being ready to explain why the problem occurred and put matters right, your manager gets the customer's viewpoint first. This may be to your disadvantage. Your manager will need time to investigate the problem. Meanwhile the customer is left dissatisfied.

Being polite and helpful to customers

Dealt with in your usual polite, helpful way, taking payment will form a natural part of your other exchanges with customers, greeting them, serving their order, etc. But because of people's attitudes to it, money has much potential for difficulty and ill-feeling.

To reduce the risk of customers taking offence:

- always say 'please' when asking for the money and 'thank you' when given it

- be ready to explain the bill if customers look puzzled or worried

Be careful to give customers the correct change.

- give customers who get their bill at the table, a chance to study it

- count the change into the customer's hand, on to the counter or table, or present it on a plate – whichever seems most acceptable to the customer

- give the change promptly – particularly when customers pay at the table and you have to take the money to the till. Delays suggest you are hoping to keep the change as a tip

- when checking notes for forgery, and lists of credit cards which have been stolen/withdrawn, do so discreetly. If the customer queries what or why you are checking, give a reason that can't be challenged, e.g. 'the banks have asked us to take more care'

- write the total on credit card vouchers – leaving it open (for a tip) irritates many customers

- if authorisation on a card is refused, tell the customer discreetly, if possible out of the hearing of other people in the customer's party

- when the bill is for a couple, present it to the woman if she has booked the table or ordered for both people (indications that she is entertaining the man)

- for groups of people where you do not know who the host is, or the bill is being shared, place it at the centre of the table.

Some customers like to show off with their money. Beware it is not a front, designed to distract you from taking the standard precautions, e.g. requiring a cheque guarantee card.

If customers query the amount charged or their change, do not take offence. Respect their right to do so. You may have made a mistake, or it may be the customer's poor numerical ability, poor understanding of English, or unfamiliarity with British currency.

Do not rush customers with sight difficulties. Offers to help can be appreciated, but the customer may worry that you are trying to take advantage of his or her disability. If your offer to help is accepted, give the customer a chance to check each coin and note (which can be done by feel and weight) before finally handing it over. When you return the change, identify the value of each coin and note so the person can put them away safely, e.g. notes folded in a particular way.

Forms of payment

The forms of payment you can accept reflect decisions by management on what is convenient for customers and encourage them to spend, yet minimise the risks of theft and fraud.

Cash

The main risk is from counterfeit money. Small businesses are favourite targets, because it is assumed the staff will not check for forged notes, especially if a time is chosen when they are very busy. To reduce the risk, some places refuse customers wanting to pay with £50 notes, giving an excuse such as shortage of change. Machines which expose the note to special light, make it easier to detect forgeries.

The police may be able to use forged notes as evidence in a prosecution. But the business gets no compensation and it takes a lot of sales to make up the profit on a £20 or £50 note which proves to be a forgery.

Suspected forgeries

If you suspect a note is forged (see illustration), ask the customer to wait while your manager checks properly. It may help to say that because of a forgery alert, you have instructions to get the manager every time a £20 or £50 note is presented – whether or not this is true.

The situation is not easy. You want to avoid:

- embarrassing the customer unnecessarily – he or she may not know the note is forged

- making a mistake – your suspicions may be wrong

- losing money for the business – by not acting on your suspicions.

If your manager is not near, get a colleague to call him or her, or use a telephone or the emergency bell. Wait with the customer and apologise for the delay. Keep the suspect note in your hand, in view of the customer. If you leave the customer's sight with the note, you could be accused of changing it. If you give the note back, and it is a forgery, the note and customer may disappear.

Cards

Many customers like to pay using a 'plastic' card. They don't have to carry a lot of cash and get other advantages depending on the type of card:

- *credit card*, e.g. Access and Barclaycard – all the customer's purchases can be paid for once a month with one cheque, or over a much longer time – although interest is charged and a minimum amount must be paid each month

- *charge card*, e.g. American Express or Diner's Club – gives the convenience of settling all payments once a month but with no extended credit

note feels crisp, not limp, waxy or shiny

thread embedded in paper

printing sharp, well-defined, no blurred edges

serial number (horizontally or vertically)

colours clear and distinct

watermark visible when held up to light

Watermarks
Bank of England:
The Queen
Bank of Scotland:
Sir Walter Scott
Clydesdale Bank:
sailing ships
Royal Bank of Scotland:
Lord Islay

Partially-sighted symbols on Bank of England notes

○ £5   ■ £20

◇ £10   ▲ £50

Message sequence on a PDQ swipe machine

SALE WIPE CARD	wipe card through card reader
PRINTING PLEASE WAIT	terminal will start printing the receipt and check the card is valid and not hot listed
SALE AMOUNT	enter amount, e.g. for £10.99 enter 1099 (no decimal point)
DIALLING	terminal is calling the authorisation centre
AUTHORISATION CODE XXXXX	briefly displays number
SALE TEAR OFF	tear off receipt and ask customer to sign it. Press ENTER key. Screen will prompt you to check signature and press YES

Other messages

CARD EXPIRED	ask customer to pay by some other means
CARD NOT ACCEPTED/ INVALID	as above (terminal not set up to accept this type of card)
MAX TIMES ALLOWED	as above (customer has used card up to the day's limit)
OVER TRANS CEILING	as above (amount is greater than allowed for this card type)
INVALID AMOUNT	re-enter correct amount or cancel
VOICE REFERRAL	lift handset (authorisation centre needs to speak to you)

- *debit card*, e.g. Connect or Switch – the amount is immediately taken out of the customer's bank account. Some customers prefer this. Unlike a cheque, the transaction is verified by the bank as it is made (usually automatically), so there is no need for a £50 or £100 limit. Provided there are sufficient funds in the customer's account, the transaction can be for any sum.

Customers may earn bonus points, Air Miles or similar incentives through using their card. Some credit cards earn money for charity each time they are used. These are called *affinity cards*, and those who benefit include Oxfam, the National Trust, as well as charitable organisations that the cardholder has a connection with, e.g. professional association, trade union, university or college they studied at.

When making the agreement to accept a particular card, and on a regular basis thereafter, the business has to pay the card company a fee. The business does not get the full amount paid by the customer (because of the card company's commission). Card companies are anxious for their cards to be widely accepted, and some offer incentives and marketing support to businesses.

Businesses which do a lot of card transactions have an electronic machine which reads the information recorded on the black band on the back of the card. Being linked to the card company's computer, an immediate check is made with the customer's account number. If credit is available, the transaction goes ahead.

With a manual machine, the card company will set a limit which can be accepted (typically in the range £50 to £100). Above this, authority for the transaction must be obtained by telephoning the card company.

Vouchers, tokens and meal/refreshment cards

These are a convenient way of paying in restaurants for employees of the company, students of the school or college, and similar situations. The voucher, token or card is exchanged for food and drink to the same value. Some work like a phonecard, decreasing in value with use. Some work like a credit card, charging the card holder's account for purchases.

Discount vouchers and sales incentive cards encourage customers to spend more. Handing over the voucher or producing the card gives the customer certain items free, or a reduction off the whole bill. Conditions may be set down, e.g. valid at weekends only.

Luncheon Vouchers are accepted as payment for food in some restaurants. Purchases over the value of the voucher(s) must be paid in cash. It is not in the customer's interest to purchase items less than the voucher's value, since you cannot give change. Check that the voucher has not expired.

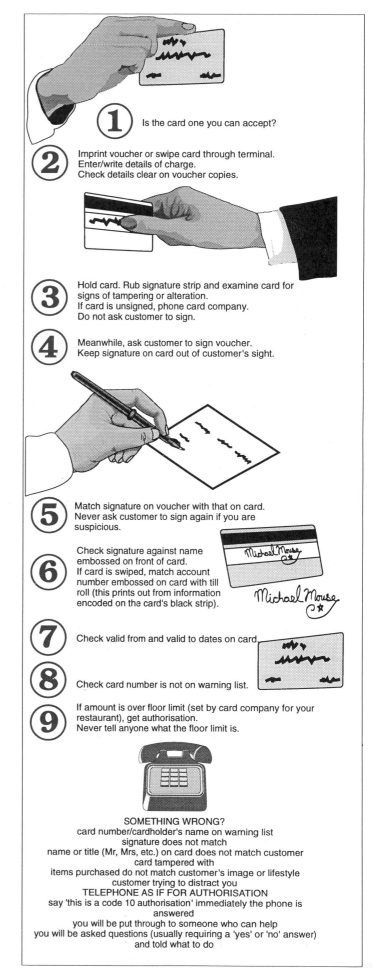

1. Is the card one you can accept?

2. Imprint voucher or swipe card through terminal.
Enter/write details of charge.
Check details clear on voucher copies.

3. Hold card. Rub signature strip and examine card for signs of tampering or alteration.
If card is unsigned, phone card company.
Do not ask customer to sign.

4. Meanwhile, ask customer to sign voucher.
Keep signature on card out of customer's sight.

5. Match signature on voucher with that on card.
Never ask customer to sign again if you are suspicious.

6. Check signature against name embossed on front of card.
If card is swiped, match account number embossed on card with till roll (this prints out from information encoded on the card's black strip).

7. Check valid from and valid to dates on card.

8. Check card number is not on warning list.

9. If amount is over floor limit (set by card company for your restaurant), get authorisation.
Never tell anyone what the floor limit is.

SOMETHING WRONG?
card number/cardholder's name on warning list
signature does not match
name or title (Mr, Mrs, etc.) on card does not match customer
card tampered with
items purchased do not match customer's image or lifestyle
customer trying to distract you
TELEPHONE AS IF FOR AUTHORISATION
say 'this is a code 10 authorisation' immediately the phone is answered
you will be put through to someone who can help
you will be asked questions (usually requiring a 'yes' or 'no' answer) and told what to do

Travellers' cheques

Restaurants patronised by high-spending tourists and business people from outside the UK will usually accept these. They are equivalent to cash, but more secure as the person using them will be refunded if they are stolen. The value will be in £ Sterling, US $ or the currency of the country that the visitor has come from. The customer is asked to sign the cheque a second time, before payment is accepted (see checklist opposite).

Cheques

For customers, cheques are easy to use and safer than carrying cash. The customer must produce a cheque guarantee card. Provided the amount is not more than the limit printed on the card (£50, sometimes £100 or £250), and conditions for use are met, the bank will honour the cheque.

A disadvantage of cheques is that the bill for food and drinks for a party of people may come to more than a £50 cheque guarantee card limit. This means asking customers to pay the balance in cash or taking a business risk, as some shops and supermarkets do. The customer is asked to produce a driver's licence, other cards, or some identification, and to write his or her address on the reverse of the cheque.

Taking payment

Some tills only add up the items sold. Others tell you what change is due. Where a limited range of dishes and drinks are sold, the till may have pre-set keys or codes which automatically enter the price of each item. Some tills record who handled the transaction, the time and date, the number of customers in the party, etc.

Another name for automated tills is EPOS or electronic point of sales systems. These may be linked to the kitchen and bar control systems, comparing the numbers of each dish and drink sold with stock issues, and producing detailed sales information.

General procedure for taking cash payment, using a till

1 Enter the price of each item that the customer has ordered, or use the pre-set key or item code.

2 When two or more of the same item are ordered, enter the price for one item, then use the multiplication key followed by the number ordered.

3 When all the items are entered, press the total. Tell the customer what this is.

4 Enter the value of the money given to you by the customer, and press the key to tell you what change is due, if any.

5 Count the change out into your hand.

6 Count the change to the customer, working up from the bill total to the amount you were given.

In self-service and take-away restaurants, payment is usually required at the time of ordering. A similar arrangement is used in some pubs and restaurants. Customers order and pay at the counter, to be given a receipt or numbered ticket, so that the food can be delivered to the right table when ready.

Presenting the bill at table

1 Fold the bill in half, so that the person paying will be the only one to see the total. Place in a bill folder, on a plate or small tray and take to the table.

2 Place the bill by the person who asked for it, the host, whoever booked the table, or took charge of the ordering of the meal. Otherwise place it in the centre of the table.

3 Leave the customer to check the details. Return when payment (cash/cheque/card) has been placed with the bill, or the customer appears to have a query.

4 Process the payment (e.g. count out the change, get the credit card vouchers signed), receipt the bill, place the receipt and change/voucher on the plate, and return this to the customer's table.

5 Do not hover as if expecting a tip. If a tip has been left, collect it after the customers have departed unless you are invited to take it earlier.

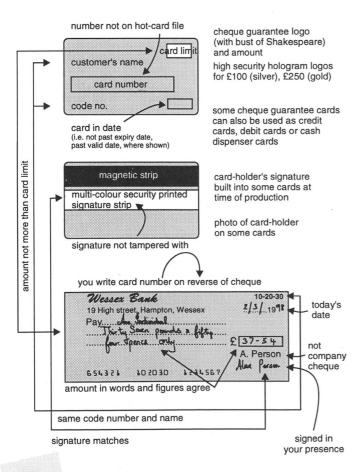

Dealing with problems

1 Remain calm, polite and respectful. If the customer questions your authority or the reason for what you are doing, say that it is an instruction from the bank, credit card company, police or your head office. If you make a mistake, apologise sincerely and do whatever is necessary to correct the problem.

2 Move difficult customers out of earshot of others. Avoid direct eye contact where this will further embarrass, intimidate or anger the customer.

3 If you have any doubt at all about your ability to deal with the situation, call your manager. Never accuse customers of wrong-doing yourself.

Here are some specific problems you might encounter and suggestions for dealing with them:

• *errors or voids* – write CANCELLED through incorrect bills and put aside for the manager. Incorrect credit card vouchers should be torn into small pieces (to reassure the customer)

• *invalid cheques, cheque cards, etc.* – explain why you cannot accept payment and suggest alternatives, e.g. 'I am afraid your cheque card has expired, Miss Cohn. Have you got the new one, or would you like to pay by credit card? We accept ...'

• *authorisation refused* – explain tactfully, e.g. 'I'm sorry, Mr Sperry, authorisation has been refused. I'm sure that if you get in touch with your credit card company they will explain. In the meantime, would you like to use another method of payment?'

• *suspected fraud* – if the card company asks you to retain the customer's card, suggest the customer contacts the company and speaks to them directly (offer a phone with some privacy). Do not give the card to the customer

• *disputed bill* – check each item carefully, where necessary referring to the original order for the table and checking with copies retained by the kitchen, dispense bar, etc.

• *customers attempt to depart without paying* – assume they have forgotten, and tactfully remind them, out of earshot of other customers

• *customer departs without paying* – inform the manager at once, giving as many details as you can remember of the customer.

There will be rules about opening the till to give change (usually discouraged), and what to do if a customer says one of the dishes was not ordered, after you have served it and rung up the amount.

Always return the customer's card.

CHECKlist
Taking payment

✔ be clear to customers what they are to pay and how the charge was arrived at

✔ be polite, say please and thank you at each step

by cash

✔ state the value of the note the customer gives you

✔ check notes for forgeries

✔ keep note outside the cash till until you have counted the change

✔ count change back to the customer

by cheque

✔ cheque details correct and customer produces a valid cheque guarantee card (see illustration)

✔ only accept one cheque per transaction

by travellers' cheque

✔ date and payee details correct

✔ customer signs cheque in your presence

✔ this signature matches other signature on cheque

✔ signature checked with passport/other identification

✔ customer given change if value of cheque higher than amount due

by card

✔ card is valid and details correct (see illustration)

✔ authorisation code imprinted/written on voucher

✔ carbon sheets from vouchers torn up in view of customer

1 What must you check when getting your payment point ready at the start of your shift?

spare till roll · pens · receipts · give-aways · stolen card list · customers bills · credit card vouchers · sufficient charge · float checked

2 What steps can be taken to reduce the loss which would occur if the till were robbed a) during service, b) after closing?

DIS IS A STICK-UP!

CANCELLED DUE TO STAFF VIGILANCE

3 What mistakes might explain why the amount of money in the till at the end of service is a) too much, b) too little?

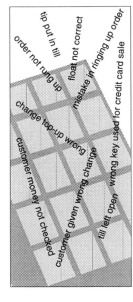

tip put in till · order not rung up · float not correct · mistake in ringing up order · order rung up twice · change too-up wrong · customer given wrong change · till left open · wrong key used for credit card sale · customer money not checked

4 What should you say to these customers? What can you do to sort out the problem?

I won't pay the service charge · I must have left my cheque card at home · My eye sight's very poor - is this a fiver? · AMOUNT DUE 32.65 · This bill is wrong. I paid cash for the drinks. · I've no money either or a credit card

5 When the meal charge is to go on a hotel guest's accommodation bill, what must you do and why?

TOTAL DUE: £960.02
Vera Bowers
Room No: 324
Express to Cashier

6 Give the main points you should check when accepting payment a) in cash, b) by cheque, c) by card.

forgery · change · £ · stolen · name · matches · Card · valid · payee · signs · date · amount · signature

Henleys Bank
Pay Minnie Moon
One hundred and
twenty five pounds
£ 125
Mickey Mouse

7 What do you do if there is a problem with what the customer has given you as payment? What special points should you consider if it is a) a forged note, b) a stolen cheque or credit card, c) you are asked to retain the card when seeking authorisation, d) the card has expired?

Keep calm
Get help
Follow instructions

Don't put yourself in danger
Avoid embarrassing customer
Try not to alert customer

8 What should you do if you a) ring up the wrong amount on the till, b) write the wrong amount on the payment voucher for a card, c) find you have got the wrong amount when counting the change back to a customer?

VOID ITEM
CREDIT CARD VOUCHER
apologise
begin again

Table and silver
service

Preparing service areas and equipment

Service goes smoothly when you are well prepared. The more that can be done in advance, the more attention you can give to customers during service.

A methodical approach works best. If checklists or work procedures are available, follow these carefully. Otherwise, make your own TO DO lists. As you get a better idea of what needs to be done, update these lists so they become really effective memory-aids.

For well-established routines, you probably won't need reminders. Avoid the temptation to cut corners. For example, most days you may not need to fill the salt pot, but if it is empty the day you don't bother checking, customers get a poor impression of standards.

Preparation activities may be organised on a rota basis, with each person doing a different set of tasks each day. Or you might work as a team, two people changing the table cloths, one putting out the knives, another the forks and so on. When team members are not available, you may have to take on extra duties.

Service areas

Everything that might be required for service is kept in the service area, where preparations can be completed, and sometimes the washing-up is done. Other small stocks of cutlery, crockery, napkins and similar items may be kept in sideboards in the room, conveniently located for re-laying tables.

Keep your preparation areas tidy, everything in its proper place, in good condition and clean. There may be a cleaning schedule which sets out when floors and walls should be washed, cupboards and shelves emptied and cleaned, etc.

MON	TUE	WED	THU	FRI	SAT
Cruets washed, dried, refilled	Clean cutlery drawers	Polish silver	Clean sideboards	Clean glass cupboard	Clean drinks fridge

OLD ORLEANS
A TASTE OF THE DEEP SOUTH

11 am checklist

1 Relishes out (corn, onion and tomato and chilli). Mustards out (French, English and American).
2 Popcorn machine assembled and first batch made.
3 Coffee machines on.
4 Hot towel machine full of 'HOT' hot towels.
5 Dessert area stocked up, desserts portioned as appropriate. Hot fudge 'hot' and ready to serve.
6 Music on at right volume. All lights working.
7 All tables set to Old Orleans standard: sugar containers clean and full (with individual portion packets); salt and pepper never less than half full; cutlery polished; table/table mats clean and fresh; never less than 15 white napkins; toothpick glass full; ashtrays and matches on every smokers' table.
8 Sideboards fully stocked.

Service equipment

When preparing what you need, inspect each item. Return any that are not clean to the wash-up area, or wash them yourself. Take out of service any that are damaged, e.g. china which has cracks or chips.

Your manager will tell you whether damaged items should be thrown away, or kept aside for the next stocktaking of equipment. There may be a scheme for recording loss through breakages.

Check that stocks are sufficient and in their proper place. Order new stocks before you run out. You may have to complete an internal order form (sometimes called a *requisition*), and have this signed by a manager. Follow safety procedures for withdrawing damaged or faulty equipment from use (see page 22).

Turn on equipment for making drinks, keeping food and equipment hot or cold in time for it to reach operating temperature. Check that refrigerators are working at the correct temperature.

Following cleaning schedules

Follow your workplace cleaning schedule or rota so that every part of equipment is kept clean. For example:

- wash tops and shelves of trolleys and hot cupboards *daily*, the wheels, door channels and shelf supports *monthly* (to prevent build-up of grease and food debris, causing hygiene and safety problems)

- keep trays clean and dry during use, put through the dishwash *daily* (to thoroughly clean and sanitise). Allow to dry before stacking.

Caring for china

Handle carefully at all times to avoid damage and accidents. Do not stack plates, saucers, cups or bowls too high. Keep the spouts of tea and coffee pots turned inwards and pointing in the same direction.

Fill dishwasher trays so that items do not vibrate against each other, rattle or turn over during the wash. Use a plastic scraper to remove food and stubborn deposits, never scouring pads, knives or abrasive powders which damage the surface.

Never heat plates over a gas flame or on an electric ring. Sudden temperature changes cause cracking.

Caring for cutlery and other silverware

Stainless steel and silver-plated items should look shiny and bright. If smears remain after washing, dip cutlery in very hot water for a few moments, then polish with a clean, dry cloth.

Caring for glassware

All glasses should be handled carefully. Dropping or knocking a glass against any hard surface may break it, or cause a crack or chip, so that the glass has to be thrown away. Sometimes the damage is not visible to the eye, but internal weaknesses lead to the glass cracking when you would not expect it to, e.g. when washing up (the change of temperature) or polishing (the extra pressure).

To reduce the stress to glasses, do not pick them up in handfuls with the fingers, overload trays or stack them one inside the other (unless they are the type made to be stacked). Glasses should never be used to scoop ice, or to store steel cutlery, even if this is only for a short time while you are drying up.

Don't subject glasses to sudden changes in temperature. Warm the glass first if you are going to fill it with a hot drink. If it has ice in, dump the ice and allow the glass to stand briefly before washing. Don't put cold drinks in glasses which are still warm from washing.

The floor should not have crumbs or debris from the previous meal.

The centre fold should run straight down the middle of the table.

The cloth should hang evenly over each side of the table.

Extra crockery and cutlery which might be needed during service should be in position.

When working as a team, agree what each person does so the tables are set in a logical order.

How tables are laid-up varies according to the style of the restaurant and the meal.

Hold cutlery, crockery and glassware by the handle, rim, stem or base.

The final result should be pleasing to the customers.

Requisitioning stock

1 Fill out the requisition book – check carbon is right way up, and between correct pages (triplicate book).
2 Before going off duty, place the book in the stores pigeon hole at reception.
3 When stores deliver (next morning), check against the requisition book.
4 When satisfied, sign the book.
5 Let the stores keep top two copies (third copy remains in book).

Condiments and accompaniments

These include:

- *seasonings* – salt and pepper, whole pepper and coarse sea salt (in mills to be freshly ground as required), cayenne pepper (e.g. with smoked salmon and trout), ground ginger (e.g. with melon)

- *sugars and sweeteners* – white and brown sugar, coffee sugar crystals, low-calorie sweeteners

- *prepared sauces and dressings* – mustards (including French, German and English), ketchup, Worcestershire sauce, vinegar, oil, mayonnaise, vinaigrette and other salad dressings

- *prepared breads* – rolls, Melba toast, bread sticks, croissants, pitta and other speciality breads.

Follow the instructions on the label for storing sauces which have been opened. Some must be kept chilled. Wipe clean the outside of the bottle and around the lip. Wash the top as necessary.

When not in use, keep sugar basins, marmalade and jams covered (with a lid or clingfilm).

Place new stock of packaged sauces and dressings, jams and marmalades so that the older stock is used first. Check the date mark. Discard products which have passed their best-before or use-by dates and tell your manager so the loss is accounted for. To reduce wastage, keep stocks of slow-moving items to the minimum.

Refuse and waste containers

Empty regularly and keep clean. Store broken glass and china in its own waste container. Otherwise wrap well in paper to prevent injury to waste handlers, and damage to plastic waste bags. Take care not to let cutlery and bones go into waste disposal machines.

If a waste disposal machine is not available, put liquid waste and waste which might ooze liquid into a solid container.

Empty ashtrays into a fire-proof container used only for this type of waste.

Preparing customer and dining areas

Approach your preparation tasks thoughtfully and in a logical order. Spend a few minutes counting on to a tray and polishing all the cutlery you need, rather than going backwards and forwards between the tables and sideboard.

Service items

Check each item is spotlessly clean before placing on the table, and not chipped or damaged.

Take special care when handling cutlery, crockery and glassware not to touch with your fingers any surface that might come into contact with food, drink or the customer's mouth.

Room layouts

Put tables and chairs in position, checking each for damage and cleanliness. Adjust the legs of any tables that wobble, or use wedges (e.g. cork from wine bottles, kept for the purpose and sliced into rings of suitable thickness).

Check with the reservations book or your manager so that you can set up tables with the right number of covers for each party booked.

Attention to detail enhances any setting, grand or modest. The arrangement of the tables, neat rows of napkins, glasses, cutlery and chairs create a pleasing symmetry.

5 Table and silver service

Table lay-ups

Follow the sequence which works best for the style of table layout. It wastes time if you have to rearrange or redo things, e.g. moving the cutlery to make room for the place mats.

1 Lay the cloth. The table top should be fully covered and between 30 cm and 45 cm of cloth hanging over each side (see illustrations). Handle the cloth as little as possible to avoid creasing or marking it.

2 Position (if used) place mats or show plates (decorative plates used in some up-market restaurants, removed once the order has been taken).

3 Lay the cutlery. Start from the inside of each setting and work outwards (e.g. table knife then fish knife on the right, table fork then fish fork on the left).

4 Place the side plate, and the side knife on the plate (if this is the style).

5 Place the napkin (see opposite page), and the glasses for water, wine or other drinks to be served with the meal. Attractive glasses boost sales by reminding customers that they might enjoy a drink with their food.

6 Position cruets, table decorations (e.g. flowers), promotional cards, etc. Table numbers should face the entrance to the restaurant.

Dishes of butter, jugs of milk and water and similar items should be kept chilled and covered, and not put on the table until just before or after the customers are seated. Jams and marmalades should not be put out in advance, unless they are in jars or containers with a lid, or in sealed, single-portion packages.

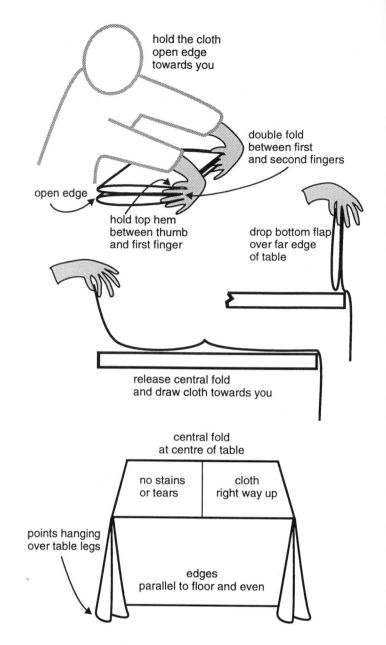

hold the cloth open edge towards you

double fold between first and second fingers

open edge

hold top hem between thumb and first finger

drop bottom flap over far edge of table

release central fold and draw cloth towards you

central fold at centre of table

no stains or tears

cloth right way up

points hanging over table legs

edges parallel to floor and even

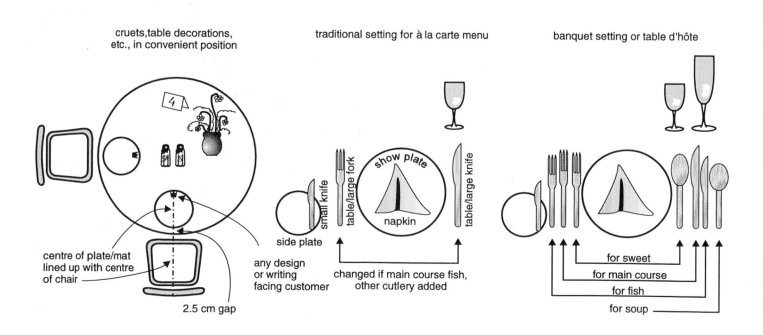

cruets, table decorations, etc., in convenient position

traditional setting for à la carte menu

banquet setting or table d'hôte

centre of plate/mat lined up with centre of chair

2.5 cm gap

side plate

any design or writing facing customer

small knife

table/large fork

show plate

napkin

table/large knife

changed if main course fish, other cutlery added

for sweet

for main course

for fish

for soup

Bar food servery set-up

- Servery cleaned daily, all dust and debris swept up and floor mopped.
- Knives and forks wrapped in white napkins and placed in centre drawer.
- Dessert spoons and dessert forks placed back-to-back in right hand drawer.
- Soup spoons placed in left hand drawer.
- Vinegar jar and bowls of ketchup, mustard and burger relish placed on small plates lined with doilys.
- Sets of cruets on top shelf.

Folding napkins

Make sure your hands and the surface you are using to fold the napkins are absolutely clean before you start.

There are many attractive ways to fold napkins. Starched linen napkins give the widest scope. With paper napkins, choose folds that do not rely on great stiffness. Experiment to see what works well and looks best for the table setting:

- the more complex the fold, the longer it takes to do
- some customers do not like folds which involve a lot of handling to make, because of the hygiene risk
- napkins can add height and colour but when the table has flowers, candles, and several glasses at each setting, a flat fold may look best.

Attractively folded napkins can add interest and style to the presentation of food and drink items, e.g. a bread roll in a rose.

Clown's hat

1 Fold napkin in half bringing bottom to top.
2 Holding centre of bottom with finger, take lower right corner and loosely roll around centre, matching corners.
3 Complete the cone.
4 Turn napkin upside down, then turn up hem all around. Turn and stand on base.

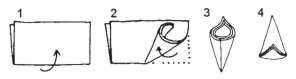

Goblet fan

1 Fold napkin in half.
2 Pleat from bottom to top.
3 Turn napkin back one-third of the way on right (folded) end and place into goblet.
4 Spread out pleats at top.

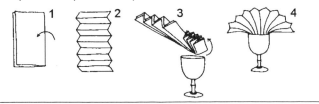

With thanks to Visa® Napery Fabrics

Menus and promotional items

To fulfil their purpose – inform customers what is available and encourage them to buy – they must be:

- up-to-date – for the correct day and meal, promoting a future event or a special offer while it is valid
- accurate – describing what is actually available and the price which will be charged
- pleasing to look at and handle – no food or grease stains, clean and undamaged.

Lay-ups for banquets and other special functions

For banquets, business lunches, weddings, cocktail parties, conferences, meetings and similar functions, the arrangements will have been agreed with the organisers in advance:

- the food and drinks to be served – from this you can work out the table lay-up
- how many people and the table plan – this may mean using tables which inter-link and banqueting chairs (designed for ease of handling and storage)
- any special table decorations and settings required, a stage for entertainment, dance floor, etc.

These details are written down on a function sheet or in the bookings book.

For large functions, form an action plan with your colleagues, deciding on which jobs can be done in pairs (e.g. laying large table cloths), and what sequence to follow for the cutlery, glassware and other items.

With long tables, position place settings carefully to give a sense of symmetry, and a pleasing overall effect. When everything is on the table, stand at one end. Are the napkins, glasses, show plates, flowers, candles, etc. in a straight line? Are the backs of chairs lined up? Do this last, as you may have moved the chairs adjusting the table settings.

Environmental systems

Customers expect a comfortable, pleasant atmosphere – not the brightly lit, well ventilated room that you might prefer for setting up. The routine, which is likely to be different for day-time and evening sessions, and vary according to the weather, may include:

- turning on decorative lights, dimming main lights
- adjusting thermostats for the central heating or air conditioning
- closing or opening and perhaps unlocking doors and windows
- turning on the music system and playing a suitable disc or tape.

Element 3

Clearing dining and service areas after service

In some hotels and restaurants, where the dining area is in regular use, clearing-up and preparation tasks are combined. All used items are removed from the table, then it is reset for the next meal.

In between use, the floors are vacuumed and light cleaning and polishing done. Once a week or thereabouts, everything is removed from the tables to allow thorough cleaning of the room and furniture.

Another approach is to clear everything from the tables after service, wipe down surfaces and stack furniture ready for cleaning.

Your job may include washing or vacuuming floors and sanitising tables, chairs, preparation and storage surfaces. Or these tasks, like the washing-up, may be done by cleaners, kitchen or food service assistants.

Clearing service equipment

Help others involved in the clearing and cleaning of equipment and yourself, by taking an organised, methodical approach:

- keep similar items together as far as possible, e.g. the table numbers back on the shelf, menus together, salt and pepper pots on their own trays, sugars on another – cleaning, replacing menus and refilling accompaniments are then much easier

- place soiled linen in different piles, one of tablecloths, another of napkins, another of service cloths – this helps sort and count them before they go to the laundry

- empty ashtrays into a fireproof container, and place apart from other washing up – for safety and hygiene reasons

- scrape off food debris, sort and throw away other rubbish before leaving items at the wash-up – reducing the risk of cutlery, paper and plastic items damaging the waste disposal machine

- put saucers and plates in their own neat piles, cups together, cutlery soaking in a bowl or sorted into the basket for the dishwasher – stacking the dishwasher trays is quicker and breakages less likely

- wipe clean bottles, jars and other containers used for accompaniments, check they are closed properly, then place those which must be kept chilled in the refrigerator – food spills on the outside of containers or trapped in lids are difficult to remove once dry, and a hygiene risk

- return bread rolls to the kitchen if they are used for another purpose, e.g. breadcrumbs, or throw away – uncovered food attracts flies and other pests.

Clearing with a tray

1 Place the tray with half on the table, and hold the tray at the opposite end with the left hand.
2 Use the right hand to clear the table.
3 When carrying large, heavy trays, hold the tray with both hands, fingers gripped firmly underneath.
4 Go through fire and swing doors sideways or backwards, so that you push the door open with your body, not the tray. Make sure first that no one is approaching from the other side.

Remember:
- put heavier items at the centre of the tray
- stack plates of the same size together
- place cutlery together on the tray
- place rubbish away from the cutlery
- clear glasses on a separate journey, if possible
- never stack cups more than two high
- never stack glasses
- never overload your tray.

Coppid Beech Hotel

Other service equipment

Turn off hot cupboards, plate warmers, hot plates, refrigerated units, drink chillers and urns when not in use. Wipe down surfaces and wash out food containers. Leave hot equipment to cool before cleaning.

Return to the kitchen, or cover and store as instructed, fruit juice, milk, desserts, cheese and other food displayed in the restaurant during service. Wipe down trolleys.

Environmental systems

Lighting, music, ventilation and air conditioning should be turned off when not required to save energy and reduce costs.

Copthorne Hotels

Cleaning standards: restaurant

All plates held by the edge and all glasses on the lower half.

All tables kept clean by wiping with a clean damp cloth and sanitiser.

All ashtrays washed *not* wiped with a cloth.

All spillages or stains wiped off all surfaces and work tops.

Floors of service areas brushed and mopped last thing at night.

All glasses washed in glass washer.

All glasses polished and replaced in correct place on glass shelves, facing downwards.

Weekly: glass shelves emptied, lining mats removed, shelves and mats washed.

Weekly: bottle shelves and fridges emptied and cleaned. Bottles wiped with damp cloth before putting them back. Ensure old stock is put in front.

Greeting customers and taking orders

A warm, friendly smile and pleasant greeting when you first meet customers will do much to help them enjoy their meal. You establish a good foundation for using all your customer care skills.

Never leave customers waiting without an explanation, an apology, and an offer to help. If:

- the person in charge of seating customers is busy, reassure the waiting customers that they will be dealt with shortly by (name the person), and apologise for the delay

- you are the only person available to greet and seat the customers, but cannot leave what you are doing, give the waiting customers a smile or other friendly gesture to show you have seen them.

If they are not greeted when they come into the restaurant, some customers will make their own way to a table. This causes difficulties if that table is reserved for another party, or hasn't been cleared yet, or is in a part of the room where the serving staff are very busy.

In restaurants where tables can be reserved

After you have greeted customers, ask if they have reserved a table. When the answer is yes, ask for the name, check with the reservations record for the size of the party, table number and any special requirements.

For customers you know by name, large parties and VIPs, you should be able to show them straight to their table without referring to the book in their presence (because you have done so before, to remind yourself of who is expected). This gives an impression of personal service, which customers appreciate.

Customers expect you to know what the dishes are on the menu and be able to answer their questions.

Customers without a reservation

When tables are or might be available, confirm the number of people. You need to do this because you may be dealing with the advance party, while others park their car or finish their drinks. But think for a moment about the customer or customers before you decide how to word your question:

- a couple who almost certainly want a table for two – 'We have a table for two by the window, or if you would prefer in the non-smoking area' (this gives the customers a chance to confirm they are on their own)

- a family arriving together is unlikely to be waiting for others – 'We have a table for 6 free, and can easily remove the extra place' (gives them the chance to say that another child or parent is on the way, and shows that you are willing to make extra effort to give the family a good table)

- a single person probably wants a table for one, but in some restaurants he or she may be asking on behalf of others waiting in the bar or outside – 'We have a nice table over there if you are dining on your own, or...' (shows that you have a table where he or she will be comfortable – not, as sometimes happens to single diners, the least popular table because it's by the door or in the middle of the room – and gives the chance to say that a bigger table is needed).

When customers have to wait for a table

If no tables are available, give an estimated waiting time. Provided this is not too long, the customers will usually welcome your suggestion that they have a drink in the bar: 'I'll bring the menu and we can take your order at the bar, if you like'.

Keep in contact with customers waiting for a table: tell them of any change to the estimated delay, see that they are offered further drinks. Never let someone else get their table first.

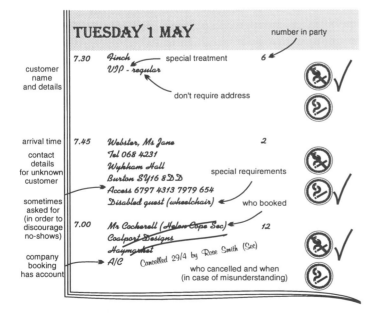

customer name and details	**TUESDAY 1 MAY**	number in party
	7.30 Finch ——— special treatment	6
	VIP - regular	
	⌐ don't require address	
arrival time	7.45 Webster, Ms Jane	2
contact details for unknown customer	Tel 068 4231	
	Wykham Hall	special requirements
	Burton SY16 8DD	
sometimes asked for (in order to discourage no-shows)	Access 6797 4313 7979 654	
	Disabled guest (wheelchair) ← who booked	
company booking has account	7.00 Mr Cockerell (Helen Cope Sec) ←	12
	Coalport Designs	
	Haymarket	
	A/C Cancelled 29/4 by Rose Smith (Sec)	
	who cancelled and when (in case of misunderstanding)	

Large parties without bookings

When a large party arrives and you need to move tables together, explain this and ask them to wait in the bar or another suitable place. Preparing their table will be quicker and easier if customers are not hovering. They get a better impression arriving at a table which is ready.

No table is available

If the wait for a table is too long for the customers, or you know you cannot accommodate them, apologise. Try to be helpful, perhaps suggesting other restaurants nearby, or offering a card so that they can book in advance for another occasion. Remember:

- some customers don't know that tables at your restaurant are always booked up well in advance – avoid speaking down to them, e.g. '*Our* customers *always* book at least four weeks ahead'

- visitors and tourists may not know it's a local festival – mention why everywhere is particularly busy so they don't go from one place to another getting more and more frustrated. Suggest a take-away, pub snack or moving on to another town

- customers may be suspicious if they see empty tables and few people around or in the bar. Give other details that will convince them, e.g. 'Sorry, but we need those tables for a conference which breaks for a late lunch at 1.30.'

If reservations are not accepted

If it is not clear, ask how many people are in the party. If a table is free take the customers to it. Otherwise, apologise and explain how long they might have to wait.

In some restaurants waiting customers have to form a queue inside the front door (or even outside as at the Hard Rock Café in London's Park Lane). When a table for two becomes free, the next couple in the queue are invited to take it, even if they are behind people waiting for a table for six.

Another system is to take the names of waiting customers and the number in the party. Later the customers can be called to their table by name. A variation on this is to give customers a numbered ticket or token, as happens at some supermarket delicatessen counters.

Customers with special needs

Help customers who have communication or mobility difficulties, e.g. by offering a braille menu, moving chairs aside for wheelchairs, bringing a high chair or cushions for children (see pages 12 to 14).

Assistance with coats and bags

Customers may appreciate help taking off their coats, especially if they are older, or the coat is a heavy one.

There may be somewhere to put customers' bags, umbrellas, etc. so they are out of the way and safe. You can direct them to the cloakroom attendant as they arrive in the restaurant, or point out the coat stand near their table. Sometimes customers will let you take the coats and bags for them. Remember what items belong to which customers.

Escorting to the table

Lead the way when you show customers to the table. You know where you are going, and by arriving first you are ready to help customers be seated, e.g. pulling chairs out for ladies and those with mobility difficulties, unfolding napkins and handing out menus.

Greeting customers at the table

If someone else is responsible for showing customers to tables, try to be at the table when the customers arrive. You can help everyone get seated comfortably.

If the customers are already seated and studying the menu by the time you arrive, welcome them, e.g. 'Good evening'. In some restaurants, staff introduce themselves by name. You might then offer drinks, or take the food order.

Banquet service

There are three main possibilities. Customers:

- make their own way to the table and place of their choice – for informal events where people want the freedom of deciding who to sit next to

- go to the table reserved for their party and choose where to sit at that table – for functions where companies book a table for their employees and partners, or groups book for their members

- find where they have been seated by the organisers or hosts of the event – for more formal events. There will be name cards at each place. Table plans at the entrance to the room and where pre-meal drinks are served help people find their way about.

At some formal events, the toastmaster or master of ceremonies announces the guest(s) of honour. Other guests are asked to stand, while the top table process into the room and take their seats.

Presenting the menu

The restaurant manager may present the menus, after showing customers to the table. You may do this. Or the menu may already be on the table. If the menu or the specials of the day are displayed on a board, tell customers this after they have taken their seats.

In some restaurants, the host is given a menu with prices, while the host's guests have un-priced menus.

When you draw customers' attention to the menu, mention any information not in the menu, e.g. what the fresh home-made soup is, or any dishes which are unavailable. This is a good time to describe dishes or special offers you have been asked to promote.

The menu
tells customers what is available

Choice of dish
organised in groups to match stage of meal
Starters • Main courses • Vegetables • Sweets
or types of dish together
Rice dishes • Grills • Specialities of the restaurant

Descriptions of dishes
encourage customers to be adventurous
explain dishes with unfamiliar names
add interest to the choice

Photographs of dishes
add impact – colour, shape, display of foods
reassure – show familiar ingredients
standardise – show consistent presentation

Prices
of individual dishes – *à la carte*
or based on the number of courses
or meal, usually with selection of dishes from each group

Set-price menus
may be extra or supplementary charge for certain dishes
e.g. smoked salmon when other starters cost less

Banquet or special event menus
usually no choice – organisers or hosts decide for guests

Two menus offered
table d'hôte menu has set price with limited choice
for two, three or sometimes as many as five or six courses
(or sometimes no choice)

à la carte menu of individually priced dishes

You should be ready to tell customers about:

- any items not available
- specialities of the day and special promotions, as briefed by your supervisor/manager/the chef
- for each dish the main ingredients and summary of how it is made
- dishes that take a long time to prepare, and those which might suit someone in a hurry
- dishes available for vegetarians (see box on page 55) and those on special diets (e.g. no dairy products) or with allergies to certain foods (e.g. nuts)
- what variations to dishes are possible, e.g. baked potato, not chips, with any main course
- price of dishes not on menu.

Taking the order

The aims are the same – whether you are using a hand-held terminal linked to a computer, a simple order pad, or relying entirely on your memory.

1 To find out what the customers require to eat and drink.

2 To pass this information on to those responsible for preparing the food and drink (computerised systems print the order out in the kitchen and dispense bar).

3 To calculate the amount which customers have to pay. If payment has been made in advance, or the meal is part of a package (e.g. hotel prices which include breakfast and/or dinner), this information helps check for discrepancies between meals served and meals paid for.

Copies of orders may also be used to:

- compare the amount of food purchased with the number of meals served
- monitor popularity of different items
- reconcile or marry up customer orders with the amount of cash taken.

In some restaurants all orders are taken by the restaurant manager or head waiter or waitress. A variation is for waiting staff to take the orders for supplementary items, e.g. sweets, cheese, coffee/tea. In some clubs the customers (members of the club) write the order down.

Order forms preprinted with dish/item names, and hand-held computer terminals are time-saving methods for taking orders. Tick or press in the code allocated to the dish. Some terminals will prompt you with selling opportunities 'Ice cream?' (with apple pie) or reminders 'How done?' (for steak).

5 Table and silver service

Customer skills when taking orders

1 If the customers are not ready to order, offer to return to the table. An enquiring pause at this stage may produce the useful response 'We'll be ready in about 5 minutes'.

2 Face the customers as they make their choice. Look at them when they speak.

3 Show respect for the customers and try to project your wish to help them enjoy their meal. This may mean a strictly upright posture and 'Thank you, ma'am', or sitting at the table with a customer dining alone, or kneeling on the floor beside a group of customers. It may mean being jovial and chatty, or quiet and respectful.

4 Decide whose order you should take first. It is usually considered polite to take women's orders before men's, and the host last. If the mode is informal, you could ask 'Who's ready to order?' Sometimes customers sort themselves out on whose turn it is to order, or one acts as the spokesperson.

5 Be patient when customers are indecisive or change their minds. Offer some suggestions, or try to gently guide them to a decision.

6 Prompt for further requirements. 'Would you like a side order of onion rings?' Done well, this will boost sales and increase customer satisfaction.

7 Don't promise what can't be delivered: 'That should be fine, but I'll just have a word with the chef.'

8 Read back the order to check you have each detail correct. Mistakes annoy customers and cause trouble with the kitchen.

FRIDAY'S
The American
Restaurant & Bar

You're a salesperson

Your most valuable tools are knowledge of products and the ability to adapt them to your guests' needs:

* memorise a repertoire of your personal favourites and suggest them to guests – *My favourite sandwich is the Deli Wrapper, fries and coleslaw*
* be visual – use your hands to describe the size of Fajita salad and 'sizzle' words liked *huge* and *fudgy* to describe an Outrageous dessert
* suggest dishes which are quickly prepared to guests with time constraints – *Why don't I put your children's orders on the ticket with your nachos so they can begin their meal right away?*
* help your guests choose by narrowing the choices – *If you're interested in seafood, the Firecracker Shrimp and the Jack Daniels Glazed Salmon are our specialities*
* use open-ended questions – *We have a house dressing, which is Italian topped with fresh grated blue cheese. We also have Thousand Island, Creamy Blue Cheese, Country Buttermilk, Italian .... Which would you prefer?*
* use suggestive selling – *I can add bacon and cheese to your baked potato for a small charge*
* don't oversell – no one enjoys a meal which they only eat half of, or leave with indigestion from eating too much.

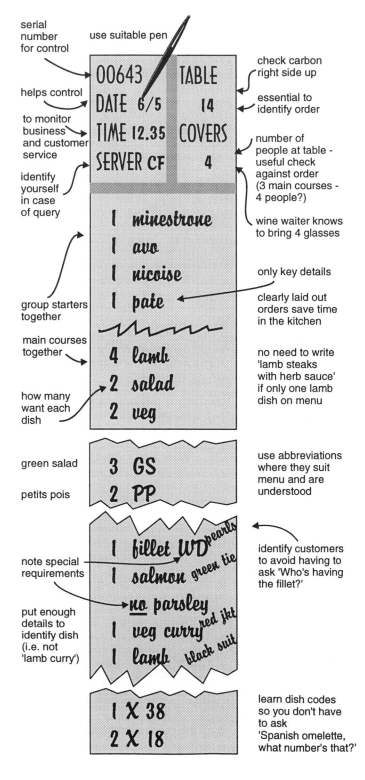

Presenting the menu

- Present the menus (open) to the ladies first, the host last.
- Explain the menu content/layout: seasonal menu, regional dishes, fixed price menu, roast trolleys, vegetable selection.

Remember:

- the guest does not know the menu, you do
- take every opportunity to sell
- check before service what the specials are and if anything is unavailable and explain these when presenting the menu.

Taking an order

- Do not leave the guest for a long time reading the menu (5 minutes is usually ample).
- Use a pink triplicate order pad and a good quality ballpoint pen. Write clearly.
- Identify each guest by clothing, never by removable items (e.g. glasses) or personal features.

More on vegetarianism

The most common reason vegetarians do not eat meat, poultry or fish is their dislike of killing for food. Religion and health are the other main reasons.

Some vegetarians will not eat any foods of animal origin, e.g. eggs, milk, cheese, honey, even though they do not involve the death of animals. Some will not wear clothes, shoes or accessories which are made from leather. Some will not eat particular vegetables (e.g. onions and garlic).

Vegetarians tend to feel that it is wasteful and/or unhealthy to eat foods which are over-refined, e.g. white flour and white rice have the major part of the protein, mineral and fibre content removed.

Some people prefer to eat *wholefoods*, i.e. as unrefined or unprocessed as possible.

Types of vegetarian

Semi-vegetarian or *demi-vegetarian* – those who eat a mainly vegetarian diet, but occasionally eat meat or fish.

Ovo-lacto-vegetarian – diet includes milk, dairy products and eggs (preferably free-range). The majority of vegetarians in the UK are of this type. Besides meat, fish and poultry, they will not eat products made from dead animals, e.g. suet, lard, gelatin and aspic (made from animal bones), animal rennet (used to produce many types of margarine and fromage frais).

Lacto-vegetarian – includes milk and milk products but excludes eggs.

Ovo-vegetarian – includes eggs, but not milk or milk products (e.g. yogurt, cheese).

Vegan – eat vegetables, fruit and other products of plants (e.g. milk, cheese and yogurt made from soya). All foods of animal origin are excluded (meat, fish, dairy products, eggs, honey, etc.).

Fruitarian or *fructarian* – diet consists of only raw fruit, nuts and berries. They usually exclude all grains and processed foods. Honey may not be acceptable.

With thanks to Mary Scott Morgan

Adjusting the place settings

If the table is set for more customers than required, remove the extra place settings. Do this quietly and with as few trips as you can. For example:

- use a small tray or the show plate if there is one
- place the side plate on the tray or plate, and the napkin on top of it
- pick up each item of cutlery one at a time, and place it on top of, or in the fold of the napkin (to deaden the noise)
- wedge the base of the glasses under the edge of the napkin.

If this will make the customers more comfortable, and not cause a lot of disturbance, remove chairs which are not required. You may also be able to rearrange the covers to give each customer more space.

Adjusting the cutlery

Once you have taken the order and passed on the details to the kitchen, return to the table with any extra cutlery customers need. At the same time remove any that will not be required.

To disturb customers as little as possible, work logically and quietly. For example:

- from your copy of the order, collect all the extra items that will be needed, e.g. fish knives and forks and steak knives
- place the cutlery on a small tray or plate lined with a folded napkin to deaden the noise (see photograph)
- proceed around the table in an anti-clockwise direction
- standing at the right of the customer, remove any cutlery from the right of the table setting that is not required, e.g. soup spoon and large knife
- place down the new cutlery on the same side of the setting, e.g. fish knife and steak knife
- move to the left of the customer, remove and replace the forks
- remove and replace the cutlery from the right of the next customer.

Serving customers' orders

What matters most to customers about the service they get in a restaurant? What do you like and dislike when you are a customer? What really impresses you? What is particularly annoying?

Most people put polite, friendly, helpful and attentive service in No. 1 position. Next might come the speed of service – no one likes to be kept waiting, or to get the next course before they have finished the earlier one. In third position might be the skills with which the food is served – serving spoons handled well, food placed on the plate attractively, etc.

Order to serve customers in

For formal occasions including banquets you will be given the rules. Etiquette is one consideration, the smooth running of service the other.

The traditional approach is to serve women before men, the hostess before the men and the host last. When the host is a woman, she might wish her male guests to be served before her.

In informal situations, there is greater flexibility. As children tend to be impatient, serving them first usually pleases the parents.

If a party of men and women seem to be treating each other as equals and there is no obvious host, serve in whatever order comes naturally and is most efficient, e.g. clockwise.

Side to serve customers from

Follow your workplace rules (see illustration for general guidelines). In some restaurants it is acceptable to serve everything from one position – standing at the end of the table, or wherever is most convenient to customers. Try to avoid:

- stretching across or in front of customers
- standing between customers who are deep in conversation
- surprising customers – there could be an accident if the customer suddenly turns in the direction you approach from.

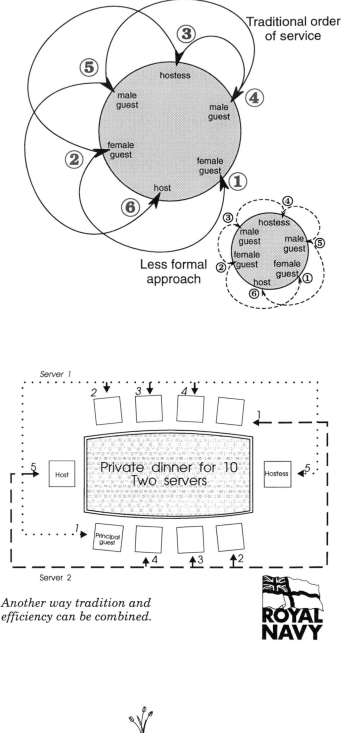

Traditional order of service

Less formal approach

Another way tradition and efficiency can be combined.

ROYAL NAVY

SERVE

FOOD from left - less likely to find glasses in the way, or customer's hand reaching for a glass

DRINKS from right - since most customers use right hand to hold the cup or glass

Adjusting the table items

Before you take the food to the table, check that each customer has the right cutlery. Even if you have done this after taking the order, customers do sometimes use the wrong cutlery, e.g. the large knife and fork for the fish, or the dessert spoon for the soup.

In some restaurants, the cutlery for any courses which follow the main course (e.g. sorbet, dessert, cheese, fruit, savoury, coffee) is put down just before that course is served. If it is a teaspoon or small knife, this can be put on the sideplate or saucer and the two put down together.

When customers are smoking at the table, change the ashtray frequently:

- place a clean ashtray upside down over the used one – this looks nicer and stops ash flying everywhere

- remove both from the table

- return the clean ashtray to the table

- place the used ashtray on your tray or sideboard to be emptied safely.

Condiments

These are spices and sauces which customers may like to flavour their food with. Some form part of the table setting (salt and pepper usually do). Some are offered with particular dishes (e.g. mustard with steak, the pepper mill with all main courses). If customers make an unusual request (e.g. pepper with strawberries), oblige without any argument!

Remove condiments from the table when customers no longer require them. Traditionally, the salt and pepper is removed at the time the main course plates are cleared, unless a cheese or savoury course follows.

Accompaniments

These are offered because they:

- improve the flavour of the food, e.g. ground ginger with melon

- provide contrast of texture, e.g. toast with pâté

- counteract the richness of the food, e.g. apple sauce with pork

- are traditional, e.g. gravy with roast meat.

You may be responsible for preparing some, like freshly-made English mustard, hot toast, buttered brown bread. Others you may collect from the kitchen (with the food), the service area, or your sideboard.

To improve presentation and cut risks of spills, sauceboats are usually placed on a small salver or plate, perhaps with a dish paper (for savoury items) or doily (for sweet items).

Guest service

The manager will meet guests and escort them to the table. Watch your tables and approach as guest is seated.

If for any reason you are unable to go directly to the table acknowledge the guest with a smile and *I'll be right with you* or similar.

If the manager is unable to be at the door, approach the waiting guests, wish them good morning and having enquired how many are in the party, escort them to a suitable table.

There are regular guests who prefer a particular table. The guest history index will remind you of these guests.

Ladies should be seated first and all guests should be assisted with their seating.

Unfolding napkins

Unfold napkins for all guests: lift napkin from right, open and place over guest's lap from left.

At breakfast

Explain the service system that is in operation. Invite guests to help themselves from the buffet. The guests may prefer you to collect all items for them – never refuse.

Ask if guests would prefer white or brown toast, and if they would prefer it straight away or with their cooked breakfast.

Clear all breakfast dishes, toast racks, etc. as guests finish with them. Do not wait for the whole table to finish. Clear from the right, using a silver salver with napkin liner.

Every time a guest gets up from the table (e.g. to go to the buffet), fold their napkin into a triangle shape and place to the side of their side plate. If the napkin has fallen to the floor, replace it with a fresh one.

Taking the order

Number the guests as seated going clockwise around the table. At the bottom of the order sheet make a clear note of which guest is number 1, e.g. *lady in blue = No 1*.

On small tables, identify guests by letters, e.g. G for gentleman, L for lady, YG for young gentleman.

Serving the food

Customers expect their food and drinks to be served in a certain order. This order combines tradition and the way in which the palate reacts to different flavours and textures. At breakfast, for example, fruit juice at the beginning of the meal sharpens the palate. Drunk after a strong beverage like coffee, the juice tastes unpleasant.

Menus are built around the accepted order of dishes, moving from the light and delicate to the more substantial. The dessert or sweet course will be designed to finish off the meal. But because customers' appetite will depend on what they have eaten, the sweet order is not taken until the preceding course has been eaten. With set menus that offer no choice, careful planning will take account of likely preferences.

As in so many other aspects of food and drink service, tradition and tastes are changing. This is partly the influence of visitors to Britain. Many Americans like to drink coffee throughout their meals, and insist on iced water. The French take cheese before their dessert.

Quality service

Customers want food which is:

- well presented – appetising and pleasing to look at

- at the right temperature – e.g. ice-cream not melting, hot soup not warm or cold, cold meat not warm, toast warm not cold

- safe to eat – your fingers not in contact with food or those parts of service dishes and crockery which come into contact with food.

Much depends on good timing. The general rules are:

- serve drinks before food – many customers enjoy a drink while they are waiting for the food, and with their food. The wine for a particular course should be served immediately before or after the food

- collect the food when it is needed – too soon and hot food becomes cold, while cold food gets warm. It is a hygiene risk to have food waiting at the wrong temperature

- collect plates before or with the food – otherwise the food has to wait around

- collect and serve cold food before hot food – cold food will be unaffected by a short wait, but hot food quickly drops in temperature

- serve the main item of any course first – meat or fish before vegetables. This gives a better presentation. Rice is sometimes served before the meat

- pick up dropped items as soon as you can – but avoid unnecessary interruption to the service. Don't leave cutlery which has been retrieved from the floor where it might be mistaken for clean items.

Keep fingers well clear of the food. Warn customers of very hot plates.

In some restaurants, the chef may present a special dish (paella in the photo).

Where many hundreds of customers have to be served in a short time, different service techniques have been developed.

Offering ground pepper from a large pepper mill provides a personal touch to the service.

Attractive trolley displays boost sales of desserts (and cheese).

Whatever the surroundings, customers appreciate friendly, efficient service.

Removing the silver domes (called cloches) at the same time when there are two or more customers, adds a touch of theatre to the meal.

Seating of top table?
Toasts?
Speeches?
Dancing?
Entertainment?

The Lord Mayor's Banquet

Whittington Room

What drinks?
When offered?
Who pays?
Any limits?

Where is your station?
What are you serving?
How many?
Silver or plate service?
Order of service?
Signals to serve and clear?

WINES   MENU

What each dish is?
What accompaniments?
Alternative for special diets?

Serving cheese

You may be responsible for preparing the cheese board, as well as its service.

1 Bring out cheese from refrigerator about one hour before use.

2 Arrange the cheeses so that there is a variety of shapes, colours and flavours. Decorate with celery, grapes, apples, radishes, etc., but don't swamp the cheese.

3 Use a large surface so each cheese can keep its flavour and crumbs apart from the other.

4 Use a separate knife for blue cheeses. (Some restaurants provide a different knife for each cheese.) A fork will be useful to help pick up cheeses.

5 When cutting a whole cheese, a horizontal slice should be taken, leaving the top surface as even as possible. Scooping is wasteful.

6 Wedges should be cut lengthways from nose to crust. Never cut across the nose of a wedge.

7 Remove pieces of cheese that have become so small they look unappealing.

8 Provide the customer with a clean side plate, side knife (and sometimes fork) and a fresh dish of butter. Cruets should be available. Biscuits, bread, celery, radishes and fruit may be offered or left on the table.

The cheeseboard can be heavy, and some cheeses are hard to cut. Rest the edge of the board on the table to get firm support.

Element 3

Maintaining dining and service areas

Keeping tables cleared and the room looking tidy gives customers a good impression. But sometimes it is difficult to balance priorities. Do you serve some customers who have just arrived, or clear tables?

Make the most of each journey to or from the service area. It takes only a few moments to clear some things from the table you are at, or an adjacent one, before you go off to collect the next part of the order.

Clear as quietly as possible. Handle the cutlery gently but firmly. Do not bang plates when scraping or piling them, even if there are no customers in the room.

Clearing during the meal

Customers do not want to feel hurried (although all appreciate prompt service). Leave a slight pause after everyone at the table has finished that course.

Sometimes it is better to clear the plates as customers finish, for example. Observe what is going on. Remove a plate which has been pushed aside, or is being hit noisily by a child.

Clear quietly yet efficiently. To take not more than two plates at a time, and stack them on the sideboard or out of the room, is the quietest method. It is often more practical to stack them in your hand, as you move around the table (see illustration overleaf), or to use a tray.

Plates are normally removed with the right hand, from the right hand side of the customer. Glasses, cups and saucers are also removed from the right.

Clear tables as soon as possible after customers have left..

Brush the crumbs off so the customers have a clean table for the next course.

Stacking plates as you clear

With practice, you can stack plates as you clear them from the table (see illustration). For most people eight main course plates is the maximum that can be managed at one time, three or four if bones or unwanted food have been left.

For clearing side plates (e.g. after the cheese course) it may help to take a clean dinner plate to the table. Use this as the first plate, to stack cutlery and collect debris.

For soup plates with liners, collect two plates at a time and take them to the sideboard for stacking. Clearing more than this is difficult and noisy, as you have to keep rearranging the piles of liners, bowls and cutlery.

Crumbing down

This is done in the more traditional forms of food service. After clearing the main course, use a folded napkin to brush the crumbs from the table surface on to a plate. Some restaurants use a brush instead of a napkin, or even a special table crumber (like a hand-held mechanical carpet sweeper).

Once customers have left the table

Use a tray, unless there are only a few items to remove. Remove napkins, extinguish candles (take care that hot wax does not drip over you or the table linen). Wipe any spills. Leave cloth-covered tables covered. Replace the cloth with a clean one before the table is reused (see page 48).

All cutlery and crockery left on the table should be collected for washing (even if unused). Do the same for linen napkins. As these may have been touched during the course of the meal, this avoids a hygiene problem.

Before returning condiments and accompaniments to storage, check their condition. Customers may have used the sugar spoon to stir their drink, then returned it to the bowl.

Keep rubbish aside from items which are reused. Do not allow the contents of ashtrays to fall into food.

Spillages and breakages

For the comfort of customers and reasons of safety, clear these up as soon as possible, taking great care.

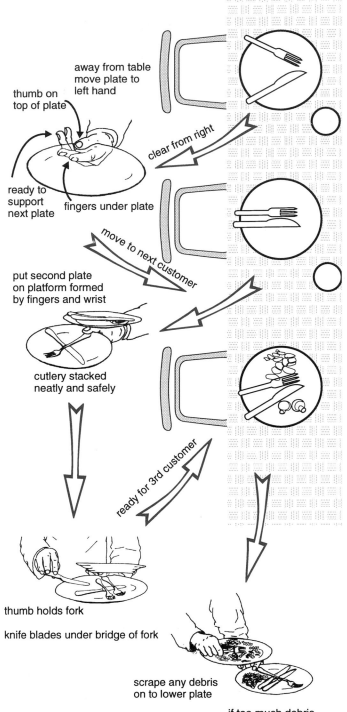

away from table move plate to left hand

thumb on top of plate

clear from right

ready to support next plate

fingers under plate

move to next customer

put second plate on platform formed by fingers and wrist

cutlery stacked neatly and safely

ready for 3rd customer

thumb holds fork

knife blades under bridge of fork

scrape any debris on to lower plate

if too much debris, don't attempt to clear more plates on this trip

Providing silver service food

Here your technical skills come into their own. Silver service done well adds great style to the occasion. Your customers can enjoy the ceremony of transferring the beautifully presented food from service dish to plate.

Service operations

In silver service, you transfer the food from the serving dish to the customer's plate using a serving spoon and table fork, sometimes a spoon only or two forks.

Restaurant silver service

In the restaurant, the serving dish is taken to the customer. The customer's plate is on the table, in front of the customer, and you hold the serving dish nearby.

In a variation of this, sometimes called guéridon service, a trolley is positioned by the customer's table, where the serving dish is also placed. This gives you two hands free to hold the spoon and fork.

Sometimes the serving dish is presented to the customer then placed on the sideboard, perhaps on a dish warmer, and the food served on to the plate there.

Banquet silver service

In banqueting you could be serving 10 or 12 from the same dish. You must move quickly from one person to another so the food is served as hot as possible.

Buffet and carvery silver service

In buffets and carveries (see Section 6), customers come to the food. If it is quite a long buffet arrangement, the customer holds the plate and moves down the table, choosing dishes which you serve. Usually you have two hands free to hold the serving spoon and fork or more appropriate equipment.

Presentation of food for silver service

With skill, careful arrangements of food created in the kitchen will look as impressive after you have transferred the food to the customer's plate.

Portioning

Be clear before you start serving what the portion size is per customer. This may be:

- common sense, e.g. when there are 3 pieces of stuffed courgette for 3 customers

palm of your hand outstretched

large dishes resting on wrist and lower arm

neatly folded serving cloth to protect from heat of dish and stop dish sliding

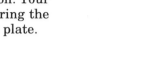

curve of fork in bowl of spoon comfortably balanced in hand

finger acts as lever to open

apply pressure to open

bring dish to customer's plate

approach on left of customer

tilt dish so sauce or gravy collects and can be served

close to plate just over rim

ask if the customer would like the sauce or gravy over the meat or to one side

sauce boat near customer's plate

pouring side facing plate

- clear from the arrangement and/or decoration of the food on the dish, e.g. meat grouped in layers of 3 slices, each with a garnish

- a matter of judgement (and practice, e.g. with dried peas): a dish of peas and 4 customers to serve.

You shouldn't have to decrease the serving size as you move around the table.

Silver service skills

The sequence of service is:

1. collect plates (hot for hot food, cold for cold food) and assemble on the sideboard, or take direct to the table

2. position a plate in front of each customer

3. collect and serve the food.

For a small party of customers, you may be able to bring everything from the kitchen in one journey: plates, serving dishes of food, sauces, etc. Hotplates are useful for keeping serving dishes of hot food warm while you position the plates.

If using a trolley or guéridon, put the plates in front of customers after you have served each plate of food.

5 Table and silver service

Posture

This assumes you are serving from the left.

Stand slightly behind and to the left of the customer to be served, back straight, feet together, serving dish just above waist level.

Step forward with your left foot, into the space between the customers. As you do this:

- lower the serving dish between the customers
- bend forward so that the dish just overlaps the edge of the customer's plate
- keep the serving dish at a height of 2 to 3 cm above the level of the customer's plate
- keep the serving dish horizontal (but tilt slightly when there is gravy or a sauce to serve).

Depending on how tall you are, you may need to bend your back to get the serving dish to the right height. Some people prefer to bend at the knees, keeping the back straight.

When you have served the food:

- rise as you gently pull back out from between the customers
- lift the serving dish out between the customers' shoulders (not over their heads)
- shift the weight of your body on to your right foot
- withdraw your left foot and the serving dish into the aisle space, keeping the spoon and fork over the dish to avoid drips.

Placing the plates

1 Hold the pile of plates resting on the palm of the left hand, which should be covered with one end of a serving cloth, the cloth wrapped around and over the top of the pile.

2 As you approach the customer, pick up the plate by the rim (see illustration).

3 Keep the plate horizontal.

4 Lean forward slightly and gently slide the plate on to the centre of the place setting in front of the customer.

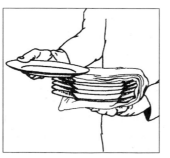

Placing clean plates in front of customers. Note how the thumb is kept well clear of the centre of the plate, from which food will be eaten.

Presenting the food

At the sidetable, remove the dish cover (if there is one). Lift carefully, tilting the cover as you do so. Any condensation will be caught in the lid, not drip on to the tablecloth or the food.

Present the serving dish to the customers before any is served. Everyone at the table can admire the dish in its entirety.

Order of service

Serve the main item first. This would be the meat, fish or vegetarian special in the main course, followed by the potatoes and other vegetables.

Service equipment

Have a neatly folded service cloth underneath the serving dish. The cloth prevents the serving dish from slipping. For a hot dish it provides protection against the heat. For a large dish, the cloth should be folded so it lies up the lower portion of your arm, where the dish will be resting.

If the serving dish is of a shape or size which makes it difficult to carry, place it on a larger, flat serving dish, preferably lined with a doily or dish paper.

Use a clean serving spoon and fork (or equivalent) for each dish you take to the table. When you are serving two or more vegetables from the same serving dish, you may need extra serving equipment to avoid spoiling the appearance and flavour of the different items.

For practical reasons, soup is usually served at the trolley or sidetable. This avoids having to carry a heavy tureen around the table. When the soup plate is resting on a liner, it can be carried more easily, with less danger of your finger coming into contact with the soup.

Using a serving spoon and fork

The curve of the fork should lie in the bowl of the spoon (see illustration on previous page).

Hold the two together so that the palm of the hand and all the fingers are over both handles. Make sure that both are comfortably balanced.

Insert the first finger midway between the spoon and fork handles. This acts as a lever so that the fork prongs and spoon bowl can be opened and closed to hold the items securely.

To serve a stuffed tomato, or a similar shaped, rather delicate food, you may find it easier to turn the fork the other way around, so that it curves around the food.

The curve of the fork lies in the bowl of the spoon. The first finger acts as a lever, to help open and close the spoon and fork.

For some foods it is better to hold the fork with the curve outwards.

Positioning the food on the plate

Place the principal item (e.g meat or fish) lower centre on the customer's plate, with vegetables top left and potatoes top right. Gravy, sauce and/or accompaniments go at the top right-hand side.

When serving dishes with a pastry crust, portion the pastry, place to one side, spoon the filling on to the plate, then add the portion of crust.

Although it should not happen, if you find a portion of food (e.g. fillets of fish) too large to lift elegantly with a spoon and fork, you may find it easier first to cut the food across the middle with the spoon. Never drag the food off the serving dish on to the plate.

Place portions of sweet or savoury flans which are triangular in shape with the point towards the customer. The bones of cutlets and chops should point away from the customer.

For sauce, gravy or cream, ask whether the customer would like it beside or poured over the food.

Silver service from the buffet or carvery

In this form of service, the emphasis is on:

- providing a personal service, with the chance to explain the various dishes available, and serve the customer's choice expertly

- assisting with portion control, since most customers will accept what you give them as the right amount. Left to serve themselves, they might have several slices of smoked salmon, for example

- helping to keep the presentation of the dishes looking attractive.

Whether you hold the spoon and fork in one hand, just a spoon, or use some other cutlery such as a gâteau slice, will depend on the food you are serving. Choose whatever will hold the food most effectively and that you feel comfortable using.

St John's College Fellows' Dinner

1 Soup/starter served. Soups are dished up at the hotplate, other starters silver served or plated.

2 Wine served. Draught beer and Guinness are available as alternatives. Collect from the buttery bar at about 7.25 p.m. Some Fellows drink only white wine, fruit juice or mineral water, and are served from the buttery bar supply when other Fellows have red wine.

3 Bread offered. Toast is placed on the tables beforehand.

4 Soup/starter cleared.

5 Vegetable dishes placed on table.

6 Main course silver served.

7 Second round of wine/beer served.

8 Main course cleared.

9 Sweet served. Usual choice is between specified sweet/ savoury, fruit pie (dished up at hotplate), or cheese (choice of cheese board or Stilton), or fresh fruit.

10 Sweet cleared.

Between steps 5 and 7, the Butler clears away the sherry from the Green Room and lights the candles ready for coffee service. Coffee is set out between steps 8 and 9.

Element 2

Clearing finished courses (in silver service)

The procedures are the same as other forms of table service (see pages 59 to 60). As silver service tends to be used in more formal situations, follow rules carefully on which side you clear plates (usually from the customer's right).

1 What types of waste are there? What is done with each? What hygiene and safety points should you remember?

2 Why do you check service equipment? What do you look for?

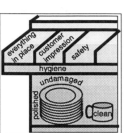

3 Describe your preparation routine. When should each task be done?

4 If you run out of stock of equipment during service what might have gone wrong? How do you avoid this happening?

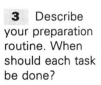

5 Where is each service item kept? How does this help efficient service?

6 What cutlery is required for the dishes served in your restaurant?

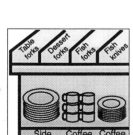

7 Comment on the sort of menu and type of service each of these table lay-ups would be appropriate for. Identify the items.

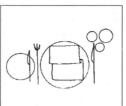

8 Identify each of these items and name a dish it would be used for.

9 Identify as many of these items as you can. Comment on the table lay-up.

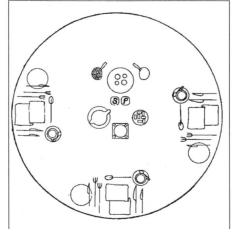

10 Identify each of these items, and what they are used for.

11 If the decision were yours, what napkin fold would you use for a) breakfast, b) private celebration dinner, c) banquet for 250. Why? Name the folds shown.

12 How do you avoid this sort of accident?

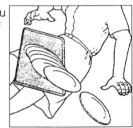

13 What is done to ensure the room is comfortable for customers during service? What happens at the end of service?

Cool not hot
Odour free
Music not loud
Fresh not stuffy
Optimum lighting
Relaxing
Turn off

14 What equipment should be turned on for service only? What should be on all the time?

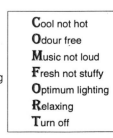

Illustrations with thanks to Coppid Beech Hotel (questions 7 and 9) and Lockhart Catering Equipment (question 8)

NVQ SVQ

Skills check
Prepare and clear areas
for table/tray service
Unit 1NC1

level 1

Element 1

Prepare service areas and equipment[†]

Get service areas ready for use, hygienic, clean, free from damage	☐ PC1
Get service equipment ready for use, correctly located, clean, undamaged	☐ PC2

⚠ Hot/cold beverage containers, refrigerated units, heated units, service utensils, trolleys

Get service items ready for use, sufficient stock, clean, undamaged	☐ PC3

⚠ Trays, crockery, cutlery, ashtrays, disposable table coverings & napkins, linen, decorative items, promotional items, menus

Prepare and store condiments and accompaniments ready for use	☐ PC4
Get refuse and waste food containers ready for use, clean, hygienic	☐ PC5
Deal with unexpected situations effectively & inform appropriate people	☐ PC6
Do your work in an organised, efficient and safe manner	☐ PC7

Element 2

Prepare customer dining areas[†]

Check dining area is ready for use, clean, furniture positioned	☐ PC1
Check service items located ready for use, clean, undamaged	☐ PC2
Lay up tables/trays	PC3 ☐
Check menus/promotional items	PC4 ☐
Deal with unexpected situations, etc	PC5 ☐
Work in organised manner, etc	PC6 ☐

Element 3

Clean dining & service areas after service

Gather or store service items for cleaning	☐ PC1
Prepare used and soiled linen for laundry, dispose disposables	☐ PC2
Store/dispose of food items, condiments, accompaniments, as required	☐ PC3
Dispose of rubbish/waste food	PC4 ☐
Clean, store, turn off equipment	PC5 ☐
Clean dining furniture for use	PC6 ☐
Leave dining/service areas tidy ready for cleaning	☐ PC7
Deal with unexpected situations, etc	PC8 ☐
Work in organised manner, etc	PC9 ☐

[†] for table/tray service

NVQ SVQ

Skills check
Prepare and clear areas
for table service
Unit 2NC1

level 2

Element 1

Prepare service areas and equipment for table service

Get service areas ready for use, hygienic, clean, free from damage	☐ PC1

⚠ Restaurant table service, banquet service

Get service equipment ready for use, correctly located, clean, undamaged	☐ PC2

⚠ Service cutlery/silverware, glassware, service dishes/flats, hot plates/plate warmers, refrigerated units, hot/cold beverage service containers, trays/trolleys, sideboards/sidetables

Store linen, table items and menus, sufficient stock, ready for use	☐ PC3
Prepare and store condiments and accompaniments ready for use	☐ PC4

⚠ Dry seasonings/flavourings, mustards and sauces/salad dressings, prepared bread items

Get refuse and waste food containers ready for use, clean, hygienic	☐ PC5
Deal with unexpected situations effectively & inform appropriate people	☐ PC6
Prioritise and do your work in an organised, efficient and safe manner	☐ PC7

Element 2

Prepare customer and dining areas for table service

Check dining furniture, linen and table items clean, undamaged	☐ PC1

⚠ Table items: crockery, cutlery and silverware, ashtrays, menus or menu holders, table decorations, condiments and accompaniments, napkins and table coverings

Position restaurant furniture for service	☐ PC2
Lay tables correctly for à la carte, table d'hôte, buffet	☐ PC3
Check menus are ready, information accurate	☐ PC4
Get condiments ready for use, clean and full	☐ PC5
Set/check environmental systems	☐ PC6

⚠ Heating, ventilation/air conditioning, lighting, music

Deal with unexpected situations effectively & inform appropriate people	☐ PC7
Prioritise and do your work in an organised, efficient and safe manner	☐ PC8

Element 3

Clean dining and service areas after table service

Assemble table items used in service areas for cleaning/storage	☐ PC1

⚠ Table items (see Element 2) in customer dining areas, sideboards, sidetables, trolleys, service preparation areas

Prepare table and service linen for laundry, or clean down and store	☐ PC2
Store food items and accompaniments for future use	☐ PC3
Dispose of rubbish and waste food	☐ PC4
Clean, store, turn off service equipment	☐ PC5

⚠ Hot plates/plate warmers, refrigerated units, hot/cold beverage service containers, trays/trolleys, sideboards, side tables

Leave dining and service areas tidy, ready for cleaning	☐ PC6
Turn off/set environmental systems	☐ PC7
Deal with unexpected situations effectively & inform appropriate people	☐ PC8
Prioritise and do your work in an organised, efficient and safe manner	☐ PC9

Customer service quiz

What can you say to a customer instead of:

- I don't know
- I'm new here
- I've just come on duty
- I'm not sure I can help you
- We haven't got it
- I don't think I can do that
- There's nothing I can do about it – it's head office policy
- We have a problem

1 What can you do to give customers a good impression of your workplace?

2 What questions might customers ask you about the menu? Why must you give accurate answers?

Well, I never knew that plaice **had** goujons!

3 Select 3 dishes which you might need to describe to a customer. Run through what you would say about each.

No, neither come from Kiev. The chicken's from Norfolk and the garlic comes from our own kitchen garden.

4 How can you tell that a customer is ready to order?

5 What should you remember when writing the order? Why is it important to remember what each customer ordered?

TABLE No. 1   COUVERTS   4
Bow Tie
Leeks + Potato   Swordfish
Soup
Silk
Grilled Tuna   Spiced
+   Cabbage
Avocado
Host   Grilled
Wild   Sirloin
Mushrooms   Rare
Pearls
Grilled   Chicken
Italian
Vegetables
DATE...........   INITIALS...........
    3 | 21

6 What do you need to adjust the table setting for the order in question 5? How do you do this?

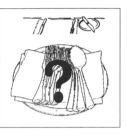

7 When carrying what the customers need to the table, what should you consider?

hygiene

presentation

noise   hot plates!

women first?
    side of service

timing

disturbance

safety

speed of service

8 If the order includes hot and cold food, which do you serve first? Why?

9 Give the rules for safe use of trays.

10 What side do you a) serve from, b) clear from? When would you do this differently?

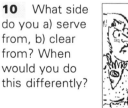

11 Mark on these items the side which should be nearer the customer.

12 Describe the procedure for clearing between and after courses.

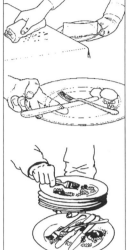

13 Comment on what is shown in these illustrations.

14 During service, what can you do to keep the dining and service area tidy? Why is this important?

I suppose I _could_ clear Susan's table, but...

15 When should you ask customers if they are satisfied/ enjoying their food?

Garçon!

16 What are the special requirements of these customers?

single diner
woman alone
business lunch
couple celebrating
tourist: no English
boisterous group
non-smoker
drunk

17 What occasions can be used to promote food and drink sales? For each, give an example of how you might do this.

Element 1

Greet customers and take orders

Greet and attend to customers
politely, helpfully, promptly ☐ PC1

Provide customers with appropriate
dining area, and assist as necessary ☐ PC2

Give accurate information to meet
customer needs ☐ PC3

△ Dishes available, dish composition, prices,
special offers and promotions

Accurately identify, record and
process customers' orders ☐ PC4

Deal with unexpected situations
effectively & inform appropriate people ☐ PC5

Do your work in an organised,
efficient and safe manner ☐ PC6

Element 2

Serve customer orders

Serve customers helpfully,
politely and without delay ☐ PC1

Provide service items, condiments
and accompaniments as appropriate ☐ PC2

Serve food and drink with
appropriate equipment ☐ PC3

△ Hot & cold plated items, cold & hot drinks

Deal with unexpected situations
effectively & inform appropriate people ☐ PC4

Do your work in an organised,
efficient and safe manner ☐ PC5

Element 3

Maintain dining and service areas

Deal with customers politely
and helpfully ☐ PC1

Keep dining and service areas
tidy, free from rubbish/debris ☐ PC2

Clear dining areas of soiled
and unrequired service items ☐ PC3

△ Trays, crockery, cutlery, glassware, ashtrays,
linen, disposable table coverings and napkins,
decorative and promotional items, menus

Maintain stocks of service items,
condiments & accompaniments ☐ PC4

Empty refuse/waste food containers
as required ☐ PC5

Deal with unexpected situations
effectively & inform appropriate people ☐ PC6

Do your work in an organised,
efficient and safe manner ☐ PC7

Element 1

Greet customers and take orders

Greet and deal with customers
in polite and welcoming manner ☐ PC1

△ Children, those with mobility/communication
difficulties, customers with/without bookings,
large parties

Identify customers' needs/requirements
and check booking records ☐ PC2

Escort customers to table/waiting area,
assist with coats and bags ☐ PC3

Present menus to customers,
translate where applicable ☐ PC4

Give accurate information on dishes
to meet customer requirements ☐ PC5

△ Dishes available, dish composition and method
of cooking, prices, special offers and
promotions
Requirements: correct number of place
settings, dietary and special seating
requirements

Politely guide customers to their choice,
record and deal with orders accurately ☐ PC6

Deal with unexpected situations
effectively & inform appropriate people ☐ PC7

Prioritise and do your work in an
organised, efficient and safe manner ☐ PC8

Element 2

Serve customer orders

Deal with customers helpfully and
politely ☐ PC1

Provide table items for customers'
orders for service at appropriate times ☐ PC2

△ Crockery, cutlery and silverware, glassware,
ashtrays, condiments and accompaniments

Serve food with clean, undamaged
service equipment ☐ PC3

△ Dishes, liners, flats, trays/trolleys, service
cutlery and silverware, service cloths/linen

Use appropriate method to serve food
of type, quality and quantity required ☐ PC4

△ Plated items, served items

Carry out work with minimum
disturbance to customers ☐ PC5

Deal with unexpected situations
effectively & inform appropriate people ☐ PC6

Prioritise and do your work in an
organised, efficient and safe manner ☐ PC7

Element 3

Maintain dining and service areas

Deal with customers politely
and helpfully ☐ PC1

Keep dining and service areas
tidy, free from rubbish/debris ☐ PC2

Clear tables of soiled
and unrequired service items ☐ PC3

△ Crockery, cutlery and silverware, glassware,
ashtrays

Deal with spillages and breakages ☐ PC4

Remove and replace soiled table linen
and keep stocks of clean linen ☐ PC5

Remove leftover food, condiments &
accompaniments, and deal with ☐ PC6

△ Dry seasonings and flavourings, mustards,
sauces and dressings, prepared bread items

Empty refuse/waste food containers
as required ☐ PC7

Carry out work with minimum
disturbance to customers ☐ PC8

Deal with unexpected situations
effectively & inform appropriate people ☐ PC9

Prioritise and do your work in an
organised, efficient and safe manner ☐ PC10

MORLAND
EST'D 1711
OF ABINGDON

Service checklist

☐ was the restaurant clean and tidy
☐ were daily specials appetisingly
described
☐ were the staff suitably dressed, neat
and tidy
☐ were all menu items available
☐ was the meal served promptly
☐ was all tableware clean
☐ were accompaniments available
☐ was the food at the correct
temperature
☐ was the presentation of the meal
appealing
☐ were tables cleared promptly
between courses
☐ were you encouraged to order a
sweet or coffee
☐ were you asked if your meal was to
your satisfaction
☐ were tables clean after people had
eaten

Activities
Provide a silver service

NVQ
SVQ

Skills check
Provide a silver service
Unit 2NC5

level
2

1 Describe how to hold the spoon and fork.

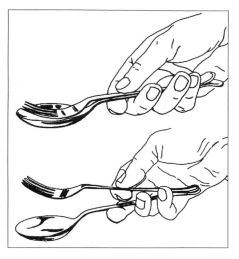

2 What sort of foods would you serve like this? Why?

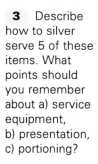

3 Describe how to silver serve 5 of these items. What points should you remember about a) service equipment, b) presentation, c) portioning?

Asparagus soup

Home-baked rolls

❧

Grilled fillets of sole
Salmon steak
Hollandaise sauce

❧

Roast lamb
Mint sauce
Gravy
Roast potatoes
New season peas
Cauliflower mornay

❧

Chicken Kiev
Braised rice

❧

Apple pie
Apricot flan
Bread and butter pudding
Fresh fruit salad
Lemon pancakes

❧

Cheese board

4 Choose another 3 items and describe how to silver serve them in each of these situations:
a) table service,
b) banquet,
c) buffet,
d) carvery.

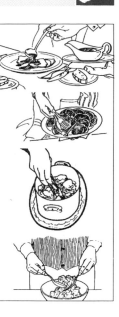

5 Describe how to put the clean plates down. What is the purpose of the serving cloth?

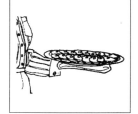

6 Describe how to hold the serving dish.

7 Comment on this.

8 What might have caused these problems, and what can you do to avoid them?

FOOD SPILLED ON CUSTOMER
FOOD BROKEN UP
uneven PORTION sizes
hot food not hot

Provide silver service food

Deal with customers helpfully, politely and identify requirements correctly ☐ PC1

Get service equipment ready for use, in position, clean, undamaged ☐ PC2

▲ Dishes/liners/flats, service cutlery and silverware, service cloths/linen
For banquet/restaurant/carvery silver service, buffet service

Check food is of type, quality & quantity required, arranged for easy service ☐ PC3

Portion, serve and arrange food items using appropriate service equipment ☐ PC4

▲ Soups, gravies/sauces, bread rolls/potatoes/ other solid items, sliced meat/poultry, rice/ vegetables/other small chopped items, pies/ tarts/flans/gâteaux, puddings/spooned desserts, cheese

Deal with surplus food and used service equipment ☐ PC5

Carry out work with minimum disturbance to customers ☐ PC6

Deal with unexpected situations effectively & inform appropriate people ☐ PC7

Prioritise and do your work in an organised, efficient and safe manner ☐ PC8

Clear finished courses

Clear finished courses from table at appropriate time ☐ PC1

▲ Starter, main course, dessert

Clear finished courses, used crockery and cutlery systematically (with help) ☐ PC2

Check table items and remove or replace as appropriate ☐ PC3

▲ Crockery, cutlery, ashtrays, glassware, condiments and accompaniments, table decorations

Clear table of food debris/waste service equipment ☐ PC4

Deal with customers' requests helpfully, politely ☐ PC5

Deal with unexpected situations effectively & inform appropriate people ☐ PC6

Prioritise and do your work in an organised, efficient and safe manner ☐ PC7

Carvery and buffet service

Unit 2NC4, Element 1

Preparing and maintaining a carvery/buffet display

Carvery service gives customers a choice of their favourite roasts and the pleasure of seeing the joints carved for them. They feel they get good value for their money – particularly if there is no restriction on portion size.

Like carveries, buffets give the opportunity for impressive displays of food. For some or all meals, and events such as a dinner dance or conference lunch, buffets provide a fairly fast, efficient means of service. Sometimes buffet service is combined with table service, for example, at breakfast when customers help themselves to cereals and fruit from a buffet table and serving staff bring the toast, hot dishes and beverages to the table.

Preparing customers' tables

The procedures are similar to the preparation of dining areas for table service (pages 47 to 49).

1 Position tables and chairs, checking they are clean and undamaged. Refer to the bookings book or function sheet for details of large groups and special bookings.

2 Lay tablecloths and/or placemats. What cutlery is put on the table depends on the menu, the type of buffet (see box on page 73) and your restaurant's policy. A typical lay-up is: large knife on the right of the setting, large fork on the left, small knife on or by the side plate. Other cutlery is added once customers have ordered. Place a napkin at each setting, wine and/or water glass.

3 Put salt and pepper pots on each table, mustards and sauces (unless these are displayed with the food, or brought to the table on request). Ensure menus and promotional material are in good condition and place on tables with no-smoking signs, flowers, table numbers, etc.

Buffet table arrangements

What is best depends on the size and shape of the room, number of customers to be served, quantity of food to be displayed on the buffet and, in a meal with two or more courses, how many courses are placed on the buffet at one time. Maintaining a smooth flow of customers is the priority.

The buffet table itself should be positioned so that customers can readily reach it from their tables, move along the table to make their selection and return safely with their plates of food. If a queue is likely to form, people returning to their tables should not have to excuse their way through those still queuing for food.

There should be enough space for staff to serve in comfort, and to move around as necessary to replace dishes of food.

Preparing the carvery counter

1 Stock the carvery counter with plates, having checked that each one is clean and not chipped or cracked. Turn on the plate warmer or hot cupboard in time for the plates to warm before service starts.

2 Ensure that all surfaces of the counter are clean, with no smears. Promotional displays must look attractive if they are to be effective. Menus should be accurate, e.g. with correct details for the roast of the day. If you write up the menu board, use plain, clear lettering and the correct spelling (see page 95).

3 Have paper napkins or wooden liners available for customers to hold hot plates with.

4 Put out sufficient service utensils for the vegetables, spoons and ladles for the sauces.

5 Place sauces and accompaniments on the counter.

6 Collect vegetables, salads, gravies, hot sauces, Yorkshire puddings, etc. from the kitchen and position on the counter just before service begins.

Generally chefs will be responsible for bringing out the joints of meat and for carving. You need to know what roasts are available, so that you can advise customers.

Preparing the buffet table

The traditional buffet table covering is a white tablecloth, which falls almost to the floor at the front, and is pinned around to cover or 'box in' the sides of the table. Other options are:

- purpose-made buffet cloths – in various designs, colours and decorative frills, these provide a quick way of 'dressing' the front and sides of the table

- banquet rolls – in effect a very long disposable tablecloth, you cut the length to suit the table size.

Slip cloths placed over the top of the buffet provide attractive colour contrast, and check-patterned cloths bring informality.

If a number of cloths have to be used to cover a long table, the overlaps should all be in the same direction, preferably away from the main approach to the table. Do check that the cloths are level at the bottom.

Plates and serving equipment

Customers should not find themselves selecting food without a plate on which to put it. Position:

- plates at one end of the buffet table, in piles along the table, or on a smaller table nearby

- dessert plates near the desserts, hot plates near hot food.

Where customers might choose both hot and cold food, it may not be appropriate to have hot plates.

If staff are serving all the dishes, put the plates out of reach of customers, but convenient for staff.

Place a serving spoon and fork (or other appropriate equipment) at each dish. With hot dishes (as the spoon will get too hot to handle) and large dishes (as the spoon may fall into the food), it is better to leave the serving equipment by the dish on a small plate.

Each dish should have its own serving equipment.

Presenting and displaying food

If you are helping to arrange the display of serving dishes, consider:

- *colour* – variety and contrast adds interest to the display, but overdone looks too fussy. If you are using flowers, avoid colours that clash with the food

- *height* – flat arrangements look dull and lifeless. Try to mix the shape and height of serving dishes. Or use tiered tables, put some dishes on stands, blocks or even upturned saucers – but make sure the arrangement is stable

- *shape* – introduce variety with the position of different shaped serving dishes, e.g. a square dish of stuffed eggs among round bowls of mixed salad

- *focal point* – the eye is drawn to this, and then out to the surrounding display. The focal point could be the main dish, e.g. decorated ham on a stand, or a flower display, basket of fruit, candelabra, or even an ice or fat carving

- *simplicity* – over-elaborate arrangements distract attention from the food

- *clarity* – avoid over-crowding, allow customers to appreciate the choice

- *ease of service* – put dishes which are difficult to serve where the server/customers can easily gain access, e.g. individual fruit tartlets (firm, fairly easy to pick up) beyond the pavlova (rather crumbly)

- *palatability of food* – place hot foods at the end of the buffet service line. Otherwise the food will cool off while customers make further selections of cold foods. Place sauces and dressings next to the items they are intended to accompany, so customers can match them to the right foods

- *menu order* – if the arrangement includes starters, main course items and sweets, cluster the various dishes making up each course together

- *portion control* – expensive items, e.g. Palma ham, are sometimes placed where access is more restricted, or at the point of the display where customers have already filled their plates.

Food safety and hygiene

To reduce the risk of the food becoming harmful to eat:

- handle dishes carefully so that your fingers do not touch the food. Keep fingers away from surfaces which will come into contact with the food, e.g. bowls of serving spoons

- keep food covered on its journey from and back to the kitchen, and protected as much as possible while on display – dangers include customers sneezing over the food and touching the food with their hands

- check that equipment is operating at the right temperature: hotplates, chilled cabinets, etc.

- put food on display at the last moment. At the end of service, return food promptly to the kitchen
- ensure that sufficient serving spoons, etc. are available throughout service.

The temperature range at which bacteria multiply rapidly is above 5°C and below 63°C. Where possible, food should be displayed in chilled cabinets or hot display units. Otherwise there must be a strict control over how long the food is on display, and what happens to food left over after service (see page 17 for a summary of the food safety regulations).

A variety of shapes and sizes adds interest.

Replenishing the display

Replace or remove serving dishes regularly. This may be done as soon as the dish is half empty, or left until there is less than an average serving left. Customers shouldn't have to chase around a huge dish to find enough peas. On the other hand, the gâteau dish might be left until the last portion has been served.

For quality reasons and food safety, dishes prepared first should be used first. Follow a control system for recording the time dishes are on display.

If separate tables are used to display different courses, clear these once the customers have finished eating that course.

Each dish that customers serve themselves to must have its own serving equipment.

Preparing the dining area

For fork and finger buffets (see box on page 73):

- position occasional tables, cover with tablecloths, place ashtrays and perhaps supplies of napkins
- arrange informal seating.

Table buffets

Fully laid-up tables, with cutlery, side plates, glasses, etc. are the most convenient arrangement for customers (see page 69). Other combinations include:

- table knife and fork, napkin and cruets. Customers collect other items as required from the buffet table, e.g. dessert spoons
- tablecloth and cruets only. Customers collect cutlery from the buffet (often wrapped in a napkin). This is ideal when a number of customers may eat at each table during the course of the meal, or in informal settings (e.g. a buffet lunch by the swimming pool, or in the lounge or garden of a pub) where customers can take the food to their seats.

If the buffet is part of a large function, and there is a table plan so that guests sit at specific seats, the table numbers should be easy to see as guests enter the room. Familiarise yourself with the room layout, so that you can help guests who have trouble finding their table.

Table settings should suit the style of service, and complement the displays of food.

Setting up the breakfast buffet. This counter keeps the food chilled.

The temperature of food displayed on carveries must be checked regularly.

Serving customers at the carvery/buffet

Customers leave their table to choose from the dishes and roast joints of meat on display. Chefs may do the carving. Sometimes the first course and sweets are brought to the customers' table by serving staff.

Customer care

Be ready to invite customers to go and make their choice of food. In a breakfast buffet arrangement, customers sometimes do not realise that they should serve themselves to fruit juice etc.

On other occasions you may have to exercise some modest 'crowd control', so that long queues do not form at the buffet. This can be as simple as reassuring a party of customers that you will invite them to go to the buffet table in a few moments.

Offer to help customers who have difficulty getting to the buffet table, making their choice or carrying the filled plates back to their table (see page 14).

Serving the food

Agree with colleagues what dishes each person will serve – to avoid getting in each other's way, yet allowing flexibility so that customers are not kept waiting.

Use separate serving equipment for each dish.

Do not over-fill customers' plates. Position items so that the food looks as attractive on the plate as it did on the serving dish – with variety of colour, height, etc.

Ask before giving customers sauce, cream, etc. If you spill any on the rim of the plate, wipe it off with a clean serving cloth.

When serving hot dishes:

- use a serving cloth to hold hot plates
- warn customers when plates are very hot
- replace the lid during quiet periods to keep the food hot
- lift lids carefully, so that condensation is caught in the lid (not dripping on to the food or buffet cloth).

The restaurant

Tables clean and polished. Each cover set with large knife on right of table mat, large fork on left, dessert knife on folded napkin on side plate, wine glass on right hand side above large knife.

In centre of table: salt and pepperpots, ashtray (on smoking tables), bud vase with flowers.

Dumbwaiters, wine racks, coffee area fully stocked.

Lights switched on and working. Background music on. Temperature in restaurant comfortable. Restaurant toilets clean and tidy.

The carving table

The carving table must look inviting and attractive.

Before service

Head chef advised of numbers of customers expected, any large groups and when they are due.

Restaurant staff advised of soups of the day, special joint of choice, vegetables and potatoes, sweets of the day, regional cheese, availability of all foods.

Chef turns carving table heat on (at least one hour before service), checks base plates and lights are working and presentation (e.g. carving knives sharp and clean). Joints should not be displayed until 15 minutes prior to service.

Restaurant staff check carving table:

- no grease marks, no food debris in vegetable well
- serving spoons in position (one set for each dish), supply of hot main course plates
- soups, sauces, croutons, bread rolls, accompaniments, vegetables and Yorkshire puddings in position.

Throughout service

Kitchen:

- kept informed of extra bookings, parties, etc.
- given feedback on compliments or complaints made by guests
- told in advance of any dish running short.

Carver is responsible for checking presentation:

- lids removed as customers arrive, so they can see what is available
- food only handled with utensils – separate utensils must be used for each joint being served
- carving pads kept free from debris, all spills wiped up
- table tidied after each group of guests and lids replaced to maintain freshness of food
- sufficient sauces and accompaniments, dishes of vegetables replaced – do not top up foods on display but replace with hot food in a clean container
- service utensils checked and replaced if they have become too hot for customers to touch (keep handles away from the heat)
- internal temperature of joints checked and recorded each hour. Hot food must always be kept at a temperature above 63°C. If the temperature begins to decline, adjust the thermostat on the unit and reposition the joints under the heat lamps.

Never attempt to reheat foods on the carving table.

At end of session

- food returned to the kitchen
- carving table cleaned and made ready for next session
- power to carving table switched off.

Portion control

One of the reasons buffets are popular with customers is that they can help themselves to as much (or as little) as they like. The price charged reflects this.

But there are occasions when restrictions have to be made. An example is when customers want more expensive food yet accept that some form of portion control is necessary to keep the price reasonable.

In a purely self-service arrangement, there are only two ways to limit how much customers take:

- by the size of the plate – small plates hold less food than large ones
- by limiting the number of times customers can go to the buffet table.

When some dishes or all the food is served by staff, there are more options:

- specifying quantity, e.g. two slices of meat per person, or each flan or pie to be cut into six
- using particular size serving equipment, e.g. two tablespoons of peas per person
- arranging the garnishes to indicate each portion, e.g. eight slices of lemon on a paella for eight.

Types of buffet

Table buffet – customers sit at tables to enjoy the food which they have chosen and collected from the buffet. Staff may stand behind the buffet table to serve some or all of the dishes to customers. Staff can serve the food more quickly, with greater care for its presentation, and better portion control.

Some buffets are completely self-service, e.g. for a small business meeting, when the buffet is set up in an adjacent room, with everything that is required including cutlery, napkins, crockery, wine and other drinks. Staff do not enter the room until the customers have returned to their meeting.

Fork buffet – usually a stand-up affair, although some seating may be provided, this would not be at a laid-up table. Customers collect their food, a napkin and fork from the buffet table. Staff circulate throughout the room collecting plates which have been finished with, refilling drink glasses, etc. You might also be offering second helpings in this way, or new dishes.

Finger buffet – no cutlery is provided. The food is a size which can be easily popped into the mouth in one go. Customers help themselves to food from a buffet table and/or staff circulate with dishes. Some chairs may be provided for customers who find it uncomfortable to stand. Otherwise those attending can circulate freely among the other guests.

The breakfast buffet

Decide who is going to be the 'runner' to order items from the kitchen and keep the chafing pans stocked with food.

If you are serving on the buffet, do not abandon it to chase up the runner. If you are the runner, and a queue forms at the buffet, do not help with the service. Once roles have been decided, keep to them!

A small queue at the buffet when it is very busy is not a bad thing. It regulates the speed of service and allows the supply of food from the kitchen to keep up with the demand at the buffet. Food cannot be served quicker at the buffet than it can be supplied from the kitchen.

Replenishing the buffet

Throughout service, keep an eye on the buffet table. When you notice any item running low, remove the jug or bowl and take it to the back of house area:

- milk – fill the jug from the machine
- dried fruit and cereals – fill the bowls from the stores
- fresh fruit and yogurts – give the bowls to the chef to fill
- porridge – ask the chef for a tureen of fresh porridge to pour into the chafing pan at the buffet table.

Dismantling the buffet

When it appears everybody has finished, begin clearing:

- collect all service gear and take to the wash-up
- take a clothed trolley to the buffet, load with the fruits, yogurts, cold meats, etc. and return these to the chef
- return with the empty trolley and load with the cereals and dried fruit – leave the trolley outside the still room for the bowls to be filled ready for the next day.

When all the guests have left the restaurant:

- return the flowers
- place the white cloths in the linen basket, the tartan cloths and drapes on hangers in the cupboard
- fold down the tables and return to the chair store.

Element 3

Maintaining customer dining areas

Customers have considerable control over the timing of their meal. When they wish, they can leave their table to collect food from the carvery or buffet.

Be aware of what is happening, in order to:

- clear from the previous course (see page 59) by the time customers return to the table
- assist customers who don't have the cutlery they need, e.g. because they used the wrong items for an earlier course
- clear up spills or breakages (see page 22)
- remove empty wine and drink bottles, used napkins and similar items that are no longer required
- serve drinks as required, wine, coffee or tea at the appropriate time
- clear tables at the end of the meal, ready for the entertainment, speeches or dancing.

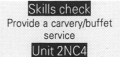

NVQ SVQ | **Skills check** Provide a carvery/buffet service Unit 2NC4 | **level 2**

Use this to check your progress against the performance criteria.

1 What are the main safety hazards and how can they be avoided?

2 What should you check when a) setting up the food display, b) laying-up customer tables? Why?

3 What can be done to keep the display of food looking attractive throughout service?

4 What can you do to keep the dining area looking tidy during service?

5 How should you handle and dispose of the different types of waste? What can go wrong if you don't do this correctly?

6 How could you help these customers at your buffet table?

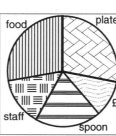

too short to see buffet
children misbehaving
in wheelchair
has difficulty walking
has put pudding on same plate as main course
severely impaired vision
very shaky hand
wants food brought to table
likes none of the dishes
is allergic to nuts
wants low-fat dishes
wants extra large portion
doesn't speak English

7 Give the reasons portion sizes may be controlled. How can this be done?

food | plate | £ | spoon | staff

8 To whom do you report: a) customer incidents, b) breakages? Why is this important?

Tell me about... So I can...

...INVESTIGATE COMPLAINTS...
...DEAL WITH CLAIMS...
...MONITOR STANDARDS...
...CONTROL COSTS...
...FIGHT PROSECUTIONS...

Element 1

Prepare and maintain a carvery/buffet service

Deal with customers in a polite and helpful manner — PC1 ❑

Keep carvery/buffet table clean, free from damage, correctly positioned — PC2 ❑

Check table items are clean, free from damage, arrange correctly — PC3 ❑
△ Crockery, cutlery/silverware, glassware, table coverings, napkins, decorative items, flowers

Check service equipment is clean, free from damage, positioned for use — PC4 ❑
△ Dishes/flats/plates, service cutlery/silverware, service cloths/linen

Present and display food items appropriately for food service — PC5 ❑

Store and display food items hygienically and safely — PC6 ❑

Replenish food items, keep carvery or buffet tidy during service — PC7 ❑

Deal with unexpected situations effectively & inform appropriate people — PC8 ❑
△ Equipment faults, shortage of table items

Prioritise and carry out your work in an organised, efficient and safe manner — PC9 ❑

Element 2

Serve customers at the carvery/buffet

Greet and deal with customers politely and identify requirements accurately — PC1 ❑

Give accurate information to meet customers' needs, promote products/services — PC2 ❑

Serve food correctly with clean, undamaged food service equipment — PC3 ❑

Serve food items of type and quality required — PC4 ❑

Portion, serve and arrange food to operational/customer requirements — PC5 ❑

Deal with unexpected situations effectively & inform appropriate people — PC6 ❑

Prioritise and carry out your work in an organised, efficient and safe manner — PC7 ❑

Drink and wine
service at table

Taking customers' drink orders

A drink is part of enjoying the meal for most customers. They appreciate knowledgeable advice on what is available – including drinks that are in fashion, different ways of serving all-time favourites, and interesting options for those who don't want alcohol.

Preparing for service

Keep storage and preparation areas spotless. Pay particular attention to the interiors of refrigerators and chillers. Regularly check the temperatures of drink chilling equipment.

Store fresh cream and milk, and fresh fruit juices in the refrigerator. Keep covered, away from strong smells.

Check glasses, water jugs, ashtrays, etc. are clean and polished. Put aside chipped or cracked items to be disposed of.

Service runs smoothly when sufficient stocks are available.

Opening checklist

HUDSON'S
A Tradition of Excellence

1 Beverage and back room areas tidied and made functional.
2 As suppliers deliver orders, orders are put away.
3 Mall and restaurant tables positioned according to table plan.
4 Table stability checked and flowers positioned.
5 Till turned on, change and bills checked.
6 Waiting stations checked and made operational.
7 Newspapers placed on canes.

Copthorne Hotels

Stock control and rotation

• Shelves fully restocked first thing in morning using reserve stock in dispense bar.
• Requisition form completed to replace used stock.
• All old stock pulled forward and new stock put at back. Date mark on all stock checked: items past their date withdrawn from use.
• All bottles wiped with a clean damp cloth and stacked with labels facing outwards.

Taking the order

The order may be taken while customers are choosing their food, at the same time as the food order, or at a later stage in the meal (see page 53 for guidance).

Greeting and dealing with customers

If you have not already done so, greet the customers (see page 52) and offer a drinks (and food) menu if there is not one on the table.

Some customers want to order at once, others enjoy taking time to choose. After telling them about the specials, say that you will be back as soon as they are ready to order.

Providing quality service

Drink requirements cannot be taken for granted. What one customer enjoys, another does not. Suggestions are usually welcome, high pressure selling is not.

Be sensitive to what customers are prepared to spend Suggesting an expensive wine with a modestly priced salad is unlikely to be appreciated. If customers have avoided alcohol in their choice of drinks before and during the meal, don't recommend a Cognac or liqueur at the end of the meal.

What places can sell alcohol

To sell alcohol requires a licence. There are various types, each with certain restrictions.

In **England** and **Wales**, the four you are likely to encounter are:

- *on-licence* – permits the sale of alcohol for drinking on and off the premises. Pubs, bars and many hotels have this sort of licence. Restricted versions of the licence permit the sale of wine only, for example

- *restaurant licence* – alcohol can be served as an ancillary to a table meal (i.e. before, with and after the meal)

- *residential and restaurant licence* – alcohol can be served at any time to those staying in the hotel or guesthouse (and the guests of residents), and with a substantial meal to non-residents

- *residential licence* – alcohol can be served with meals and at any other time, but only to those staying in the hotel or guesthouse or their guests.

In **Scotland**, the equivalents are:

- *public house licence* – allows pubs and bars to sell alcohol for drinking on and off the premises

- *hotel licence* – for hotels with four or more letting rooms in towns and cities, and two or more in country areas, permits sale of alcohol for drinking on and off the premises

- *restaurant licence* – allows alcohol to be served with a meal at the table only. Restaurants which serve drinks in a bar area before customers go to the table (or after their meal) must have a public house licence

- *restricted hotel licence* – alcohol can be served to residents at any time, their guests, and with a substantial meal to non-residents. There must be no bar counter

- *refreshment licence* – allows cafés and similar places to sell alcohol. There must be no bar counter and no off-sales. Young people are not allowed on the premises after 8 p.m. At other times they must be with an adult.

Unlicensed premises can allow customers to bring their own alcohol to drink with the meal. Some licensed restaurants also permit customers to bring their own wines, for example, but they usually charge a fixed amount per bottle (corkage) as compensation for loss of revenue from sales of their own stock.

> *You commit an offence – and put the licence of your workplace at risk – if you serve alcohol to anyone who is under-age, or drunk, or who has been declared a habitual drinker by the courts. If customers are drunk, disorderly or violent – such behaviour is illegal on licensed premises – tell your manager at once.*

When alcohol can be sold

Known as *permitted hours*, these are from 11 a.m. to 11 p.m. on weekdays and 12 noon to 10.30 p.m. on Sundays. Good Friday hours are the same as a Sunday. In Scotland, Sunday hours are 12.30 p.m. to 2.30 p.m. and 6.30 p.m. to 11 p.m.

These hours can be extended (with permission) for special occasions, e.g. a wedding reception, and on a regular basis, e.g. when meals and live entertainment are provided, or when a music and dancing or an entertainment licence is held.

When drinks have been served with a meal, customers are allowed a further 30 minutes beyond the permitted hours in which to finish them.

Who can and cannot be sold alcohol

It is against the law to sell alcohol to anyone under the age of 18. However, in restaurants and areas of a pub set aside for eating food, 16 and 17 year olds can be sold beer, cider or perry as an ancillary to a meal.

In Scotland, 16 and 17 year olds can buy wine with a table meal (as well as beer, cider and perry). It must be a substantial meal.

Young people below the age of 18 (16 and 17 for the drinks mentioned above) may drink alcohol in a restaurant which has been bought for them by an accompanying parent or guardian.

The licensee has the right to refuse to serve any person. No reason need be given.

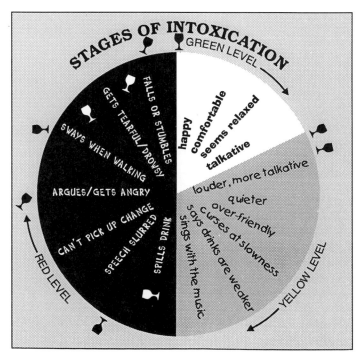

Selling skills

Rather than saying 'Would you care for a cocktail?' or 'Something from the bar?', pick up on the guests' initial response and guide them towards a speciality drink that will be value for money for them.

The American Restaurant & Bar

Be creative. Almost all our speciality drinks can be made without liquor. 'We also have a wide variety of fruit juices, and carbonated drinks as well as coffee and iced tea.' We ensure endless refills of carbonated drinks, tea and coffee are provided. By using this approach you are relieving the guests' pressure of having to drink something alcoholic and influencing the guests into making a decision.

Quality and quantity of drinks

You must serve the drink (e.g. diet coke, sparkling mineral water) and brand requested (e.g. Pepsi, Perrier), or offer an alternative. If the drinks list says Cognac, you must serve a Cognac (from the designated area of that name in France) not another brandy.

When customers do not specify the brand, e.g. 'large whisky, please', you can serve any available one. There may be a preferred or house brand, which is served in these situations because it gives the best profit margin.

You must serve the advertised measure (stated on the price list, bottle or can). The law specifies what measures (or multiples of these) can be sold for:

- *wine by the glass* – 125 ml and 175 ml

- *whisky, gin, rum and vodka* – 25 ml or 35 ml (unless sold as part of a mixed drink, e.g. a cocktail containing two or more other liquids)

- *draught beer and cider* – half-pint or pint (imperial measures remain legal).

The system, measure or glass used for spirits and draught beer and cider must carry the government stamp to show that the quantity is accurate. For wine, the maker's mark on the glass is sufficient.

Providing information on drinks

Be ready to answer customers' questions on:

- particular types of drink available, e.g. low alcohol beers, decaffeinated coffee, mineral waters, cream sherries, premium ciders, alcoholic lemonades

- what a drink they do not know is like, e.g. the house red, an organic wine, the quality of a vintage year for clarets, Van der Hum liqueur

- what is suitable for children, a celebration, to go with the curry or the fish.

Some wine and drink lists give quite a lot of detail, a guide to sweetness or dryness, and the alcoholic content. Even then, some customers prefer to ask you for this information.

More specific knowledge is helpful when your restaurant specialises, e.g. in cocktails, wines of particular countries, teas and coffees, malt whiskies, draught beer, freshly-squeezed fruit juices.

Promoting drink sales

Clarifying what customers want also provides a sales opportunity:

- 'Straight whisky, madam, or with a mixer? We have dry ginger, lemonade.... I could also recommend some delicious whisky-based cocktails'

- 'There is the house blend, sir, or we have a range of Indian and China teas. And, ideal for a lovely day like today, there is iced tea'

- 'Would you prefer sparkling or still mineral water and would you like a slice of lemon, lime or orange in it? Alternatively, we have some excellent herbal drinks...'

Listen and look for clues to what customers want. Ask questions. Try to match what you say to what they want. Don't irritate customers by giving what is obviously a standard sales pitch.

The tone of your voice will say much about how interested you are in what your customers want – often more than the words you use. Be knowledgeable and enthusiastic about your range of drinks and food, and which drinks go well with which food, and you will contribute positively to customers' satisfaction. Satisfied customers are the ones who return and recommend their friends to come.

CHECK list
Promoting drink sales

✔ know what drinks you can offer

✔ keep up-to-date with what is popular to drink

✔ listen and watch for clues to what customers want

✔ ask questions to clarify customer needs

✔ make what you are saying personal to the customer

When you can sell

✔ you are asked for advice

✔ customer is not sure what to order

✔ brand, style or strength not specified

✔ product/brand asked for is not available

✔ clearing the table

✔ presenting the menu

✔ serving or clearing away food

✔ opportunity arises in conversation

✔ responding to compliment

Element 2
Serving drink orders at table

If customers have not finished their drinks at the bar when the table is ready, offer to carry the glasses for them. Arrange the glasses on the tray so you remember which belongs to which customer.

Service procedure

1 Glasses for cold drinks must be cold. Do not use ones which are still warm from being washed. When a second round of drinks is ordered, bring clean glasses.

2 Line the drinks tray with a doily or napkin (if this is the style). Besides looking good, this stops the glasses slipping around the tray.

3 Serve guests before their host and/or hostess, and women before men (see page 56). Get as close to the table as possible before putting the drinks down.

4 Avoid stretching over or in front of people – if someone moves suddenly and knocks you, the glass or the tray, there could be an accident.

5 Hold glasses by the base or the handle, your fingers well away from the rim and the inside of the glass. Hold bottles by the base. Use the saucer to pick up cups. Do not allow the neck of the bottle to touch the glass and always keep it above the level of the liquid in the glass as it fills.

6 Put drinks down to the right of the customer, or directly in front if the customer is not having food. A handle should be turned to the right.

7 Load and unload your tray carefully, so that it does not over-balance (see page 50). If it is too heavy or too large to hold safely in one hand, put the tray down before unloading.

Serving spirits

Usually bar staff dispense or measure whisky, gin, vodka, brandy, rum and other spirits for you. Add ice and lemon as required, and place the glasses on your tray with the rest of the order (e.g. bottles of mixers, jug of water).

In some restaurants, brandy and malt whisky are also served from a drinks trolley, with the liqueurs (see below).

Serving draught beer and cider

These are usually poured by bar staff. By law, the quantity must be not be less than a pint or half-pint (see page 77). Many beers have to be poured with care, so the head of beer is right.

Serving after-dinner drinks from a trolley

1 Wheel the trolley to the customers' table. Help customers make their choice.

2 Select the appropriate glass. Measure the drink by filling the glass to the correct level (your manager will say what this is) or by using a thimble measure:

- hold the measure over the centre of the glass
- carefully pour the spirit into the measure, right up to the brim
- tip the contents into the glass in one quick movement so nothing spills
- let the measure drain before putting aside.

Pouring bottled and canned drinks at table

1 Hold the bottle by its centre, turned so the customer can see the label.

2 Pour the drink into the glass, steadily and without splashing or causing too much froth or head to form. For mixers with a spirit, ask the customer how much to add. Alternatively, pour just a little into the glass so the customer can add the desired amount.

3 Place the glass down in front of the customer, and the bottle by it if there is drink remaining. Position the bottle so the label faces the customer.

In some restaurants, the opened bottle and glass are put on the table for the customer to pour.

You may be able to pour mixers and soft drinks into the glass before you remove them from the tray.

Where the drink is poured into the glass depends on the style of service and how the drink is dispensed.

With coffee and tea, don't forget to offer sugar and milk or cream.

Always check if the customer would like ice with the drink.

In some restaurants, for some drinks, the measure is judged by eye.

A well organised dispense area makes your job easier and speeds service.

Drinks service at table

Coppid Beech Hotel

1 Approach table. Ask if ready to order.	
2 Offer alternative where appropriate.	'Would you like Booth's or Plymouth Gin, Sir/Madam?'
3 Offer appropriate accompaniment.	e.g. ice and lemon.
4 Repeat the order to guest.	To confirm that you took the order correctly.
5 Leave the table.	Don't forget to thank the guest first.
6 Print guest bill on till.	Check all items are correct before printing bill.
7 Collect drinks from dispense bar.	Use a tray.
8 Serve drinks from the right. Ladies first.	Say 'Here is your gin and tonic, Sir/Madam.'
9 Leave the table.	

Hold the glass in position until the spirit has stopped flowing and the sight glass is empty. For a double, allow the measure to refill, push the glass against the release arm or button for a second time.

Draught beers have to be poured with skill to get the right head of foam.

Pouring bottled beer

Some bottled beers need careful pouring to avoid too much head forming. You need both hands free:

- hold the glass by the base or stem, at an angle of about 45° and the bottle in the other hand, with the neck just inside the glass

- tilt the bottle so the beer runs down the inside of the glass, steadily and without stopping

- gradually bring the glass upright as it fills.

For more head, raise the bottle above the beer and pour into the centre of the glass. If too much head forms, apologise to the customer, put the glass and bottle down for a few minutes, then continue pouring.

Some types of beer finish maturing in the bottle, leaving a sediment.

1 Handle the bottle gently and keep it upright, so the sediment remains undisturbed.

2 Hold bottle and glass at eye level when pouring, to see the beer moving through the neck of the bottle.

3 Stop pouring as soon as you see sediment enter the neck. Done carefully, you will leave only a small amount of beer in the bottle.

Wine by the glass

To give customers more choice, many restaurants offer wine by the glass. Customers can enjoy a glass of sparkling wine or Champagne before their meal, as well as a bottle of red or white with their meal, and perhaps a glass of dessert wine with the sweet.

The wine will be served from the bottle, kept on the bar counter or in a chiller, and recorked or restoppered between use. Special stoppers keep sparkling wine from going flat. For still wines, some types of stopper extend the drinking life of the wine by replacing the air in the bottle with a vacuum or a special gas.

In bars where white wine by the glass is a good seller, it may be dispensed from a tap at the bar counter, connected to a bulk container in the cellar (red wine is not suited to this method). Wine display cabinets are another option, holding bottles of white wine at drinking temperature. Into the neck of each bottle, which fits through a hole in the bottom of the cabinet, is fitted a push bar or button dispense measure similar to those used on spirit bottles.

The quantity of wine served must be 125 ml or 175 ml (see page 77). This can be measured by:

- filling a wine glass to the maker's capacity line – good-quality wines should then be poured into a larger glass so the bouquet can be appreciated

- dispensing the wine through a measure (fitted to the bottle or the supply line from the cellar).

Dealing with an intoxicated guest

The American Restaurant & Bar

1 First and foremost, notify the manager.

2 Do not serve an already intoxicated customer who enters the restaurant. Offer to call a taxi or offer to call a friend. Do not simply refuse service.

3 Discontinue drink service. That decision must be final.

4 Do not argue with the guest. Remain in control of yourself. Do not over react or retaliate to what a person says to you.

5 When dealing with a group, enlist support from other members who are more sober.

6 Do not use judgmental statements, such as 'You are drunk' or 'You're too smashed!' Do not use the terms 'intoxicated' or 'inebriated'. Instead explain why you will not serve the guest, with tact and diplomacy (and, if possible, taking the customer aside):

> *I'm concerned about your safety*
>
> *I cannot serve you any more liquor. May I suggest some Potato Skins or a Club Sandwich?*
>
> *I want you to have a pleasant evening, and I'm concerned that you may be stopped by the police. They are running an anti-drink-driving campaign...*

7 Do not let the person drive. Offer to call a taxi. Or suggest that a friend or someone else who is sober drives the person home.

Sutcliffe

Service of drinks: essential points

- variety of drinks and beverages available, including herbal teas and decaffeinated coffee

Where unit has licence to sell alcohol

- trading hours
- legal restrictions on serving alcohol to young people
- differences between low-alcohol (not more than 1.2% alcohol by volume) and alcohol-free (not more than 0.05%)
- measure of spirits sold (usually 25 ml)

Tea and coffee service

- how the boiler (or still) works: safety points
- cleanliness of equipment
- method of making and quantities to be used
- importance of always making fresh and never re-heating or mixing with old brew
- checking supplies of sugar, milk, stirrers

Serving hot drinks

Serve tea and coffee freshly made. Tea needs between three and five minutes only to infuse. Coffee becomes bitter in taste when kept hot for too long (more than 30 minutes), or if the holding temperature is too high (85°C is best).

1 Warm tea pots before use, with a little very hot or boiling water. Coffee pots filled from a bulk container (as in the photograph on page 75) should also be pre-warmed.

2 Measure quantities accurately. For tea, the general rule is one teaspoon or bag per person and one for the pot. Ground coffee, once opened, should be used within a day or so. Use the correct coffee for the method you are using. Never pour brewed coffee back through spent grounds to strengthen, or add more tea leaves to the pot. Never re-use tea bags or coffee grounds.

3 Use freshly-drawn, freshly-boiled water – take the tea pot to the kettle. For coffee, the water should be just off the boil.

4 Do not overfill pots or cups – this would make them difficult to handle without spilling. Place jugs or pots on the table with the handle towards the customer, sugar bowls, milk, cream, etc. within easy reach.

If a customer would like a fresh cup of coffee and the first, only half drunk, has gone cold, offer a clean cup. When using the small coffee cups (called demi-tasse) for after-meal coffee, the coffee keeps its temperature better if the cups have been warmed before use (e.g. in the hot plate).

Methods of making fresh coffee

Espresso – check temperature and pressure of machine. Discard old grounds and rinse coffee holder well. Re-pack tightly with coffee. Wipe rim before inserting in machine (to ensure a good seal). Warm the cup before filling with coffee.

Vacuum pot or Cona – fill the lower bowl with cold water and put over heat. Place glass rod (or other filter mechanism) into top bowl (on its stand at this stage) and add coffee. When water has boiled, insert top bowl into lower bowl, twisting to ensure a good seal. When the water has all risen into the top bowl, lower the heat, stirring gently once or twice. Allow the coffee to infuse for 1 to 2 minutes. Remove from the heat. When coffee has filtered back into the lower container, put top bowl aside.

Filter method (with machine) – check machine is on. Place fresh filter paper in the holder. Add the coffee (usually a pre-portioned pack). Pour cold water into the top part of the machine. Place clean pot under filter. Do not remove pot until coffee has stopped dripping through the filter (or quickly place a fresh pot in its place). Do not leave almost empty pots on the hotplate – they are likely to boil dry and then the glass will crack.

Filter method (with funnel) – place fresh filter paper in the funnel. Add coffee. Place funnel over pot, then pour over not-quite boiling water. Use a circular motion, so you moisten all the coffee. Do not add too much water at once, otherwise it will overflow and take coffee grounds down into the pot.

Plunger (cafetière) method – place coffee in the bottom of the jug. Pour on not-quite boiling water and insert the plunger. Allow the coffee to infuse for 4 minutes or so, then push the plunger firmly down.

How to serve coffee from a tray

Approach the customer from the side the cup is positioned, usually the right. Place a small coffee cup, saucer and coffee spoon just to the right of the customer. The handle of the cup should point to the customer's right hand.

If this is the practice, place a small doily under the cup, and a small side plate under the saucer.

Return with the coffee tray. Approach the customer from the right:

- enquire if the customer would like sugar and if so, brown or white
- rotate the tray so that the spout of the coffee pot is pointing towards the customer's cup
- enquire if milk or cream is required – never say 'Would you like black or white coffee?' (which may be offensive)
- if the customer wants milk or cream, pour the coffee until the cup is two-thirds full – tilt or pivot the pot on the tray
- if milk or cream is required, serve this in a similar way.

In less formal service, the sugar, milk or cream are left on the table. The coffee pot is held in the hand. If both coffee and milk (or cream) are poured for the customer, the coffee pot is held in the right hand, milk in the left.

Preparing bottled wines for service

Your customers may have a choice of several red and white wines, as well as some rosés and sparkling wines. Some restaurants and hotels have hundreds of wines on their list, including very expensive bottles.

To ensure these wines are enjoyable to drink, they must be stored and served carefully. The guidelines depend on the type of wine and style of restaurant.

Preparing wines for a banquet (in the hall photographed on page 47).

Preparing wine service area and equipment

Larger restaurants may have a dispense bar where colleagues issue you with the bottles ordered by customers. Otherwise the wine will be kept on racks, or in chillers or refrigerators, where you have convenient access.

Before service starts, check that sufficient stocks of each wine are available (see below for storage and service temperatures). Tell your manager when a wine needs re-ordering or you find faulty wines (e.g. leakage from the cork).

Service equipment

For serving wine you are likely to require:

- *ice buckets* – to chill white, rosé and sparkling wines. Silver-plate and stainless steel buckets should be well polished, with no fingerprints or smears. Fill when required with half to two-thirds ice, the rest water, so the body of the bottle is submerged. Do not overfill, to reduce the risk of spilling. Some ice buckets are on *stands*, so they can be put by the customer's table

- *wine coolers* – these have insulated sides to keep white and rosé wines at their correct, chilled temperature. There is no need to fill with ice and water, so the bottle remains dry. The wine does not get over-chilled (as it does if left too long in ice), and no condensation forms on the outside (as happens with ice buckets, when water drips on to the table or the floor)

- *carafes* – for wines sold in this way (of table quality typically), purchased in a bulk container. By law, carafes should hold one litre, half a litre (50 cl), 75 cl or 25 cl. A range of sizes may be used

- *decanters* – traditionally used for fine red wines which have a sediment. The wine is very carefully poured into the decanter, usually through a filter, so that the sediment is left in the bottle. Decanters are sometimes used to encourage red wines to breathe, and to help them reach drinking temperature (see below)

- *corkscrews* – to remove the cork from the bottle. The so-called 'waiter's friend' folds to fit in the pocket. Other types are bulkier and do not have a knife, although some people find them easier to use. Some corkscrews also have *bottle openers*, for removing crown tops (more likely on bottles of mixers than wine)

- *service cloths* – to dry a bottle which has been chilled in an ice bucket, to protect yourself when opening the bottle, and to catch drips when serving

- *wine lists/wine menu* – tell customers what is available and the price of each wine. Many also give information about the character of each wine, the shipper and the alcoholic content.

Storing wines

Wine bottles sealed with a cork should be stored on their side, so the wine is in contact with the cork, keeping it moist. The design of wine racks used in cellars and dispense bars ensures this. Look for the arrow on boxes of wine indicating which way up they should be stacked.

The best temperature for storing wine is between 10°C and 12°C. If it is kept warmer or colder than this for days or weeks (e.g. in a warm service area or the refrigerator), the quality is spoilt. Rapid changes of temperature are also harmful – so you should not put red wine in the hot cupboard to warm it, or white wine in the freezer to chill it.

A practical solution is to keep a small stock at serving temperature, replenishing this in sufficient time before service begins, about:

- four hours for red wines (in a warm room at around 20°C)

- one hour for white and rosé wines (in a refrigerator or wine cooler) and 1½ hours for sparkling wines and Champagnes.

Your manager will say what quantities of each should be kept ready for service. Check the details of functions and other special parties for the wine requirements.

Serving bottled wines

Most restaurants serve wines with some ceremony, because it adds to the enjoyment of wine and customers expect it. There are practical advantages too:

- presenting the wine reduces the risk of opening the wrong bottle because you have misheard the name

- opening the bottle in view of the customers reassures them about the quality of the wine

- allowing the person who ordered the wine to taste a little, gives a chance to correct problems before the glasses are filled, e.g. chill the wine for longer.

Dealing with customers

Wine drinking is on the increase. Some customers know a great deal about wine, others want to give that impression. Some enjoy trying different wines, others keep to what they know.

You must try to please all types. It helps to know enough about the wines you sell not to contradict the knowledgeable and be able to give information to those who appreciate it. At the same time, you can do your part to promote drink sales by suggesting and describing appropriate wines.

Providing information on wines

To choose a wine, customers need to know what is available and the price. They will look at the wine list or ask you. Often they do both. They appreciate your suggestions, as well as questions you ask so as to give them the best advice, e.g.:

- would you prefer red or white, or perhaps a rosé?

- we have some oaky Chardonnays that go well with the pasta you have ordered, or would you rather a fruity white, or perhaps a medium dry?

- for the festive occasion, yet good value, there are some excellent sparkling wines from Spain and South Africa

- the house wines, on special promotion this month, are from a prize winning winery in Portugal.

How customers choose wine

Customers arrive at their choice in any number of ways. Some look for a name they know:

- the grape, e.g. Cabernet Sauvignon – many New World producers (e.g. New Zealand, California) and the traditional wine-growing countries of Europe use the grape variety to describe the style of wine

- the producer or shipper, e.g. Torres (Spain) and Hunter's Valley (Australia) – well established names, may be widely advertised

Good wine service adds to the enjoyment of restaurant dining.

- the country, e.g. Greece – perhaps because customers have been to that country on holiday, or they generally enjoy wines from there, or have read or heard about them

- the region, e.g. Moselle – this may reflect more detailed knowledge about wine or the wines of particular countries, or the power of traditional wine-growing regions, e.g. Chianti, Bordeaux.

From the wine list (and/or the label on the bottle) you should find sufficient information to help such customers make their choice.

Other customers begin with the colour and style of wine. They know or have some idea of what is appropriate for the situation and choice of food. They may have preferences, e.g. for a light-bodied wine, or a rich, spicy one. They appreciate suggestions from you which meet these requirements.

Sometimes customers do not know as much as their use of names suggests, thinking for example that Fitou is a Spanish wine. Try to guide them without saying directly that they are wrong.

Promoting wines

By giving helpful advice, you promote wine sales. As a result of your suggestions, customers may order wine when they would otherwise have had nothing, or a better quality wine (at a higher price) instead of their choice of the house bottle.

Your aim must be to please the customers (see checklist on page 78). You want them to feel that the better wine was worth the extra it cost, not that they were the victim of high-pressure selling.

Who can be served alcohol

You cannot serve wine (unless the non-alcoholic type) to customers under the age of 18 in England and Wales and 16 in Scotland (see page 76). Adults can order and serve wine to youngsters and children below these ages (but not younger than 5) who are eating with them.

Serving red, white and rosé wines

For most customers, seeing their bottle of wine opened for them is part of the experience of drinking wine (see illustration below and page 87).

Temperature

Red wine is served at room temperature (a warm room, that is), white, rosé and sparkling wine chilled (see illustration below). But if a customer says a wine at these temperatures is too cold or not properly chilled, you should do your best to correct the situation.

If a customer orders a bottle which needs:

- *warming* – warm a decanter or carafe for a few minutes in a hot cupboard, then transfer the wine to this. Alternatively, wrap around the decanter a clean cloth soaked in hot water and well rung out

- *chilling* – put in a bucket of ice and water for 15 to 20 minutes. If you add salt and move the bottle from time to time, 5 minutes may be sufficient.

Information on the label

By law:
country wine made
alcoholic strength
contents in litres, cl or ml
standard size: 75 cl (750 ml)
bottler or brand owner and address
(for EU wines) quality of wine

Crocodile Tears
of 1995
Australian wine of unusual quality
Handmade and bottled by the owner
at his estate from Amber Nectar grapes
Best served at 10°C
as an accompaniment to most barbequed food

13% vol   Michael Dundee   75cl
Darwin   Northern Territory   Australia

Other information:
vintage (year grapes harvested)
region or area wine made
grape variety
where wine bottled
quality testing number
style of wine & serving suggestions

20°C   medium and full-bodied reds

17°C   light reds, Beaujolais Nouveau

10°C   whites and rosés

7°C   sparkling wines and Champagnes

1 show the bottle to the customer to confirm that it is the one ordered

2 cut off the top of the plastic or foil capsule which protects the cork – this looks neater than removing all the capsule, or leaving a torn edge

3 check for any dirt on the top of the bottle and the cork – likely on older bottles

4 wipe clean with a moistened napkin – paper to avoid stains to linen ones

5 remove the cork (see also page 87) the shaft of the corkscrew should go into the centre of the cork, deep enough to get a good grip, but not right through the cork – you don't want to find the cork has broken, leaving some stuck in the bottle, or bits floating in the wine

6 ask 'Would you like to taste the wine?' some customers say no

7 if so, pour a little wine into the glass of the person who ordered it

8 when you get approval, pour some wine for all the customers who are drinking it

9 fill the glasses not more than two-thirds full to allow the bouquet of the wine to be enjoyed

Preparing service areas, equipment and stock (for wine service)

Customers expect their wine to be served without delay. This is easier when you are well prepared, equipment in place, and a sufficient stock of each wine is at or near serving temperature (see beginning of this section).

More on storing wines

The wine inside a bottle goes through a continuous process of change. Some wines improve with age to reach a peak, and then the quality spoils. The deterioration in quality may be very slow for six months to a few years, depending on the wine, so that it is hardly noticeable, but after that the wine soon becomes undrinkable.

The right conditions and temperature (see below) help keep wines in the best condition for as long as possible.

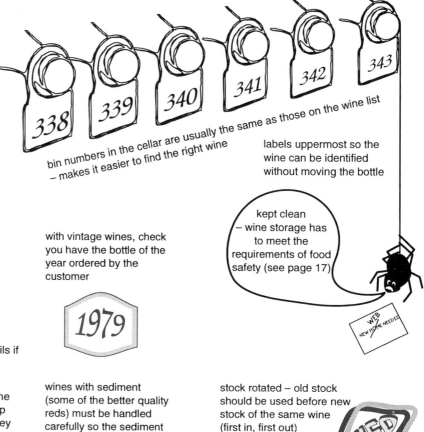

size and shape to concentrate aroma (bouquet)

clear, colourless glass so natural colours of wine can be appreciated

if different glasses used for white wine, bowl is slimmer and overall size smaller than red

good quality, thin, plain glass feels good in the hand and on the lips; some restaurants use cut-glass

tulip or flûte shape for sparkling wines shows bubbles to advantage, and they last longer than in saucer-shaped glasses

large enough to hold reasonable amount of wine (about one-sixth of a bottle) yet not more than two-thirds full

moderate length stem so glass can be held without the hands warming a chilled wine

narrower at lip than in bowl

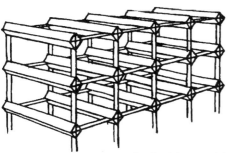

bottles lying on side so wine keeps cork moist

bin numbers in the cellar are usually the same as those on the wine list – makes it easier to find the right wine

labels uppermost so the wine can be identified without moving the bottle

on racks in cellar: dark, slightly humid cellar or room where temperature is fairly constant and cool (10°C to 12°C)

with vintage wines, check you have the bottle of the year ordered by the customer

1979

kept clean – wine storage has to meet the requirements of food safety (see page 17)

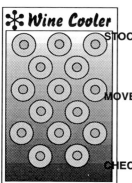

✳ Wine Cooler

STOCK with sufficient to cover day's sales – wine spoils if kept too long at low temperatures

MOVE the bottles already in the chiller to the front or top when restocking, so they are used first

CHECK temperature regularly

wines with sediment (some of the better quality reds) must be handled carefully so the sediment slips to the bottom of the bottle, not mixed in with the wine

stock rotated – old stock should be used before new stock of the same wine (first in, first out)

FIFO

Determining customer requirements for wines

There is a wider choice of wines in the UK than virtually anywhere else in the world. The range available in your workplace will be selected for its appeal to customers, providing interest and good value.

Dealing with customers

When customers obviously know a lot more about wine than you, show that you respect their greater knowledge. Treat it as an opportunity to learn more, not a competition to prove who is the most expert.

Nor is there anything to be gained by challenging the accuracy of what customers say about wine. If they wish to give fellow customers (and you) the impression they are experts, find things to say which go along with this. Faced with what you are sure is a wrong choice, suggest alternatives and why they would be suitable, then respect the customer's final decision.

Maintaining a rapport with your customers

Build up a repertoire of something to say about each of the wines on your list. A few words that convey the style and characteristics of the wine are usually all that is required.

Try to link what you say to what will catch the interest of customers. What style of wine would they like? What would go with the food they have ordered? Have they heard about the wine's success in a recent competition or tasting on the TV? Do they have favourite countries or regions or grape varieties?

Dealing with their queries helpfully

Prepare for questions from customers by linking what you can offer to the points they may consider when choosing wine (page 83).

As you develop your knowledge of wine, you'll get better at matching the style and character of wines you don't sell, to those you do. Asked for Beaumes-de-Venise, you can suggest an Australian dessert wine, describing its luscious quality and strong orange blossom nose (or bouquet).

Wine with food

Remember, the choice of wine is up to the customer, not you. That said, there are some widely accepted guidelines which form a good starting point for advising customers:

- dry wines before sweet wines – if sweet wines are drunk first they tend to overwhelm the taste of the medium or dry white wines

- white wines before red wines for the same reason

- white wines go well with light dishes such as salads, and with fish and most white meat

- red wines complement red meat and cheeses

- full-bodied reds are better for game and other strongly flavoured foods

- sweet white wines go well with desserts

- avoid wines with food which contain acid (e.g. fresh grapefruit as a starter). Vinaigrette dressings, strongly spiced dishes and hot curries can overwhelm wine.

Presenting the wine list

Handing the wine list to customers is usually a good time to tell them about promotions and special features, e.g. the excellent value Riojas or the recently arrived stock of an acclaimed vintage.

Taking orders

Take care to avoid mistakes over which wine has been ordered. This may happen with names that are difficult to pronounce or spell, when there is more than one wine with a similar name (e.g. of the grape), or different vintages of the same wine.

Write the order details clearly (see page 54) and then confirm the order with the customer. If the wine has a number on the list, say both the number and the name of the wine to the customer.

Presenting and serving wines

Most customers expect to have the bottle presented to them, and to see it opened. Doing so adds to the sense of anticipation and the subsequent pleasure from drinking the wine. It also has practical advantages (see page 83).

Check your preparation is complete before you reach this stage. Are the correct glasses on the table? Is an ice bucket or wine cooler available? Have you a corkscrew?

Handling and presenting wine

Handle bottles with care and respect – customers are paying for the wine. Shaking a sparkling wine causes frothing when you come to open it, and the cork may shoot out. Any sediment in red wine will get disturbed.

Presenting the wine

Show the bottle before opening to the person who ordered it. Hold it so that the label can be clearly seen.

If the wine is already cooling in a bucket, bring both to the table. Lift the bottle out of the bucket, wipe dry with a clean napkin or service cloth, and then present it.

Opening and serving wine

Open white and sparkling wines when the customer is ready to drink them. Red wines can be opened after they have been approved.

Opening a bottle of still wine

1 Remove the top of the plastic or metal capsule which covers the cork. Use a small sharp knife (the blade of the waiter's knife is ideal – in use in the photographs). Do not rotate the bottle – with experience you will be able to cut round the capsule in one movement.

2 Wipe the top of the bottle with a moistened napkin.

3 Pinpoint the centre of the cork with the tip of the corkscrew, then raise it directly above the bottle.

4 Keeping the corkscrew upright, twist firmly twice.

5 Hold the lever of the waiter's friend against the rim of the bottle. With the other hand, lever the cork out a short distance. Then give the waiter's friend another two turns and lever the cork a second time until it is almost out of the bottle.

6 With your fingers, pull the cork out gently and quietly.

7 Remove the cork from the corkscrew.

8 Wipe the neck of the bottle with a moistened napkin.

The ring of the bottle provides a natural guide for the knife blade.

Aim the tip of the cork-screw dead centre in the cork.

Hold the lever of the waiter's friend firmly against the bottle.

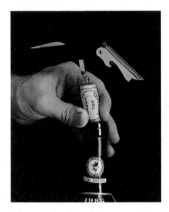

The cork should not make a sound as you pull it out the bottle.

Three senses are involved in the appreciation of wine: sight, smell and taste, in that order.

Grip the lever in a way you feel comfortable and safe with.

Smelling the cork is more of a ritual than a guaranteed test.

Opening a bottle of sparkling wine or Champagne

Safety should be your first consideration. People have lost an eye through carelessness when opening sparkling wine. Always cover the top of the bottle with a napkin and keep your finger over the cork.

1 Grip the bottle firmly with one hand. Hold the bottle at an angle of 45°, pointing away from anyone or anything that might be damaged should the cork suddenly shoot out.

2 Locate the ring of the wire muzzle with the fingers of the other hand.

3 Untwist the wire muzzle to break it.

4 Take a firm grip of the top of the cork (with the muzzle and foil still in place) with one hand. With the other, firmly grip the bottle. Gently twist the bottle in one direction, the cork in the other.

5 As you feel the cork begin to move, ease it out between your finger and thumb. Continue to hold the napkin over the top of the cork. The cork should come out with a hiss.

If the cork won't budge, don't peer at it – it's likely to hit you in the eye. Call your manager or a colleague to help, in the meantime keeping your finger over the cork.

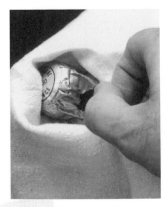

From the time you pick up the bottle until the cork is released (step 5 above), hold your thumb securely over the cork to prevent it flying out the bottle. The napkin is also a safety precaution.

Once the bottle is open

The cork is sometimes left with the customer, on a small plate, in the wine basket or the ice bucket.

Pouring and letting customers taste the wine

Stand behind the customer's right shoulder to pour the wine. When the service style is less formal, you might be able to fill everyone's glass standing in one position at the table. Avoid stretching in front of anyone.

Offer the person who ordered the wine the opportunity to taste a little before you begin pouring (see page 84).

The neck of the bottle must not touch the glass as you pour (for hygiene and safety reasons). Twist the bottle slightly as you lift it from the glass. This prevents wine dripping on to the table. For the same reason, wipe the neck of the bottle with a napkin after each pouring.

Pour wine for each customer who requires it. To allow the bouquet to be enjoyed, no wine glass should be filled more than two-thirds full. Some experts recommend between one-third and one-half full. Pour sparkling wine slowly, so the wine does not froth too much.

When some wine is left in the bottle

When everyone has been served, place the bottle near the person who ordered it, or in the centre of the table:

- white, rosé and sparkling wines in a wine cooler (or ice bucket, but this may over-chill the wine)
- red wines standing on a coaster or small plate, or lying in a basket.

If you return the wine to an ice bucket, leave the napkin hanging over the top of the bottle, or on the handle of the ice bucket. It is then handy to wipe the bottle when you or the customer wants to refill the glasses.

Replenishing glasses

In some restaurants, customers are expected to (and prefer it this way) to help themselves to more wine as they wish. In others, the bottle is left within reach of the customers, but serving staff regularly refill glasses. Or the bottle is kept on the sideboard and serving staff refill glasses (but they should not wait to be asked).

Pause for a moment before pouring, so customers who have had enough can say so. Take empty bottles away promptly, asking if the customers would like another.

Serving another bottle

When serving another bottle, present and open it as before, then pour a little into a clean glass for approval. If the wine is different, give everyone a clean glass. Even when it is another bottle of the same wine, some restaurants will provide clean glasses.

Dealing with faults

By knowing what to look out for, you can often prevent a faulty wine being served, or at least being tasted by the customer. But if it is the customer who first notices the fault, a knowledgeable response from you will keep the customer satisfied.

These are the general rules:

1 Apologise and remove the faulty wine and any glasses into which it has been poured.

2 Offer another bottle of the same wine or invite the customer to choose a different wine.

3 Bring fresh glasses with the new wine.

4 Recork the faulty wine or seal the bottle with clingfilm, and put aside for your manager to deal with. Generally the offending bottle will be returned to the supplier.

The condition of the bottle

Any sign that wine has leaked out (e.g. stickiness around neck) indicates a faulty cork. Do not serve.

If the wine has been stored in a damp cellar, the label will looked aged. This is not usually a problem, unless there is doubt over the identity of the wine.

The appearance of the wine in the bottle

Crystals (of tartar) in white wine are harmless and do not affect the taste. They probably mean the wine has been stored at very low temperatures at some stage.

If a still wine appears to be fermenting in the bottle (small bubbles form, especially when it is moved), do not serve. Remember that some wines are made to sparkle slightly in the bottle (e.g. Lambrusco, Vinho Verde).

If the wine is cloudy, stand the bottle upright. If it does not clear within 24 hours, it should not be served.

In a mature red wine, some natural sediment is to be expected. Wines of this age are often decanted.

The end of the cork

Crystals on the end of the cork are harmless.

A dry cork on an older wine is a sign that the bottle has been stored upright. This will not necessarily spoil the wine, but the cork may be difficult to extract cleanly.

If the cork is very dry and has shrunk so much you think air has got to the wine (which will ruin it), get another bottle, or recommend a replacement.

Giving service

The basis of good service is where:

• the giver is **happy** to give the service
• the giver is **confident** in what he or she is doing
• the giver is **at ease** in the service situation.

Dealing with complaints

Be very positive, friendly and genuine – the customer will quickly pick up if you're not interested or up-tight about dealing with the situation.

Own the problem – take the attitude that it is **my** problem, I want to be the one to sort it out and make this customer happy again.

Listen – to find out the facts, to allow the customer to let off steam.

Apologise – 'I'm sorry to hear that' followed by 'thanks for telling me' is very effective in calming angry customers.

Deal with the problem – to make the customer satisfied as soon as possible.

Sound friendly – avoid a monotonous, expressionless tone in your voice. Do not use sarcasm or sound superior.

The wine itself smells unpleasant

Some wines give off a mildly unpleasant smell after the bottle is first opened. It is the result of many years of storage in the bottle and should disappear quickly, leaving the wine unaffected. With some red wines the smell in these first few moments is dank, while some white wines smell of sulphur.

A genuine 'corked wine' is rare (although some people use the expression incorrectly, to describe wine which has pieces of cork in it). It has a strong, pungent and unpleasant dank smell of mushrooms. The smell may go after the wine has been opened for a short time, but if not, do not serve.

The wine will also taste (and probably smell) unpleasant if the glass it is served in has not been washed correctly, leaving traces of detergent or grease.

Appearance of the wine in the glass

If a still wine fizzes or has bubbles (not noticed before the bottle was opened), do not continue serving.

If the wine is darker than it should be, this is a sign of oxidation (probably because the cork has dried out and shrunk, letting in air).

If crystals, sediment or bits of cork have got into the glass, remove the offending glass and apologise. Depending on how much wine is lost, customers may expect a replacement glass from another bottle – your manager will advise.

Customer finds the wine faulty on tasting it

Report it to your manager who will pour a little into a clean glass, smell and if necessary taste the wine. If the wine is faulty, it will be replaced without question.

1 Describe the preparations you make for service.

2 Give the safety and hygiene points you should follow when carrying and handling glasses.

3 When unloading a tray of drinks, how can you prevent the tray over-balancing?

4 How can you remember which drink is for which customer?

5 What information must you write on the drinks order?

6 What is the measure of spirits sold in your restaurant? When wine is sold by the glass, what quantity can you offer?

7 What accompaniments should you offer for a) gin, b) brandy, c) vodka, d) whisky, e) rum?

8 What drinks might these glasses contain? How would they be poured at table? Comment on the way the tray is loaded.

9 What is wrong about this, and why?

10 Give the rules for making tea.

boiling
pre-warm
amount
infuse
(not stew)

11 Describe one method of making coffee. Say what should and should not be done.

12 What should you do if a drink is spilled over the customer's table?

soak up spill
don't risk staining
apologise
to customer
get manager
cover damp area of cloth

13 Say when you should **not** try to sell an alcoholic drink.

NO ALCOHOL SERVED

NO THANKS I'M DRIVING

NO ALCOHOL SERVED

NO THANKS

14 What would you do (and say to the customer) in each of these situations?

under-age wants alcohol
customer trips
drunk wants drink
customer argument
complaint

15 What would you say to these customers? Why is it important your information is accurate?

Something non-alcoholic please.
Glass of sweet red... Fruit tea...
XXX
Martini - no olive...
lager...
Bottle of bubbly...
Just water, thank you...

1 Why are these problems? How can they be avoided?

2 What safe practices should you follow when carrying out these tasks?

3 Mark the serving temperature for each type of wine.

4 Describe the best way to get each type of wine to its serving temperature. What can you do to quickly a) warm, b) chill a wine?

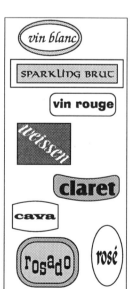

5 Which of these wines could you serve each of these customers and why?

6 What is wrong about this information given to customers? How would you avoid making similar mistakes?

7 What are the good and bad points about these glasses for wine? Mark the best glass for each type of wine and where it should be filled to.

8 What could go wrong here? Describe how the bottle should be opened.

9 Describe 5 wines from your list, as you would to customers.

10 Choose and describe a wine to recommend to these customers.

11 What should you do about each of these situations, and what would have helped avoid the problem?

12 What information should be on the label? Say something about this wine.

Element 1

Take customer orders

Check service equipment and get ready for service ☐ PC1

▲ Glassware, trays, service linen, pen, note paper

Greet and deal with customers politely and helpfully ☐ PC2

▲ Those who: comply with licensing legislation; act in drunken manner; violent or disorderly; under-age; under exclusion order; requesting service outside hours

Identify, record and deal with customers' requirements ☐ PC3

Promote drinks to customers at all appropriate times ☐ PC4

Give customers accurate information ☐ PC5

▲ Price, special offers, ingredients, alternatives, relative strength

Deal with unexpected situations effectively & inform appropriate people ☐ PC6

Prioritise and carry out your work in an organised, efficient and safe manner ☐ PC7

Element 2

Serve orders to table

Deal with customers politely and helpfully ☐ PC1

Keep service equipment clean and free from damage ☐ PC2

Serve drinks to meet customer requirements ☐ PC3

▲ Draught & bottled beers/cider, wine, spirits, soft drinks, minerals/juices, hot drinks

Serve alcoholic drinks only to permitted customers ☐ PC4

Give customers accurate information on drinks ☐ PC5

Deal with unexpected situations effectively & inform appropriate people ☐ PC6

Prioritise and carry out your work in an organised, efficient and safe manner ☐ PC7

Element 1

Prepare bottled wines for service

Prepare the wine service area ☐ PC1

Maintain wines at correct temperature ☐ PC2

▲ Red, white and rosé wines

Select clean, undamaged bottles for use ☐ PC3

Check service equipment is clean and ready for use ☐ PC4

▲ Ice buckets, wine coolers, carafes, decanters, corkscrews, serving cloths, wine lists/menus

Deal with unexpected situations effectively & inform appropriate people ☐ PC5

Do your work in an organised, efficient and safe manner ☐ PC6

Element 2

Serve bottled wines

Deal with customers in a polite and helpful manner ☐ PC1

Give accurate wine list information to meet customer requirements ☐ PC2

▲ Flavour, price, country of origin

Serve only permitted persons ☐ PC3

Promote wines at appropriate times ☐ PC4

Identify customer requirements, present and serve wine ☐ PC5

Serve wine at correct temperature using appropriate equipment ☐ PC6

Deal with unexpected situations effectively & inform appropriate people ☐ PC7

Do your work in an organised, efficient and safe manner ☐ PC8

Element 1

Prepare service areas, equipment and stock for wine service

Get service equipment, table items and wine lists ready ☐ PC1

▲ Glassware, trays, service cloths/linen, cork-screws/opener, ice buckets, chillers/coolers

Check wines are available, ready for service ☐ PC2

▲ Red, white, sparkling, semi-sparkling, rosé, low/non-alcoholic wines

Deal with unexpected situations effectively & inform appropriate people ☐ PC3

Prioritise and carry out your work in an organised, efficient and safe manner ☐ PC4

Element 2

Determine customer requirements for wines

Greet and deal with customers in welcoming, polite manner ☐ PC1

Identify host and present wine list PC2 ☐

Give accurate wine list information PC3 ☐

▲ Name and type of wine, prices, main characteristics, alcohol content, country of origin

Establish rapport with customers PC4 ☐

Deal with queries correctly PC5 ☐

Record/deal with customers' orders PC6 ☐

Deal with unexpected situations, etc PC7 ☐

Prioritise and carry out work, etc. PC8 ☐

Element 3

Present and serve wine

Prepare service areas, equipment and wine for service ☐ PC1

Serve customers in polite, helpful manner ☐ PC2

Handle and present wine in appropriate style ☐ PC3

Serve wine at correct temperature using correct equipment ☐ PC4

Identify and deal with faults PC5 ☐

Replenish glasses regularly PC6 ☐

Deal with unexpected situations, etc PC7 ☐

Prioritise and carry out work, etc. PC8 ☐

Counter and take-away service

Preparing areas for counter/take-away service

Customers want to enjoy their food and drink in pleasant surroundings. Attention to detail, from the arrangement of napkins to the general comfort of the room, shows customers that you care.

Preparing the work areas

Everywhere should look tidy and be clean. Check that everything has been left in its proper place by the cleaners, and that no rubbish or cleaning equipment has been forgotten, e.g. under seats or tables.

Approach each area as your customers will:

- *waiting area* – while queuing and deciding what to eat and drink. Are menus, price lists, etc. the correct ones? Do promotional displays look attractive?

- *service area* – at the counters, choosing and taking their order. Are the front of counters clean? What about the floor and wall areas customers can see from their side of the counter?

- *seated area* – finding a table and sitting at it. Are non-smoking areas well signed? If an area is closed off for some reason, or tables reserved for special parties, is this clear to customers?

Promptly report broken equipment, damaged fittings, light bulbs not working, etc. Cordon-off unsafe areas and remove any furniture or equipment which is a safety hazard. Check that fire escapes are clear.

Top-up brochure racks. If newspapers are supplied, check these are in place. Tidy noticeboards and displays of promotional material.

Preparing service equipment

One of your first tasks may be to switch on equipment that needs to get hot or cold before it is stocked with food. Some refrigerated and cold display units are always left on, e.g. for canned and bottled cold drinks. Check these are at the correct temperature.

Check glass panels, sneeze screens and shelves of display units. Use a polishing cloth to remove any smears or fingerprints. (Sneeze screens have this name because they protect the food should a customer sneeze or cough in the direction of the display.)

Preparing service items

Examine each item carefully. Return to the wash-up or wash yourself any that are not clean. Put aside any which are damaged or faulty.

Refill the *cutlery* containers. Stack *trays* at the beginning of counter runs or the entrance to the serving area. Put glasses, cups and saucers, plates and other *crockery* where they will be needed. Some counter units have lowerators for storing plates. Each time a plate is taken, a spring mechanism pushes up the pile of plates inside the cabinet. Trays, cups and sauces may be stacked in dispensers, to look neater, make them easier for customers to handle and reduce breakages.

Refill dispensers or containers which hold napkins, drinking straws, disposable drinking containers, stirrers for tea/coffee, etc. Top-up supplies of food containers, boxes, cartons, bags, drink cups and lids and other *packaging* required for take-away orders. Other items used in take-aways include disposable cutlery (e.g. plastic spoons with ice-creams), wet wipes or towelettes, tray mats, and coupons, scratch cards or similar promotional material.

After finding out what is on the menu, collect and position spoons, ladles, serving tongs, food slices and other *serving utensils* that will be needed. Some dishes require particular utensils to help with portion control (see below). For hygiene and food quality reasons, and to avoid delays in service, each dish should have its own set of serving utensils.

Place *ashtrays* on tables where smoking is allowed. You may have to set tables with place mats, tablecloths, cutlery, glasses and other items (see page 48).

Refuse and waste food containers

Waste in the wrong place is a safety and hygiene risk. It makes customer and service areas look untidy.

Customers are less likely to leave their rubbish lying around when there is somewhere convenient to dispose of it. They are more likely to use bins that look tidy and clean, and seem to be emptied regularly.

Promotional materials

Display the day's menu, check prices and remove any out of stock items. Confirm that you have the appropriate vouchers or coupons for special promotions, and that the advertising material is well displayed.

Promotional material must look good to get customers' attention, encourage them to spend more, try new dishes and drinks. The spelling must be right, the words accurate (see illustration on opposite page).

Storing and displaying food for service

Carefully stored, attractively displayed food encourages sales. Hot food kept on the counter too long looks dry and unappetising. Customers find over-crowded counters confusing. Serving is difficult from containers which are too full or too close to other foods.

Poor practices are a hygiene hazard, allowing harmful bacteria to multiply (see pages 17).

Keep doors of food display units shut. The equipment will work more efficiently, and there is less risk of temperature variation. Cold food which gets warm, and hot food which gets cold usually has to be thrown out.

Chilled food and drink

Bottled and canned cold drinks, fruit juice and milk dispensers can be stocked well in advance, provided the equipment has reached the correct temperature. Also put out packaged food that does not need chilling, e.g. biscuits, crisps and sweets. Check all date marks, and arrange items so that the older stock is used first. Withdraw any stock which has passed its date.

Bring cold food (sweets, starters, salads, etc.) from the kitchen before the hot dishes. Place them in the chilled cabinets without delay. If you do not know, check where each item should go before you collect the food.

Do not block the intake or outlet air vents of refrigerated displays with dishes of food or decorations.

Hot food

Immediately before service, collect hot dishes. The kitchen will usually cook these in batches when service is over an extended period, so the quality remains high.

Some fast food and other restaurants have a system for controlling the time that food is on display. Records are kept for each batch, the temperature of the equipment and wastage (food which has passed its maximum display time).

Condiments and accompaniments

In staff restaurants, salts and peppers, sugar, tomato and other sauces may be put on customers' tables. In motorway restaurants, single-portion sachets are usually placed at the cutlery dispense point or other convenient place. In fast food and take-away restaurants, sachets are given to the customer with the food, or containers put on the counter.

Before each service, check that pots and jars are clean and full.

Food safety and hygiene

Keep food covered as much as possible, or protected behind glass display panels. Cover hot dishes with a lid when there is no one at the counter. Follow workplace rules on wearing gloves and uniform.

When customers can serve themselves to dishes, check that serving utensils are available. Remove and replace any that fall in the food, or which you see customers use for another dish.

Promoting sales

In counter service, customers see the food. You can add impact to the display (see also page 70) with:

- *colour* – contrasting colours help to offset each other, e.g. carrots between containers of green vegetables

- *shape* – a variety of shapes adds interest, e.g. filled rolls next to sandwiches

- *texture* – contrasts increase appeal, e.g. chocolate mousse next to fruit salad

- *portion size* – match portion size and plates. An overcrowded plate looks messy and too large a plate makes the portion look mean.

Remember that you are dealing with food. Don't:

- mix cooked and uncooked items, e.g. a fresh trout surrounded by fillets of smoked trout

- put plants or fresh flower arrangements where they might come into direct contact with uncovered food

- display food in containers which cannot be properly cleaned, e.g. bread rolls in a wicker basket

- use artificial food in arrangements which might lead customers to think that it is fresh food, available for sale, e.g. a plastic apple among the cheeses.

GARDNER MERCHANT

Selling ideas

Take products from their usual position and create a special 'impact' display.

'Pile it high' to make a bold display – but don't overdo it and confuse the customer.

Group related products together to encourage a second purchase, e.g.:

• sandwich, yogurt, drink   • salad, bread roll, butter

With 'mix n' match' displays: balance colours together and strive for maximum eye appeal.

While your customers are waiting, catch their eye at the till – with confectionery, home-made jams, recipe books, etc. Think of the things you decide on impulse to buy at a supermarket, as you queue at the till.

People relate to people. 'Julie's Special' or 'Alan's Dish of the Day' sounds much more friendly and personal than 'Chef's Special'.

Don't just have a chilled display cabinet. Do something with it. Change the name to 'Eskimo's Larder', 'Arctic Shop', etc.

Element 2

Clearing areas for counter/take-away service

The priority is to leave everything safe and tidy, so the cleaners can do their job properly. If you are working in a 24-hour operation, clearing will take place during quiet periods. Sections of the counter and seating areas are closed off.

Wipe down equipment, tables and chairs. Change cleaning solutions regularly, and follow instructions for use carefully. Many will damage surfaces and harm you if misused.

Check under tabletops and chair seats for anything sticky (e.g. chewing gum). It may be your job to sweep up rubbish, vacuum or mop floors.

Service equipment

After removing food and food containers (see below), switch off equipment, as instructed. Leave heated units to reach room temperature before cleaning. Rinse and dry surfaces.

Remove grease and food from corners and the runners of sliding doors. Use a nylon brush or pad to remove stubborn deposits, never anything that will scratch the surface. Special cleaning solutions are required to avoid damaging or discolouring some surfaces.

Collect food containers, serving utensils, trays, cutlery, crockery and similar items, and take to the wash-up. Empty ashtrays into a fire-proof container. Wash separately from other service items to prevent contamination.

Dealing with waste

Remove rubbish from floors, tables and elsewhere. When emptying rubbish bins or removing waste bags, watch out for dripping liquid (when partly-filled drink containers have been dropped in the rubbish).

Returning food and drink items to storage

Return food to the kitchen or preparation area without delay. The chefs may deal with left-over food, while you put away butter packs, fruit juices, canned drinks, accompaniments, condiments, etc. Check date marks, keep stocks of the same age together and put aside anything which has passed its date or the packaging has been damaged on display.

8 Counter and take-away service

Units 1NC4 and 2NC12, Element 1

Serving customers at the counter

There are three variations on **counter service**:

- *un-assisted* – customers help themselves to everything. This encourages a feeling of value for money
- *partly-assisted* – some items are served, usually the more expensive, as staff can give the right portion
- *fully-assisted* – everything is served, giving better portion control, food presentation and faster service.

In **take-away service**, counter staff take the order and payment, and package the food so it can be eaten off the premises. In drive-thru restaurants, cars proceed from the order point to the cashier's window to the collection window (or payment and collection are combined).

Dealing with customers

You have a few moments only with each customer to convey friendly service and personal attention.

Greeting customers

A warm smile and a short, but friendly greeting wins over most people. Look at customers' faces, not the counter.

Taking the order

Looking at the person whose order you are taking also helps you. Watch the lip movement and facial expression and you'll find it easier to understand what the person is saying, and how he or she is reacting to what you are saying. This is especially helpful if the restaurant is noisy, or the accent is unfamiliar to you.

Be patient if the customer has problems communicating. Point out items to establish what is wanted (for more on this and mobility difficulties, see pages 12 to 14).

You may have to write the order down, or key it into a cash till or electronic terminal (see Section 4). If payment is made elsewhere, you will be given the details of what to serve.

Offer accompaniments to suit the dish, e.g. ice cream with the apple pie, chips with the burger. Say if a dish or drink is unavailable, and recommend alternatives.

Repeat the order. This gives customers a chance to confirm what they want. While doing so, you can ask if they want a regular or large portion, or a drink.

If customers are ordering from their car (in a drive-thru restaurant) speak clearly to overcome noise in and around the customers' car. Keep questions short and simple. Be polite but do not have a conversation.

Ten Golden Rules of Service

CASTLE VIEW

1 Know your menu.
2 Your counter display must look good – people eat with their eyes. Cold food is very easy to display, but don't forget to show the customers the hot food as well.
3 Take a few minutes before service to tidy up. Make sure your overall is neat and clean and always wear a cap.
4 Smile!
5 Never leave a customer waiting.
6 Never be too busy for a customer.
7 Get to know your different customers and cater for them.
8 Never eat at the counter.
9 If you think any portion of food is of a poor standard or looks cold, do not serve it – inform the supervisor.
10 Always keep food cabinets topped up. Remember – the last customer is as important as the first.

Promoting sales

You do this when you suggest other items and tell customers about special offers, e.g. free coffee if they also have a sweet. (See box opposite.)

Providing accurate information

If there are dishes on the menu you don't know, find out what is in them and how they are made, before service begins. You can then answer customers' questions quickly and helpfully.

You must be accurate about ingredients which customers may not like or cannot eat. Don't guess or try and get away with vague answers, 'Well apple pie doesn't usually have nuts in'. Tell the customer the chef does sometimes vary the recipe, and you will check immediately if they wouldn't mind waiting.

Informing customers of waiting time

Sometimes customers can't or don't want to wait. Telling them that there will be a few minutes' delay, e.g. because their dish is cooked to order, or more food is on its way from the kitchen, gives them the chance to say so. You can then suggest alternatives.

What customers don't like is uncertainty, or what proves to be inaccurate information. Saying that more soup is on its way and giving the same answer 10 minutes later will annoy customers. Find out how long the delay will be, and tell customers that it's likely to be – 5, 10, 15 minutes or whatever.

If take-aways are delivered, you will have to consider the delivery time as well as that required to prepare the order (see below).

Taking customers' orders by phone (for take-aways)

Customers telephone their order because they want it ready when they call, or to have it delivered.

1 Answer with a pleasant greeting, the restaurant name (in case the customer has dialled a wrong number) and your name (for the personal touch).

2 Speak clearly and smile. While customers cannot see you, smiling helps you sound friendly and cheerful.

3 Ask for the customer's name. Getting this now means you can use it. Customers feel they are getting more personal service when you use their name. If the name is a difficult one, politely ask the customer to spell it. Say it back to confirm you have the correct spelling and pronunciation.

4 If the customer doesn't have a menu or know the restaurant, you'll have to say what is available and the prices. Most people have some idea of what they want, and you can save time by finding out what this is and then making suitable suggestions.

5 Check details as you proceed, e.g. whether it is a large or standard pizza. Promote specials and encourage customers to order more, as you would taking an order at the counter.

6 Ask if the customer is collecting the order or wants it delivered. Check when it is required and confirm that this is possible, or agree a time which is acceptable – taking account of traffic, weather, distance and availability of delivery crew. You will get to know difficult addresses, e.g. a block of flats with a lot of stairs to climb to the front door.

7 For orders which are being collected, get the customer's telephone number. If customers are reluctant to give it, or say there is no point because they will be on their way to collect the food, explain that it is company policy to get it. If the customer is using a call box, it is still useful to have the number. Hoax calls may have come from that phone or area.

8 For delivered orders, ask for the address. Take care over each detail. For unfamiliar addresses, ask for information which will help the delivery crew, e.g. 'Can you tell me what road that is off, please?'

9 Read back the order, address and telephone number. Say how much it will cost, and any delivery charge, e.g. because it is out of the free delivery area. Confirm the time it will be ready/delivered.

To avoid problems with hoax calls, you may have to ask for payment against a credit card. Other checks are:

- call back the number with an excuse, e.g. 'I do apologise, but I should have asked if you wanted extra cheese with the pizza'

- dial 1471 to get the voice giving the time and number of the last caller. Some phones display the number of the caller and of previous callers. But callers can prevent their number being revealed.

Delivery hospitality

Greet the customer in the unit or on the phone with a smile and a personable and courteous verbal greeting.

In the unit

- for take-away obtain name, for delivery, obtain name and address
- suggest appropriate deals and promotional items
- repeat the order
- complete payment transaction
- indicate where the customer may wait if for takeaway.

On the phone

- answer within the first 3 rings, identify self and unit
- collect customer information by asking questions and suggesting value and promotional items
- repeat order and verify coupons if appropriate.

Selling by suggestion

Some customers come into your restaurant not sure what food they want. No problem! You have a full range of products to tempt them with.

Other customers rush in, knowing basically what they want. No problem either. You have a few minutes to sell the products they want, and suggest others they might want but hadn't thought of or didn't realise were available.

Yet other customers really do know what they want. They will not usually object to you offering other products but may be offended by the over-sell.

With the right selling technique you can win new customers, and keep a regular customer coming back.

1 Look directly at the customer and smile. Everyone responds to a smile. Make it natural, and let the smile reach up into your eyes.

2 Make the food you are describing sound irresistible. Use phrases which will tempt your customer. On a hot day: 'Would you like a long cool drink?' sounds more refreshing than: 'Would you like a drink?'

3 Promote larger portions or sizes. Suggest that the customer might enjoy a large size product. He or she can only say no thank you.

4 Don't over-promote yourself. People don't like a pushy person to tell them what they want. Persuasion is a gentle technique. Be natural. People respond to this – they feel comfortable.

5 Treat every customer individually. Make each customer feel special. Don't use exactly the same words with every person in the queue – you are not a robot. To one say: 'Would you like a fruit juice with your breakfast?' To another say: 'We have freshly squeezed orange or grapefruit juice, may I get you one?'

6 Keep up the sales pitch. Continue to suggest products right through the order. Just because you get: 'No thanks' to the orange juice, that is no reason to think the customer would not enjoy a large coffee.

7 Don't rush the customer by saying: 'Is that all?' If you need to ask if the customer has finished ordering, let the opportunity to do this arrive naturally.

8 Counter and take-away service

Serving the order (at counters)

A well-presented dish may persuade someone to choose that dish. Arranging it attractively on the plate – following the same rules about variety of colour, shape and texture – helps the person enjoy the food. If you spill sauce or gravy on the rim of the plate, wipe it off with a clean serving cloth or kitchen paper.

Consider what the customer is choosing. Will space be needed for vegetables? Should the rice go in a circle, so that it surrounds the main item, or to one side? Would the customer like gravy over the vegetables and the meat? What other accompaniments should you offer?

Use the correct serving utensils for each dish to serve the proper portion size (see industry examples). A perforated spoon is wrong with fruit salad, because the syrup is part of the enjoyment of the dish. Never touch food with your fingers, or the parts of plates, cups and glasses which might come into contact with the food or customers' lips.

To suit different appetites, some items may be offered in standard, small, large and perhaps extra-large portions. Check first what the customer would like.

Before serving from large containers, place the container lid below the counter. Seeing the food encourages sales and customers like to see what you are doing. Replace lids during quiet periods.

If customers change their minds – 'May I have roast instead of creamed potato?' – start again with a clean plate. Don't scrape the unwanted food off the plate.

Temperature of food

Food must be served at the correct temperature, hot food on hot plates, cold on cold plates. Use a cloth to hold plates which are very hot, and warn customers.

Serving drinks

Cans, bottles and pre-poured glasses of cold drinks are often placed in a chilled cabinet for customers to select. Hot drinks are also self-service. In some restaurants, staff serve all drinks, in others there is a combination of self-service and assisted service.

When there is a selection of flavours, different blends of tea or coffee, the option of whipped or extra strength, standard or large, ask what the customer would like. Don't wait for the customer to say 'Was that an Earl Grey bag you used?' or 'But I wanted a large shake'.

Thanking the customer

Some companies have standard closing remarks. Otherwise find your own expressions which convey to customers that you are pleased to have served them and would like them to call again.

Customers expect, and successful businesses build their reputation on, high standards of presentation and consistent portion sizes. Follow workplace guidelines exactly. Pass on to your manager any ideas of your own for presenting food so they can benefit the whole company.

Assembling and presenting orders

Assemble products carefully, so that hot food is hot, and crispy food crispy. Typical order of assembly:

Cold drink ➡ Cold dessert ➡ Hot drink ➡ Boxed hot products (e.g. bacon and cheeseburger) ➡ Pies ➡ Fries

Pack products carefully so that items do not get squashed, or packets spill their contents:

- boxed products in the base of the bag
- fries with napkin to one side
- pie on top of boxed products
- cold desserts in separate bag
- one napkin per cooked product.

Present products carefully. Logos on cups and packaging should always face the customer as you hand the order over. Bags should be double folded away from logo, with a crisp, neat fold.

With thanks to Compass Group Retail Catering Division

Why portion control?

BAXTER & PLATTS

When portioning is consistent, everyone knows where they stand. If not:

- customers get upset that their colleagues have got more or less than them
- counters run out of food – the chefs have ordered and prepared food to produce X number of portions
- the unit fails to meet budgeted costs, etc., and it can be difficult to get back on track.

What to use for portioning

ladle for stews and 'wet dishes' such as soup and sauces – normally level amount

solid spoon for other dishes with sauce, rice, pies, desserts, some vegetables like braised celery

slotted spoon for food that may need to be drained and solid vegetables (e.g. broccoli, cauliflower)

slice for fish, solid pies, bakes (e.g. lasagne), pizza, tarts

tongs for some desserts, pasta, grilled chops, etc.

scoop for chips.

It all comes down to you!
If a product is not right, don't serve it, and let your manager know.

McDonald's

Maintaining the counter and service areas

Attractive counter displays and the skills of your colleagues in the kitchen will do much to create the right impression when the first customers enter the service area. It is more difficult to maintain the presentation throughout service, so all customers get a good first impression.

The preparation and clearing procedures (see previous pages) are also appropriate for maintaining service. But because you are doing them during service and in the presence of customers, be especially aware of:

- the impression you give to customers – they may be watching what you are doing

- safety – use safety signs to warn customers (see page 21), and never leave cleaning materials unattended

- timing – make good use of quiet moments, plan ahead and help colleagues do so, e.g. by warning kitchen staff when dishes are getting low.

Keeping the work area tidy and clean

During busy service periods, it is not easy to keep the tables clear, the floor free of rubbish, and waste bins tidy. But even if customers leave behind a mess of food wrappings, trays covered with spilt drinks, etc., they don't like chaos when they arrive.

Work quickly, safely and quietly to keep on top of the situation. Stack items carefully, sorting out what is rubbish and what is to be washed – no clattering of crockery or cutlery.

Clearing by tray

Keep the weight evenly balanced and watch where you are going (see page 50).

Clearing by trolley

Take care not to bump into customers' belongings or the furniture. Stack like items together, in their proper places, and do not overload the trolley. You cause a safety hazard and waste time if things fall off.

Self-clear

Even when customers do the clearing themselves – taking the used items and trays to a service point – you need to wipe table surfaces and generally keep the customers' areas looking tidy.

Sutcliffe

Essential points during service

- tables cleaned regularly after customers have left
- chairs returned to correct position
- ashtrays clean and in smoking areas only
- trolleys clean and in correct position

Trolley clearing

- trolleys moved slowly and quietly
- bottom shelves stacked first
- plates cleared of food (into suitable container) and stacked to safe height
- cups emptied and stacked safely
- ashtrays emptied into fire-proof container
- trolleys never left unattended in restaurant

The food counter

- food served with correct equipment to ensure accurate portion sizes
- questions on menu answered accurately
- neat, clean personal appearance maintained
- kitchen given advance warning that items are running out
- empty trays replaced with full – never fill up empty containers in front of customers
- correct utensils used when replenishing food, and splashing avoided

Maintaining stocks during service

Especially after a busy period, there is a risk that you run out of certain dishes, or customers find there are no trays, for example. This is less likely to happen if everyone follows a routine for checking that all is well during service, and takes action before stocks run out.

Service items

Take those that customers or you have finished with to the wash-up without delay. Collect cleaned items and return them to their place.

Food and drinks

Serve first dishes which were prepared first. Maintain a strict rotation of containers.

Remove nearly-empty and empty containers of food and replace with fresh ones from the kitchen. Don't pour the food from one container into another.

Maintaining displays

So the displays look appealing throughout service:

- move food on shelves to the front or customers' side

- take food from the side of the dish nearest you and keep the food together as much as possible, not spread thinly over a large dish

- as the counter empties (e.g. towards the end of service), cluster the remaining food together, e.g. so that you have one full shelf not two half-empty ones, and all the food on one cold counter not spread over two

- where possible, transfer remaining food to smaller containers, e.g. moving the salad from a large, almost empty bowl, to a smaller bowl which it fills

- remove empty containers from customers' sight as quickly as possible, taking them to the wash-up or placing under the counter.

Dealing with rubbish and food waste

Dispose of this promptly and tidily, remembering that customers may be watching you. If you have to touch rubbish or food waste with your hands, wash them thoroughly before handling or serving any food.

Collect rubbish from the outside car park and pavement as necessary. Your workplace will get a poor reputation with the local community if it causes a litter problem.

Avoid obstructing pavements and roads with rubbish awaiting collection. Check that bags are securely tied at the top. If a bag has burst, place it inside another. If liquid is leaking out of the bottom of the bag, place it in a second bag, or in a cardboard box lined with newspaper.

Butlin's HOLIDAYS

Drinks dispenser checklist

1 Check drinks dispenser to ensure that it will not run out prior to service.
2 Ensure that sufficient quantities of various drinks mixtures are available for service, if required.
3 Ensure that correct drinks products are placed in correct containers.
4 Ensure water supply on and power supply on.
5 Maintain sufficient supply of tea pots, coffee pots, etc. for service period.
6 Empty slop trays frequently and clean down drinks servery.
7 Clean down dispenser at the end of each serving period in correct manner.

Closing down after service

After the restaurant has closed for the day, everything should be left tidy, safely stored, ready for overnight cleaning (if applicable) and for the staff who will be on opening duties.

Check carefully for discarded cigarette ends which have not been fully extinguished.

ISS Mediclean

Daily cleaning schedule after service

1 Refrigerated display counters emptied and cleaned, switched off.
2 All food locked in fridge. Fridge doors cleaned.
3 Stainless steel counters washed and polished.
4 Hot counters emptied and cleaned top and bottom, and clean covers put on.
5 Coffee machine emptied, coffee jugs washed. Trolley cleaned, replenished with spoons, sugar, coffee ready for morning and locked away.
6 Orange dispenser cleaned and switched off.
7 All sinks cleaned.
8 Floor swept and washed.
9 Tables in restaurant cleaned and left ready for morning service.
10 All cutlery checked and put away.
11 All cleaning cloths washed and put to dry. Buckets emptied and washed. All mops put in solution, then rinsed, dry squeezed and put to dry.
12 All bins emptied, cleaned and new bags put in.

1 State your workplace rules for using cleaning materials safely.

SAFETY FIRST
wear gloves
never mix
label containers
dilute accurately
don't leave about

2 What can you do to make sure customers get a good impression of tidiness and cleanliness?

TOMMY'S TAKE-AWAY
CLEAN OFTEN
WORK TIDILY
LOOK SMART
BE HYGIENIC
DISPLAY WELL
THINGS IN PLACE

THE RESTAURANT
FOOD TO KITCHEN
EQUIP. TO WASH-UP
HOT CUPBOARDS OFF
COUNTER CLEARED
TABLES CLEARED

3 What must be done at the end of service?

4 Give some ideas for displaying food attractively.

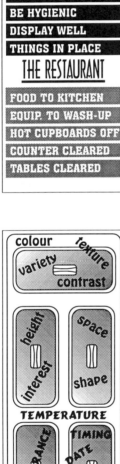

colour — texture — variety — contrast — height — space — interest — shape — TEMPERATURE — APPEARANCE — TIMING — HYGIENE — DATE — TO FRONT — FIFO — time on display — temperature probe — serving utensils — covered/protected — rubbish removed

5 When restocking food and drink items, what must you do?

6 What must you do (and not do) to ensure that food and drink are safe to eat?

7 For each method of portion control give one or two examples of food for which it is suited.

size of container

serving utensil

metered dispense

250G

purchase specification

200G

presentation guide

instructions
3 potatoes each

pre-plating

per-item charge

RASHER OF BACON 75P
GRILLED TOMATO 50P

weigh and pay

Help yourself to salad
£3 standard size

8 What sort of questions can you ask to clarify what the customer wants?

QUALITY SERVICE

Would you like chocolate or strawberry flavour? To eat in or take-away? Cream or milk with your coffee? Would you like vinegar with your chips? And salt?

9 Why is it important to tell customers when there will be a delay? How might you do this, and what would you say if the wait is a long one?

PROMOTING SALES

The cheese-burger will be 2 minutes. Do you mind waiting? 8 minutes for the cod, I'm afraid. Would you rather order something else, haddock or plaice perhaps?

10 How do you reduce the risk of mistakes when taking an order over the telephone?

Yes, that's right - The name's Forte, 4 Fawe Park Road

A questionnaire

When you next visit a take-away restaurant as a **customer**, use the following questions to assess your experience. If possible, ask a friend to visit and assess your workplace in the same way.

☑ = yes   ☒ = no

SERVICE

❑ Did the server greet you pleasantly, politely and with a smile?

❑ Did the server help you make your selection?

❑ Did the server suggest other items in addition to those you asked for?

❑ Did the server repeat your order before registering your payment and taking the money?

Write down the actual comment the server used when closing the sale:

....

How long did you wait for your order, from the time of ordering to receiving:

....

❑ Were the other staff you saw carrying out their work in a businesslike manner?

CLEANLINESS

❑ As you approached the restaurant was there any rubbish in the surrounding area?

❑ Was the advertising material in the windows clean, tidy and correctly positioned where it was easy to read from the outside?

❑ Were any wastebins outside the restaurant dirty and full to overflowing?

❑ Were the outside lights and signs working properly?

❑ Was the initial impression one of cleanliness when you entered?

❑ Had the server a clean and tidy appearance and uniform?

❑ Did the other staff you could see have a clean and tidy appearance and uniform?

❑ Was the customer area clean, tidy and free from rubbish?

❑ Was the menu display clean, tidy and the items and prices easy to read?

❑ Was the service counter clean and well organised?

❑ Were the tables and chairs provided for customers clean and free from rubbish?

❑ Were the wastebins inside the restaurant neat and tidy?

❑ Were all the lights inside the restaurant working properly?

❑ Were the toilets clean and tidy?

Skills check
Prepare and clear areas for counter/take-away service
Unit 1NC3 — level 1

Element 1

Prepare areas for counter/take-away service

Prepare work area and service equipment ready for use ☐ PC1
▲ Service area, seated area, waiting area
Display units, heated units, refrigerated units

Arrange stocks of service items ready for use ☐ PC2
▲ Trays, ashtrays, straws, service utensils, food containers, take-away food packaging, disposable serviettes, disposable/non-disposable crockery/cutlery

Switch on service equipment to reach correct temperature ☐ PC3

Store and display chilled food & drink items for service ☐ PC4

Prepare and display condiments and accompaniments ☐ PC5

Check and display promotional materials ☐ PC6
▲ Menus, posters, black/white/illustrated menu board, materials promoting special offers

Get refuse and waste food containers ready for use ☐ PC7

Display hot food immediately before service ☐ PC8

Deal with unexpected situations effectively & inform appropriate people ☐ PC9

Do your work in an organised, efficient and safe manner ☐ PC10

Element 2

Clear areas for counter/take-away

Return perishable food and drink to kitchen/storage after use ☐ PC1

Switch off appropriate service equipment ☐ PC2

Assemble reusable service items for cleaning and storage ☐ PC3
▲ Trays, crockery, cutlery, ashtrays, service utensils, food containers

Dispose of rubbish, used disposables and waste food ☐ PC4

Leave work area and service equipment clean, ready for use ☐ PC5

Deal with unexpected situations effectively & inform appropriate people ☐ PC6

Do your work in an organised, efficient and safe manner ☐ PC7

Skills check
Provide a counter/take-away service
Unit 1NC4 — level 1

Element 1

Serve customers at the counter

Attend to customers without delay, in polite, helpful manner ☐ PC1
▲ Children, adults, those with communication/mobility difficulties

Give accurate information and promote products and services ☐ PC2
▲ Items available, food composition, prices, special offers and promotions

Identify customers' requirements and process order ☐ PC3

Action order promptly and inform customers of waiting time ☐ PC4

Serve food and drink correctly ☐ PC5
▲ Hot food, cold food, hot drinks, cold drinks

Ensure condiments and accompaniments are available ☐ PC6

Deal with unexpected situations effectively & inform appropriate people ☐ PC7

Do your work in an organised, efficient and safe manner ☐ PC8

Element 2

Maintain counter and service areas

Deal with customers in polite, helpful manner ☐ PC1

Keep work areas tidy, free from rubbish and food debris ☐ PC2

Maintain sufficient stocks of service items ☐ PC3
▲ Service utensils, food containers, trays, take-away food packaging, disposable serviettes, ashtrays, strays, disposable/non disposable crockery/cutlery

Replenish food and drink items at appropriate time ☐ PC4

Store and display food and drink ☐ PC5

Clear work area of soiled and unrequired service items ☐ PC6

Dispose of rubbish, used disposables and food waste ☐ PC7

Deal with unexpected situations effectively & inform appropriate people ☐ PC8

Do your work in an organised, efficient and safe manner ☐ PC9

Skills check
Provide and maintain a take-away service
Unit 2NC12 — level 2

Element 1

Take and serve customers' orders

Greet and deal with customers promptly, politely and helpfully ☐ PC1
▲ By phone, in person

Give accurate information and promote products and services ☐ PC2
▲ Items available, food composition, prices, special offers and promotions

Identify customers' requirements and record correctly ☐ PC3

Portion and serve food using correct equipment ☐ PC4

Complete and package orders ☐ PC5

Maintain operational standards ☐ PC6

Deal with unexpected situations effectively & inform appropriate people ☐ PC7

Prioritise and carry out your work in an organised, efficient and safe manner ☐ PC8

Element 2

Maintain take-away service areas during service

Greet and deal with customers in polite, helpful manner ☐ PC1

Keep available service equipment and utensils ☐ PC2

Keep service areas tidy and free from rubbish and food debris ☐ PC3

Keep sufficient stocks of service items available throughout service ☐ PC4
▲ Serviettes, take-away food packaging, disposable cutlery, straws

Replenish food and drink items, condiments and accompaniments ☐ PC5

Store and display food and drink items ☐ PC6

Empty refuse and waste containers as required ☐ PC7

Clean and close down equipment and service areas after use ☐ PC8

Deal with unexpected situations effectively & inform appropriate people ☐ PC9

Prioritise and carry out your work in an organised, efficient and safe manner ☐ PC10

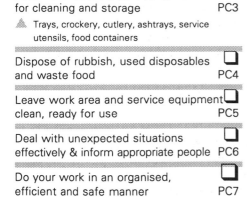

Vending service

Vending machines provide customers with a choice of food and drink items in a wide range of situations, from staff restrooms in offices and factories to hotel corridors and the crew's quarters on an oil rig. Often, vending machines are the only practical way of offering a catering service to the number of customers involved, over the hours they require the service.

Sankey

Requisitioning vending stock and supplies

Vending works well when machines are efficiently restocked. The stock should be in good condition, at the correct temperature, and within the date mark on the packaging. When customers have the full choice of products, vending is very convenient.

Deciding what you need

There are two main ways:

- looking at what is in the machine – to find out the stock level of each item, and what is required to take the stock back up to its maximum

- checking with your supervisor or workplace instructions – to find out the types and number of each product that should be stocked.

Your method will depend on the product. Typical arrangements are:

- for cans of soft drinks, packets of crisps, confectionery (i.e. sweets) and similar items that have their own section, row, shelf or space in the machine – count what is required to take the stock to maximum

- for tea, coffee, chocolate, whiteners, sugar, soups, and other powdered products – estimate what is needed to fill each canister, or check the gauge on the side of the canister

- for syrups and concentrated mixes of soft drinks, coffee, chocolate, etc. – check the level of each container

- for in-cup products – estimate the number of cups required to take the stock of each product to the recommended stock line

- for sandwiches, pies, salads, plated meals, desserts and other fresh products – follow workplace instructions on what number of each should be displayed, and in what positions.

With fresh products, there may be standard guidelines on quantities, e.g. 10 rounds of cheese and tomato sandwiches, 12 of ham and salad. If the vending machine is providing for the same customers all the time, e.g. those working in an office or factory, there will probably be a different list each day to suit the weather, the number of purchases expected, and to give customers a varied choice.

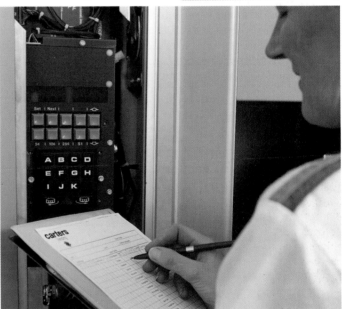

A difference between the machine's record of number of sales (being recorded here) and stock usage would be investigated by management.

When to restock

Restocking may be necessary during or after busy periods (e.g. meal breaks). Food vending machines offering a wide choice, which can only hold a limited number of each item, often need new stock. You will then have to count what is required of each item. Stock unsold from the previous day may have to be withdrawn before restocking (see overleaf) and discarded. Some snack foods have a shelf-life of five days or longer.

Restocking of products with a long shelf-life is usually done daily, as a follow-on from the cleaning routine. Once you are familiar with the pattern of demand, you are likely to know what stock is required without looking at the machine.

This form combines sales and stock control.

Completing the documentation

Be familiar with the forms and documents used in your workplace, and how to complete them. Order forms for requesting additional stock are also called *requisitions*.

1 If copies are required and you are using carbon paper, check that it is in the right place, the correct way up. Use a biro, so the writing comes through properly on to the copies.

2 Write neatly. If you make a mistake with a number, write it again and cross out the wrong number. Trying to change 7 to 1, or 4 to 8 is likely to confuse.

3 Be specific about the size and name of product you want. Writing 'coffee' is no help if there is regular, decaffeinated and cappuccino coffee.

4 Date and sign the form (sometimes your initials are sufficient). It must be clear when the stock is required and who it is for. If there are machines in several sites or different departments, you may have to give details of those.

5 Cancel forms which you decide to re-write or are not required. So there is no confusion, cross through the form and write CANCELLED across it. Forms without serial numbers (to control their use), may be torn up and thrown away.

6 Have the order authorised by your manager (if necessary). Be ready to explain why quantities are much higher or lower than usual.

7 Take the order to the person or department supplying the items required. There may be set times to do this, or orders received one day are issued the following morning.

There may be a *stock record form* which you use to write down the quantity of each item left in the machine, e.g. at the time you clean it, any which has got damaged or past its date mark, and what new stock you have put in the machine. This helps identify shortages and check stock usage against sales.

In some sites all the vending machines are linked to a computer which monitors their use. Stock requisitions are produced by the computer.

Handling and transporting vending stock and supplies

The priority is to keep the stock in good condition, undamaged and at a safe temperature. You must also take care not to injure your back. This can happen – and you may not even be aware of it at the time – through lifting or handling the wrong way, or not taking account of the conditions you are working in.

Checking for quantity, type and quality

Check against your copy (or the original) of the stock order:

- count each item – have you the number of each type requested?

- examine each item – reject any which are damaged, too near or past their expiry date.

Use a temperature probe to check the temperature of:

- chilled products – at or below 8°C (some operators work to a 5°C minimum temperature)

- frozen products – the outer layer at –12°C or lower.

Place the temperature probe against the packaging, between two products of the same type. For greater accuracy, you may have to pierce the packaging and the food itself. This would only be done for a small sample, which is then treated as wastage.

Once you are satisfied, sign the form to accept the goods. Check that any changes to the quantity of items accepted have been made before you sign.

Stock rotation

Do you know the term FIFO? It stands for FIRST IN FIRST OUT. The principle of stock rotation is that older stock – *first in* – is used before – *first out* – any more recent stock. There are three main reasons:

- *for safety* – foods which have passed their use-by or best-before date are not considered safe to eat and must be thrown away

- *for economy* – it is expensive and wasteful to have to throw food away because the quality has spoiled or it has passed its date

- *for quality* – all foods change with time. This is quite quick for fresh foods, very slow for canned products. These changes damage the appearance, flavour, texture and smell.

Food is less likely to have to be wasted when the older stock is always used first. If items with different dates are kept together, in no particular order, there is a good chance that some will sit there until beyond the date of expiry.

Transporting stock

Use the safest method available. This may mean a little more time, e.g. to go and get the *trolley*, or to park your *vehicle* at the goods delivery bay. Carrying by *hand* is normally safe for short distances and light, easily held loads (see illustration below).

Using safe methods to handle stock

1 Follow workplace instructions. Your employer has a legal duty to eliminate, or, if this is not practicable, to reduce the level of risk to the minimum. You have a duty to use the equipment and safe methods provided.

2 Plan in advance how to lift the item, and where it is to be placed. Check that your route is clear. As necessary, walk the route first (not carrying anything), give people warning, arrange for help to open fire doors, etc.

3 Test the weight of unfamiliar objects, for example by raising one end. Don't assume that you know – a canister of ingredients or the rubbish bin could be much lighter or heavier than usual.

4 Use a trolley and the goods lift where possible. Divide large loads into smaller/less bulky batches. If this means making many journeys you may need to have a break. If you can't make the load easier to handle, get the assistance of a colleague.

5 If you are lifting something from a shelf or table, first move anything that is in the way, so that you can get right up to the object.

6 To avoid confusion when working with another person, agree in advance who should give the instructions, and who will take the load.

Safe keeping of stock

Keep chilled products at a safe temperature as you transport them to restock machines. You may need insulated containers or refrigerated delivery vehicles.

To avoid damage during handling, keep stock in its original packaging as long as possible. Do not place heavy items on top of any which might be squashed, e.g. a carton of soft drinks on top of packets of biscuits.

Do not leave stock unattended, unless it is in locked storage. It might be stolen, vandalised or tampered with. Many cleaning materials are dangerous when misused – you know this, but others may not.

Employers are required by the Manual Handling Operations Regulations 1992 to avoid the need for employees to undertake any manual handling operations at work which involve the risk of injury. Where this is not reasonably practicable, the level of risk must be kept to the minimum, e.g. through training and workplace procedures.

Vending service

Every machine must be visited three times daily:

at the beginning of the day and *after lunch* – to check there is an adequate supply of cups and that the machine is working correctly

during the morning – to clean the machine and surrounding area and fill up with ingredients.

Cleaning of vending areas

All work surfaces must be thoroughly cleaned using the approved sanitiser. China used for coffees must be returned to the wash-up and the cupboard restocked with clean china.

The frontage of machines must be spray cleaned and polished. All cupboards and walls must be wiped and left free from marks and smears.

The floor must be spray cleaned using the approved all-purpose detergent and a damp cloth (use of mops and buckets to be avoided in these areas). Display a wet floor sign during cleaning and until the floor is dry.

Safe working

Wear prescribed protective clothing and stout, flat-heeled shoes.

Clear up any spillage of liquid or ingredients immediately.

Keep clear all corridors and walk-ways. Do not run in corridors or work areas.

Do not operate any equipment unless you have been instructed in its use and are authorised to do so.

Isolate equipment which is not working from the power. Report all malfunctions to the manager. Do not attempt to repair the equipment.

What you can safely handle

your physical strength – this is less if you have done a lot of carrying already, are tired or unwell or pregnant, for example

weight of object – packages of vending products are normally of a weight that can be safely handled, but always check the label and/or test the weight by picking up carefully then putting down again. You can also injure your back if you pick up a light object expecting it to be heavy

the shape of the object – a bulky item is often difficult to hold and control, it might be less easy to see where you are going

how the object can be held – smooth sides, round surfaces, greasy hands, wearing gloves, these make your grip less sure

how far the object has to be moved – to get it into a carrying position (something on a shelf at waist level is generally easier to pick up than it would be from the floor), and to take it to its destination

in what conditions you are working – outdoor delivery areas on a frosty morning, narrow, steep flights of stairs, low ceilings, uneven surfaces are typical hazards

Cleaning vending machines

To protect the drinking quality of the product, machines require regular cleaning. Once a day is the normal routine.

Cleaning vending machines

Be familiar with the instructions for each machine you have to clean, and the cleaning agents you are using. Follow the training you have been given. If you are not clear on any point, ask your manager.

Misused, cleaning agents can cause injury to you and harm to surfaces. There is also a risk that they make the drink or food unsafe, or spoil its quality. The checklist gives some reminders on safe use.

Cleaning equipment and materials

Collect all equipment and materials you need:

- trolley, spare canisters and machine parts
- plastic buckets for washing removable equipment
- disposable cleaning cloths and drying paper
- dusting brushes – on some machines, special brushes must be used to avoid damaging surfaces
- detergent solution, sanitiser and sterilant as required
- polish and cloths for cleaning outside of machine
- rubbish bags.

CHECK S list

afety with cleaning agents

✔ always wear protective gloves – cleaning agents irritate and burn the skin

✔ always wash hands before and after doing any cleaning

✔ dilute the product according to instructions

✔ use the right amount for the task

✔ prepare a fresh solution as necessary and dispose of the old – do not top up a cleaning solution

✔ use a weaker cleaning agent first – use a stronger one only if the dirt proves stubborn

✔ never mix different cleaning agents – this may produce harmful gases

✔ do not pierce an aerosol can, even if it appears to be empty – it may explode

Sankey Vending

Personal hygiene checklist
- Are your hands clean?
- Are your overalls clean?
- Is your hair covered?
- Are all cuts, open sores, etc. covered with a clean waterproof dressing?
- Do not smoke while cleaning or restocking.

The general sequence

1 Put on gloves to protect your hands, and an overall or uniform to protect your clothes.

2 Turn the machine off. If advised to do so, remove the plug from the mains socket.

3 Empty the machine. Cover the dispense nozzle of powder and liquid canisters with a cap, to protect against spillages. With in-cup drink vending machines, it is normally sufficient to remove the cup stacks once a week to clean the carousel columns.

4 Check date marks and how the stock that you have removed is looking. Put out-of-date products and any with damaged packaging in the reject food bag, ready for removal from the premises.

5 Clean the interior. Mixing bowls, nozzles, troughs, whippers and similar parts are usually removed, soaked in a cleaning solution, dried and put back in position. Compartments and shelves on which food and drink are displayed must be cleaned individually. Rinse well. Air dry, or use disposable paper.

6 Flush postmix machines with hot water from the machine after cleaning. Check that the float or probe of internal water tanks is working properly – pushing it gently down should allow water in, letting it go should stop the flow of water. Clean the air filters of merchandising machines, the cup stations and transfer arms of in-cup machines.

7 Remove the waste tray, empty and clean in detergent/sanitising solution. Dry before replacing.

8 Restock the machine (see page 108).

9 Clean the exterior of the machine (top, sides and front), inside and outside of the door, delivery area for the products, slot for accepting payment, selection panel or buttons, etc. Polish all shiny surfaces so as not to leave smears or fingerprints.

10 Close and lock the door of the machine. Put the plug back in the socket and turn it on. Turn the machine itself on.

11 Test drinks for quality, quantity and temperature. If required, check coin acceptance. Check that indicator lights are working and that product descriptions/labels are correctly placed.

12 Clean the area around the machine. Remove rubbish. If cups are the type that can be re-cycled, keep separate from other waste.

Cleaning around the ingredient canisters in a postmix machine.

Cleaning the delivery area of a drinks vendor.

Cleaning the display shelves of a food vending machine.

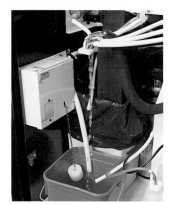

Checking the float of a postmix drinks machine.

Checking the date marks while restocking a food vending machine.

Filling the ingredients canister of a postmix drinks machine.

Loosening or feathering the cups to prevent them sticking together.

Completing documentation

Records you may be asked to make include:

- quantity and type of products that have spoilt or passed their date mark
- when each machine was cleaned
- temperature of machines which hold chilled food and drinks.

MULTI SNACK

Cleaning and hygiene – snack vending machines

This is a food machine and must be regularly cleaned to maintain hygiene standards, and to encourage customers to buy with confidence. Regular cleaning of shelves, the glass front panel and machine cabinet all pay dividends in extra sales:

- do not use detergents or polish on the inside of the machine
- wipe shelves with a clean, damp cloth
- clean the 'flight deck' of the coin mechanism with a slightly damp cloth (water only – ensure machine is switched off)
- remove the air filter weekly, and clean with a brush to remove dust and fluff.

WITTENBORG

Fresh-brew daily cleaning checklist

1 Use key to open main door. Power to machine automatically switches off on opening door.
2 Place de-tannin powder in the brewer cylinder – power on – press brewer rinse button, hold until water in – turn power off – leave to soak.
3 Check canisters and refill as necessary. Clean canister shelf.
4 Remove dispensing kit (see illustration). Clean whipper backings with sterilising solution. Soak dispensing kit in sterilising solution to remove stains. Remove pipe station block to clean. Rinse all components thoroughly and reassemble.
5 Refill the cup dispenser.
6 Remove and clean cup station: drip tray, grid, front panel, cup shute.
7 Check coin mechanism.
8 Power on – rinse brewer five times. Rinse mixing bowls using switches for bowls 1 and 2. Press cup test switch.
9 Empty and clean buckets. Clean floor of machine. Polish outer cabinet of machine.

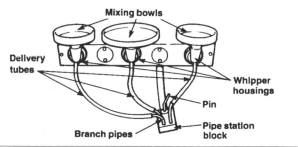

Element 3

Filling a vending machine

This is either done as part of the daily cleaning routine, or as necessary to match the pattern of demand. Follow machine instructions and workplace training carefully. The mechanism inside the machine for moving products to the collection point is often very complex. Poor loading jams the machine.

Rotating stock

The safe storage life is indicated by the use-by or best-before date printed on the packaging. Pay careful attention to these and to hygiene.

Restock machines so that food already on the shelves or racks is used before any of the fresh food. With machines where the customer selects any product from the shelf (sometimes called *shopper mode*), all the products are usually replaced with fresh products. Some machines can be switched to *FIFO mode* to dispense items in the order they were loaded.

Loading drinks machines

Some types of cups need to be loosened before they are stacked, otherwise they tend to stick together. Avoid touching the rims of cups (for hygiene reasons). Never overload with cups, as they can jam the machine.

Take care to put the correct ingredient in each canister, e.g. tea and coffee often require different whiteners. For powdered drinks, lightly tap canisters to loosen ingredients. Place cover over dispense nozzle and remove to refill or replace. Check levels of liquid concentrates. Replace as required. Replace coffee/tea filter paper if machine has a fresh brew unit.

Check the pressure gauge of CO_2 cylinders. If low, close the valve, depressurise the circuit, disconnect and replace cylinder.

After restocking postmix and fresh brew machines, do a test vend to check quality and temperature of drinks.

With in-cup machines:

- fill the cup magazines – put the cups in the correct position for the type of drink they contain

- do not force cups together as this could jam the mechanism

- cover the top cup of each selection with the lid to protect the contents against contamination.

With table-top model machines, not connected to the water supply, top up the water tank to the correct level.

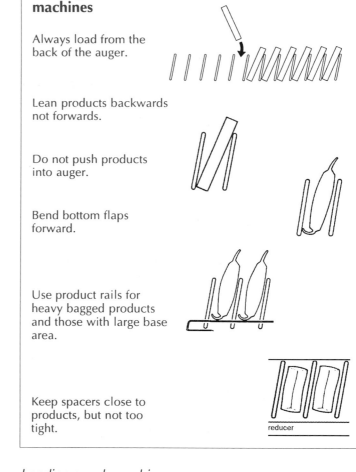

Loading snack machines

Always load from the back of the auger.

Lean products backwards not forwards.

Do not push products into auger.

Bend bottom flaps forward.

Use product rails for heavy bagged products and those with large base area.

Keep spacers close to products, but not too tight.

reducer

Loading snack machines

Load from the back of the auger (see illustration), otherwise gaps can be left. Lean products backwards not forwards and don't push them into the auger.

Use the correct rails, guides or pushers for products which might slip out of position in the auger.

With vending machines that have chilled cabinets:

- before opening, check that the cabinet is operating at the correct temperature

- you may find that condensation has formed inside the cabinet during loading – this should clear within a short time of the door being closed

- inevitably the temperature in the cabinet rises during restocking – the machine is built to deal with this, and should restore the temperature to a safe level within 30 minutes or so. If this does not happen, some machines cease vending and the lighting turns off.

Completing documentation

This will usually involve counting and recording the number of products:

- in the machine before you clean or re-stock

- that cannot be sold because they are damaged or have passed the date mark

- which you place in the machine as new stock.

Displaying vending goods

Many customers choose the product they want at the vending machine. Often the display of a product catches their eye in the first place. Display is vital for machines that sell snacks and meals, confectionery, canned or packaged drinks.

Presenting products

1 Stack displays so the label on each product faces the customer, and all the labels are lined up neatly.

2 Check which shelf the item goes on. Shelves at eye level are usually reserved for products with the highest profit margin, and for those bought on impulse. This is because most people look at eye level first.

3 Use the colours of products and their packaging to give impact and interest to the display. This can also be done with a variety of shapes, e.g. rolls on one shelf, sandwiches on the next.

4 Group similar products, e.g. packets of crisps on a different shelf from confectionery, sweets together, main course salads arranged to show the choice.

eye line is buy line

Information changes

When the machine holds products at different prices, the position of each product is crucial. After all, the machine does not know what it is vending, but it can be programmed to charge a certain price for items in row A, another for items in row B.

Some vending machines have their own mini-computer. A typical feature is the ability to charge different prices according to the time and day, e.g. allowing a discount on snack meals at the end of the day. Customers can also be given sales messages, e.g. SPECIAL OFFER 10% OFF ALL SANDWICHES.

When you set the controls of sophisticated machines like these, take care to be accurate. Key in the information, check letter for letter, figure for figure. Only press the enter or accept key when satisfied that all details (including the spelling) are correct.

SankeyVending

Merchandising

Well presented and clean vending machines attract custom. Untidy machines turn business away.

Monitor sales of each line. If interest is falling, try something else.

Build on product recognition and the popularity of well-known names. Feature brands currently promoted on television, radio, newspapers, billboards, etc.

Drinks machines

Ensure drink descriptions are correct and clearly displayed. Never alter drinks display panels (called *decals*) with bits of sticky paper (looks unprofessional, suggests poor service and quality).

Use branded decals from ingredient suppliers – these use the same typefaces, logos and colours as equivalent products sold in shops and supermarkets.

Food vending machines

With no cooking aromas to arouse the appetite, good visual display is paramount:

- use colourful vegetables (e.g. peas and carrots) or garnishes (e.g. lemon and parsley) to add interest
- keep individual items of the meal as separate as possible.

Ensure that labelling and, where appropriate, reheating instructions are clear.

Snacks machines

These are designed to let each product line advertise itself through its packaging. Make sure that:

- products are the right way round and the right way up
- the printing runs in the same direction on bars of confectionery, reading from bottom to top
- top selling lines are at eye level
- new products are placed close to top sellers.

Food display systems

Four main methods are used in food vending machines to ensure the product looks attractive and reaches the customer in good condition.

Drum and shelf – a series of shallow drums or round shelves which rotate to allow the customer to select the required item. The shelves come in various heights to suit the food, and each one can be divided into compartments of the appropriate size. These are particularly suitable for plated food, and delicate products.

Rotary conveyer feed – similar to a self-service counter display, with rows of like products together. The food containers are resting on a conveyor belt. When the product from the front of the row is selected, the others move forward.

Spiral or *auger feed* – similar to an open coil spring into which the bagged or wrapped food products are inserted. When a selection is made, the spiral revolves and the product drops out of the coil and down the dispense shoot.

Clip-in bagged conveyers – the packets of food are clipped to an overhead conveyor. Once the selection is made, the conveyor moves forward, the clip is mechanically opened and the product drops to the vend station.

A variety of shapes and colours adds interest to the display.

All food machines have a thermometer to enable the internal cabinet temperature to be checked as well as a health and safety cut-out (sometimes called a health timer).

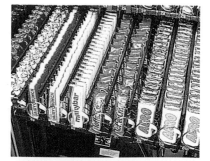

All products should be stacked facing the same way, the names reading from bottom to top.

The spiral system is used to vend a wide variety of items in different shapes and sizes.

Fault finding guide

No lights – machine switched off, door not closed, electrical fault.

Sold out sign shows – waste bucket full, no cups, cup turret/carousel not turning, disruption to mains water supply, ingredients canisters empty.

Cup delivery problems – cup carousel jammed, lack of cups, cups packed too tightly, wrong size (two different suppliers' cups used), cup chute wrongly assembled, cups fallen over in cup station, stabilising weight not in correct position.

Ingredient problem – canister not properly located, incorrect ingredients used or badly stored, blockage in system, water heating unit faulty, 'throw' adjustment required.

Condensation in machine – exhaust grill or steam extractor blocked.

Whippers leaking – incorrectly assembled, seal needs replacing.

Cold drinks warm – cooler not working.

Machine flooding – waste bucket float or switch not operating; waste bucket, pipes or housing not replaced correctly.

Carbonated drink problem – CO_2 cylinder empty, not turned on, not connected properly.

Fresh brew coffee/tea problem – filter needs cleaning or replacing, filter wiper jammed, canister not seated correctly, brewer unit not switched on.

Preparing and clearing dining areas for vending service

The only difference from counter service (see Section 8), is that customers have served themselves from a vending machine.

General preparation procedure

1 Tables and chairs should be clean and in their correct position.

2 Arrange ashtrays, placemats, salts, peppers, sauces, etc. on tables.

3 Restock tray racks, napkin dispensers, cutlery trays, crockery and glassware, etc.

4 Check that waste bins are clean and ready for use.

General clearing procedure

When staff are obviously taking trouble to keep dining areas looking pleasant, customers generally respond well. This makes your job easier.

1 Pay particular attention to table surfaces, counter tops, chairs, etc. Wipe down as necessary, using a cleaning and/or sanitising agent.

2 Keep floors free of litter. Mop up spillages promptly.

3 Empty waste bins regularly, and wipe down the lids and sides. Watch out for partly-filled drink containers – you could find a wet trail behind you as you carry away the waste bag.

4 Empty ashtrays into the special fire-proof bin provided. Use a cloth reserved for this purpose to wipe ashtrays or preferably a disposable paper cloth, moistened slightly.

Activities
Requisition, handle and transport vending stock and supplies
Maintain a vending machine, Prepare and clear areas for vending service

1 Describe the personal security measures you take when cleaning and restocking.

> **SAFETY**
> **BE** alert to the unusual
> **GUARD** stock and money
> **FOLLOW** security rules
> **KEEP** supervisor/base informed of your whereabouts
> **FIRST**

2 What is the reason for turning off (and unplugging) the machine before cleaning or re-stocking?

3 Describe how to carry a carton of vending supplies.

firm grip
close to the load
your whole body
to turn, move · using your feet
place object down, then adjust its position

4 If the interior and exterior of vending machines and the area around them are not clean and tidy, what problems can this cause?

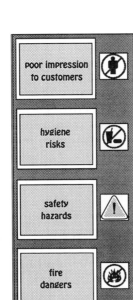

poor impression to customers

hygiene risks

safety hazards

fire dangers

5 Give the rules for use of cleaning materials.

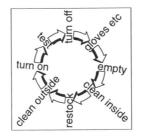

> **Vend Clean Co**
> use correct agents
> dilute accurately
> soak time right
> NO dirty solutions
> NO harsh abrasives

6 Describe the cleaning procedure for one of the machines you are responsible for.

test · turn off · gloves etc · turn on · empty · clean outside · restock · clean inside

7 Now describe the restocking procedure. What has been done wrong here?

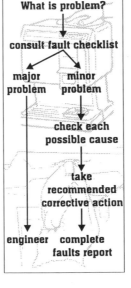

8 If you find a fault when cleaning or restocking a machine, what action do you take?

What is problem?
↓
consult fault checklist
↙ ↘
major problem · **minor problem**
↓
check each possible cause
↓
take recommended corrective action
↙ ↘
engineer · **complete faults report**

9 Why would you reject stock? What is the procedure for recording wastage?

> **BEST-BEFORE END NOV 95**
> **DO NOT CRUSH**
> **Store below 5°C**

10 What does FIFO mean? Why is it important? How do you put it into practice when re-stocking?

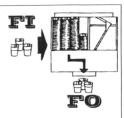

11 Comment on the way this form has been completed. What advice would you give to the person who completed it?

CASH TAKEN									
STOCK/BRAND	Open Stk	M O N	T U E	W E D	T H U	F R I	S A	Total	Close Stk
C/Pastie	7	4	11	8	4	6	–	39	5
/Mush Pie	–	2	12	5	2	15	0	31	21
S/Kid Pie	9	4	7	8	5	31	2	65	64
/Onion Pie	14	11	9	6	2	10	11	50	10
Onion Pastie				Wk					

12 Give the rules for displaying products in a vending machine.

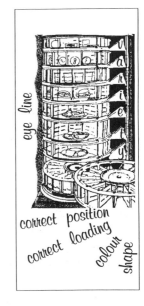

eye line
correct position
correct loading
colour
shape

13 What can go wrong if the information about the products available or the price is wrong?

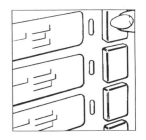

14 What's wrong here? How could such errors be avoided?

Illustrations with thanks to Four Square and Klix (divisions of Mars GB Ltd) (question 13), Electricity Association Services Ltd (question 12), Sankey Vending (question 14) and Wittenborg UK Ltd (questions 7 and 10)

NVQ SVQ

Skills check
Requisition, handle & transport
vending stock/supplies
Unit 1NC8

level 1

Element 1

Requisition vending stock and supplies

Calculate vending stock and supplies
to meet requirements ☐ PC1

▲ Food, drinks, confectionery, cleaning materials,
cleaning equipment

Communicate stock requirements
to appropriate people ☐ PC2

Requisition stock and supplies ☐ PC3

Complete documentation and
store records ☐ PC4

▲ Requisition/order form, stock record sheets

Deal with unexpected situations
effectively & inform appropriate people ☐ PC5

Do your work in an organised
efficient and safe manner ☐ PC6

Element 2

Handle and transport vending stock and supplies

Check stock and supplies for
quantity, quality and type ☐ PC1

Follow stock rotation
procedures ☐ PC2

Segregate and store stock during
transportation ☐ PC3

▲ By trolley, by hand, by vehicle

Transfer stock under safe and
secure conditions ☐ PC4

Secure stock and supplies against
theft while in transit ☐ PC5

Lift items using safe,
approved methods ☐ PC6

Deal with unexpected situations
effectively & inform appropriate people ☐ PC7

Do your work in an organised,
efficient and safe manner ☐ PC8

NVQ SVQ

Skills check
Maintain a
vending machine
Unit 1NC9

level 1

Element 1

Clean a merchandising vending machine

Isolate electricity safely ☐ PC1

Select cleaning equipment and
materials, and prepare for use ☐ PC2

Wear protective clothing ☐ PC3

Follow work routines/sequences ☐ PC4

Clean machine ☐ PC5

▲ Chilled food/ambient machine, can venders

Leave interior and exterior clean ☐ PC6

Test vend machine ☐ PC7

Complete documentation ☐ PC8

Clean & tidy area around machine ☐ PC9

Deal with unexpected situations etc. ☐ PC10

Work in organised manner etc. ☐ PC11

Element 2

Clean a drinks vending machine

Isolate electricity safely ☐ PC1

Select cleaning equipment/materials ☐ PC2

Wear protective clothing ☐ PC3

Follow work routines/sequences ☐ PC4

Dismantle internal parts to clean ☐ PC5

Clean machine ☐ PC6

▲ In-cup/sachet/cartridge/dispenser; instant
machines; fresh brew

Re-assemble internal parts ☐ PC7

Leave interior and exterior clean ☐ PC8

Complete documentation ☐ PC9

Test vend machine ☐ PC10

Deal with unexpected situations etc. ☐ PC11

Work in organised manner etc. ☐ PC12

Element 3

Fill a vending machine

Isolate electricity safely ☐ PC1

Remove stock past expiry date ☐ PC2

Stock to meet demand ☐ PC3

Follow stock rotation procedures ☐ PC4

Test vend machine ☐ PC5

Complete documentation ☐ PC6

Complete machine outputs ☐ PC7

Deal with unexpected situations etc. ☐ PC8

Work in organised manner etc. ☐ PC9

Element 4

Display vending goods

Place correct quantity and types
of items in machine ☐ PC1

Display items to maximise sales ☐ PC2

Replace unavailable items ☐ PC3

Make information changes ☐ PC4

Deal with unexpected situations etc. ☐ PC5

Work in organised manner etc. ☐ PC6

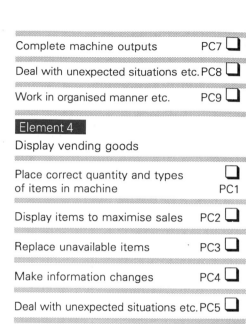
NVQ SVQ

Skills check
Prepare and clear areas for
vending service
Unit 1NC13

level 1

Element 1

Prepare dining areas for vending service

Check and position dining furniture
ready for customer use ☐ PC1

Get ready sufficient stocks of service
items, clean, free from damage ☐ PC2

▲ Trays, disposable crockery, disposable/non-
disposable cutlery, glassware, condiments and
accompaniments, ashtrays, napkins

Get refuse and waste containers clean
and ready for use ☐ PC3

Deal with unexpected situations etc. ☐ PC4

Work in organised manner etc. ☐ PC5

Element 2

Clear dining areas for vending service

Deal with customers in polite and
helpful manner ☐ PC1

Clear and clean dining furniture ☐ PC2

Assemble service items for cleaning ☐ PC3

Dispose of rubbish and waste ☐ PC4

Deal with unexpected situations etc. ☐ PC5

Work in organised manner etc. ☐ PC6

Tray and
trolley service

Preparing and clearing for tray service

Tray service is provided where customers prefer not to, or cannot eat their meal at a restaurant table. It is used in a range of situations, including:

- hospitals – for delivering patients' meals to their bedside

- airlines – for providing meals to standard and business class passengers (first class are usually served from a trolley). Some train operators use tray service so that passengers can remain in their seats instead of going to the restaurant car

- conferences held in concert halls (e.g. London's Albert Hall) or theatres, where there is not sufficient restaurant seating – the meal is delivered to delegates at their seats, on a tray or in a specially designed box

- hotels – for guests willing to pay extra for room service. In the top luxury hotels, trolleys (which fold out to become tables) are used for main meals, while some economy business hotels deliver a standard continental breakfast (fruit juice, rolls or croissants with butter and jam and fresh fruit) to guests' rooms in a box. The guests make their own tea or coffee using the kettle in the bedroom.

Preparing for tray service

The tray is a miniature table setting. While you can bring extra items to a table in the restaurant as the meal progresses, you usually cannot add to the tray. Everything for the meal must be on the tray when it is taken to the customer.

Your service area may be part of or near the place where meals are prepared and distributed, or its own room, e.g. on one of the bedroom floors of a hotel. The more you can prepare in advance, the quicker the orders can be delivered.

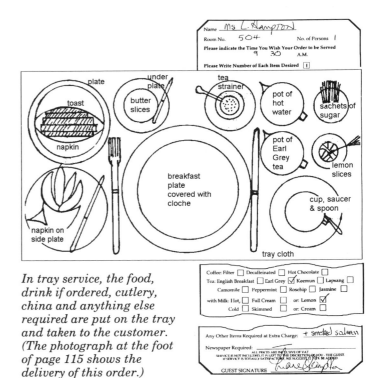

In tray service, the food, drink if ordered, cutlery, china and anything else required are put on the tray and taken to the customer. (The photograph at the foot of page 115 shows the delivery of this order.)

General procedure

1 Collect everything that you will need. You may have to go to the wash-up area for more cutlery, collect flower arrangements for trays from the delivery area, napkins and tray cloths from the linen room, disposable items from the stores.

2 Examine each item of equipment to see that it is clean and in good condition. Trays need to be washed regularly. Allow to dry before stacking.

3 Check the day's schedule or instructions for details of any special orders. In a hotel, the guest arrivals list will tell you which rooms are occupied and the names of the guests. It gives you some idea of how many room service orders for breakfast can be expected. When the list includes conference delegates or groups, check their itinerary to see what the arrangements are for breakfast.

4 You may be able to partly set up the trays in advance (see page 115). Some service areas have a rack system, which can take as many prepared trays as may be required. Tall items like stemmed wine glasses have to be put on their sides, or added later.

5 Where trays are prepared in advance, cups and glasses should be left upside down, as protection against dust. If possible, cover the trays with a suitable cloth. Use sachets of sugar and single portion-size pots or containers of jam, etc. Cover other sauces with lids or clingfilm (or place on the tray at the last moment).

Clearing after service

In a hotel, breakfast trays are usually collected from rooms after guests have left for the day. Housekeeping staff may do this, or move the trays into the corridor. Trays from other meals should be collected when guests ask, or by knocking on the door once you think they have finished.

When guests or housekeepers have put trays in corridors, they must be cleared without delay:

- to reduce the risk of accidents and breakages, e.g. someone stepping on to the tray

- not to give a poor impression to guests and visitors passing by – especially if the tray has clearly been there some hours

- for security – china and cutlery might go missing.

Plan your routine so that you regularly check along corridors where guests have had room service. If you see a tray outside a room on your way to deliver an order, return that way so you can pick up the tray. If this is not possible, make a note of the room number so you or a colleague can collect the tray as soon as it is convenient.

Before you lift the tray, check that everything on it is secure. Sometimes guests stack things neatly, but more usually you have to do this. Watch out for cups or glasses left full, or a plate which has been put on top of a crumpled napkin waiting to slip off on to the floor.

Use your knees to bend down to collect the tray, not your back.

Using a trolley to clear trays

In a hospital (or perhaps on a train), where everyone has tray service, you usually collect all the trays at the same time. This is easier when specially-designed trolleys are used, with racks to hold the (unemptied) trays.

Reposition anything which might get in the way or fall off when you stack the tray in the trolley. When the trolley is full, or all the trays collected, wheel it to the wash-up area. Here you, or your colleagues, can separate waste food, paper napkins and other rubbish for disposal, and stack washable items in the dishwasher baskets.

Unit 1NC2, Elements 1 and 2

Providing a tray service

Customers want their order delivered efficiently, with everything on the tray that is required:

- customers' enjoyment of the meal is spoiled if they have to contact you because the knife is missing, or the coffee has been forgotten

- putting right the omission disrupts your other work, perhaps leading to further complaints about poor service

- in a hospital, putting the wrong dish on the tray of a patient on a strict diet could cause great problems

and delivered at the time requested, or with minimum delay after ordering:

- delays seem much worse to people waiting in their room for the knock on the door by room service – in a restaurant, things are going on to distract them

- for breakfast service, most people's early morning routine depends on punctuality – they may have a long journey ahead of them, meetings to get to, appointments to make.

Taking the order

Customers order using the form provided or telephone. Well-designed forms are ideal for breakfast, where most people only expect a limited selection of dishes and drinks. In hospitals, a form is the most practical solution, although some private hospitals offer an extensive à la carte menu and the order is taken by a member of the restaurant or housekeeping staff.

Dealing with written orders

Hotels which offer room service for breakfast usually provide an order form that can be hung on the outer door handle of the bedroom or suite, once completed. The guest is asked to do this before retiring, and the forms are collected by the night staff in the early hours of the morning.

If this is your task, as you remove the form from the door handle, check the guest has put the room number on it.

Arrange the forms in the order in which they must be served. To give you some leeway, most hotels ask guests to indicate a preferred time band, e.g. 7.00 to 7.15 a.m. When a number of orders are for this time, you can deliver the first at 7 a.m. sharp, the others as soon as possible thereafter. When there are many orders for the same time band, deliver the first one 5 minutes early – most people prefer this to being late.

Note the partly-prepared trays on racks in the background.

Always knock and clearly announce who you are before entering the room.

In private hospitals, like this one, patients expect – and get – the best.

Taking orders by phone

1 Answer the phone with an appropriate greeting, e.g. 'Good evening, room service, Paula speaking, how may I help you?'

2 If you are busy at the time the phone rings, break off from what you are doing to answer the phone promptly, and explain that you will be available in a moment if the caller could please hold on.

3 Allow the caller to say what it is he or she would like, e.g. 'I want to order dinner in my suite.'

4 Ask for the guest's name and room number (see illustration below).

5 Write down the order on the check pad. Offer advice and promote appropriate dishes and drinks (see page 53).

6 Repeat the order, the guest's name and room number. As you confirm these details, check how many people the meal is for. Be tactful! The guest in a single room who orders two main courses may be extra hungry, or entertaining. This is not your business, but you do want to know whether one or two wine glasses are required.

7 Thank the guest. Give an estimate of when the order will be delivered, or confirm that it will be delivered at the time the guest has requested.

Trolleys set up for breakfast service in guest suites at the Conrad Hotel.

Arrival of the scrambled egg and smoked salmon breakfast (see page 113).

Confirm that the order is to the guest's satisfaction.

Note the friendly, yet respectful posture of the waiter.

Lloyds Hotel

Room	Name	No of guests	Arrival date	Departure date	Comment
201	Dr Howells	1	18/5	20/5	Double as single
106	Colin Neil	1	18/5	19/5	Regular/VIP
220	Anne Johns	2	18/5	23/5	Vegetarian
221	— REDECORATION —				
162	Mr C Yapp	5	18/5	19/5	Cash for extras

Getting the name at the beginning rather than the end of the call means:

- you can use it as you confirm the details of the order – providing more personal service
- you have warning if it is a VIP, or perhaps a regular guest in which case you can suggest the person's favourite items
- it is a security check: it might be a hoax call (e.g. no person of that name in that room), a problem guest (e.g. someone who has had noisy, late night parties), or a guest who must pay cash for any extras.

Room 232 Castle(VIP)
7.15 PROMPT

2 O Juice
2 EBMT
2 brown toast
1 Coffee

Making up the order

A well organised, methodical approach will pay dividends. Guests should not find their food has gone cold because you have misjudged the timing, or forgotten something.

1 Advise the kitchen without delay of what chefs need to prepare, and by when. This might be done on the telephone, using a computerised system, or by taking a copy of the order to the chef responsible.

2 Prepare the trays as far as possible in advance. For breakfast service, you have probably done this as part of your preparation routine. Last minute adjustments may be required, e.g. adding a fish knife and fork when the guest has ordered kippers.

3 You may be able to collect wine and other bottled drinks in advance from the bar. Or if the order includes draught beer and other dispensed drinks, collect them just before getting the food.

4 Butter, milk for tea and cereals, cream for coffee, etc. are best put on the tray at the last minute, so they remain cold.

5 When you are ready to deliver the order, add the items which must arrive hot: tea/coffee, toast, cooked breakfast, etc. You may have to collect these from the kitchen, or have them sent up in the service lift.

6 Immediately set off for the room by the quickest route. Some hotels have service lifts for delivering room orders, but when these are busy tell room service staff to use the guests' lifts.

Coppid Beach Hotel

Selling over the phone

Suggest other food and drinks that might go well with what the guest has ordered. When making your recommendations, consider what the guest wants, e.g. a light snack, an alternative to eating in the restaurant, something to drink.

Guest order	Recommendation		
	No 1	No 2	No 3
Soup	sherry	salad	tea or coffee
Soup & salad	wine	tea/coffee	dessert
Main course	soup/salad	dessert	wine
Starter	main course	coffee/cognac	dessert
Dessert	salad	tea/coffee	dessert wine
Champagne	strawberries	canapés	
Wine	mineral water	canapés	
Coffee	sandwich		

The final check

When checking a tray, imagine you are about to eat the meal and go through in your mind all the stages. For an English breakfast this might be:

- a knife and fork for the egg and bacon
- cup and saucer for the beverage
- teaspoon to stir the beverage
- butter and marmalade or jam for the toast
- small knife for cutting and buttering the toast
- side plate for the toast
- napkin to keep crumbs off the bedding and for wiping the mouth
- salt and pepper to season the food
- sugar (white/brown) or saccharin to sweeten the beverage
- milk or cream to accompany the beverage.

Delivering the order

Guests appreciate punctuality, courtesy and a respect for their privacy (see industry examples).

1 Knock before you enter the guest's bedroom or the patient's private room, and announce in a clear voice who you are, e.g. 'Room service.'

2 When you get a response, open the door slightly, pause and listen for a moment before entering the room. If you hear guests rushing for a dressing gown or a towel, pause for a while longer.

3 When all seems well, proceed into the room, quietly close the door behind you, and greet the guests. This time use the guest's name, or if you do not know it, sir/madam.

4 Place the tray down on a convenient surface. Get to know the layout and furnishings of each room, so you are not left wondering where to put the tray. Have a reserve plan for the occasions you find every surface cluttered with guest belongings. Asked politely, most guests will help clear a space or indicate somewhere convenient.

5 Reassure the guest that the items on the tray are what was ordered, e.g. 'Here is your continental breakfast with coffee, Mr Wilson.'

6 Open bottles which require a cork screw or crown top opener (as wine and beer might). Twist the top on screw-top bottles enough to break the seal (some guests have difficulty doing this, e.g. if arthritis has weakened their wrists).

7 If the meal has been ordered by phone, ask the guest to sign the order, so the charge can be put on the bill.

8 With an appropriate departing remark, e.g. 'Enjoy your dinner, Mrs Finch', leave the room quietly and promptly.

Using a trolley (in luxury service)

A trolley is used instead of a tray for full breakfasts and main meals in top hotels. Once in the guests' suite or bedroom, the trolley is folded out to become a table, which the guests can sit at. They have the comfort of the restaurant yet complete privacy.

The procedure described for tray service requires some adaptation:

- place everything on the centre area of the trolley when you prepare it, with the flaps of the trolley hanging down (see photograph on page 115)

- carefully push the trolley to the sitting area of the guests' room, or on to the balcony if this is preferred and the weather is fine

- move the place settings into position

- open the flaps on each side of the trolley and lock into position

- place chairs around the trolley (which is now, in effect, a dining table)

- invite the guests to be seated.

Sequence of service for breakfast

1 Report to room service on time and in correct uniform.

2 Check you have enough mis en place. If not prepare more. Check that we have fresh coffee. If not make fresh.

3 Arrange door knob orders in correct time order, i.e. the earliest first and the latest last.

4 Pick up orders to be delivered and arrange tray/trolley.

5 Deliver the order as follows:
   - each order must leave room service 3 to 5 minutes before order should arrive
   - use only service lift
   - before entering guest room, knock firmly 3 times and announce 'Room service, good morning'
   - when guest answers the door, greet warmly using his/ her name, i.e. 'Good morning Mr Jones, your breakfast, sir'
   - if you are using a trolley make sure to set it up properly for the guest putting the first course in front of the guest
   - when serving hot dishes remove from hot box and place above fork
   - ask if guest would like chairs placed around the trolley
   - when using tray place on table or desk, make sure the guest has plenty of elbow room
   - offer to pour coffee/tea, open curtains, turn on light, etc. Be sure to ask first
   - present check to guest for signing, offering hotel pen
   - enquire if everything is satisfactory and depart by saying 'Thank you Mr Jones, I hope you have a nice day'.

6 Return to room service straight away collecting any dirty trays/trolleys along the way.

BMI The Clementine Churchill Hospital

Patient meal service

1 Check board for any dietary or other specific room serving instructions, e.g. requested serving time is different from normal, food needs cutting up, nurse must be told when/before meal is served.

2 Check that ALL items ordered on the menu are presented on the tray, and that the tray is fully set up.

3 BEFORE knocking on the door, look at the name on the door. If there is a DO NOT ENTER display, return to the room service pantry and check with the nursing staff when the patient's meal can be served. Follow procedure for disposal of patient's food.

4 Knock on the door and wait for a response. If no reply, knock once more, pause for several seconds before **slowly** entering the room.

5 Greet the patient: 'Good morning/afternoon/evening Mr/Mrs/Ms...' If you cannot pronounce the surname, or no name is apparent on the door, simply address the patient using Sir or Madam.

6 Introduce yourself at this point if you are meeting the patient for the first time. Never ask the patient about his/her reason for admission.

7 Place the tray on the over-bed table such that the patient can eat/drink comfortably.

8 Do not leave the room before asking the patient if the tray is positioned to his/her satisfaction. Point out that the metal lid over hot food items is extremely hot and offer to remove it.

9 If the menu does not indicate a post-meal beverage, check that the patient has not simply overlooked this item.

10 When you return to collect the tray, ask the patient if he/she enjoyed the meal.

11 If the patient has not finished when you return, ask if he/she is enjoying the meal/beverage and, if necessary, reassure the patient that there is no need to hurry.

12 Any significant patient comments you receive during your visits to a room, must be passed on to the duty supervisor at the earliest convenient moment.

Liaising with reception/the bill office

Let whoever is responsible for making up the bill of hotel guests have the details of room service orders without delay. When guests settle their bill (often immediately after they have had breakfast), receptionists will usually ask if they have had room service. To avoid embarrassment, delay while you are contacted, and the possibility of a dishonest answer, keep reception fully informed about who has had room service.

Providing a trolley service

Trolleys are used to provide a snack and drink service on some trains where there is no buffet car, or as an additional service to the buffet car. They are sometimes used in offices, theatres, at sports events and in similar situations where people are seated, standing in a queue, or gathered in a room and might enjoy something to eat or drink when it is brought to them.

Preparing the trolley for service

Think of your trolley as a mobile café without tables or chairs, or as a catering shop on wheels. As you are going to wheel the trolley to where the customers are sitting or standing, you need to prepare everything you require before you set off:

- the trolley itself clean and in good order, wheels running smoothly, brake working efficiently

- price list up-to-date and on display

- the food attractively displayed so customers are encouraged to buy – typically a range of wrapped sandwiches and filled rolls, packets of crisps, salted nuts, biscuits, fruit cake, perhaps doughnuts and Danish pastries

- packets of sweets, bars of chocolate and other confectionery

- various canned and bottled drinks, perhaps kept on a chilled shelf if the trolley has a refrigerated unit

- hot water dispenser filled and turned on ready to make tea, coffee and hot chocolate (using disposable cups, factory-filled with the powdered instant drink)

- sachets of sugar, milk (usually long-life) and coffee creamer

- ice in an insulated container if this is offered with whisky, gin and similar drinks

- disposable plates, paper napkins, stirrers or spoons for hot drinks, plastic glasses for cold drinks

- cash box with a small float so you can give change

- credit card printer if you accept this type of payment, and vouchers

- receipt pad should customers require evidence of payment (e.g. to claim expenses)

- bag or container for collecting rubbish.

When loading the trolley, examine the date mark on each product. Put aside as rejects any which have passed the sell-by or use-by date. Check that you have the full range of products, and the quantity of each is correct according to your opening stock list.

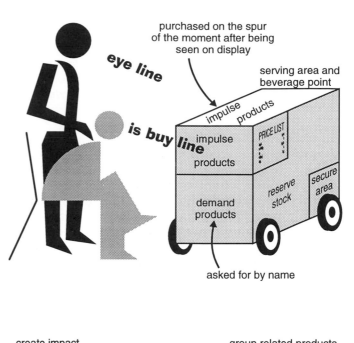

Displaying products to promote sales

Pack the trolley carefully so customers can see what's on sale. The display should look interesting with a variety of colours and shapes (see page 70) so that people are tempted to:

- buy more, e.g. when their initial intention was to have a drink, to buy a sandwich, biscuits or cake to enjoy with it

- choose the products which make the best profit, e.g. beers and spirits (providing they are aged 18 or over) instead of tea or coffee.

Serving products from the trolley

As you approach customers, greet them cheerfully. Match what you say to what you think the customers will appreciate. Most young people prefer informality, e.g. 'Hi there, would you like anything to eat or drink from the trolley?' A group of executives engaged in a serious discussion probably respond best to a polite 'Good morning, sorry to disturb you ladies and gentlemen. Would you like coffee or tea...'

Don't forget to offer sugar and milk (or creamer) with hot drinks.

Winning extra sales

As you serve the order, suggest a snack with drinks, or if the order is for food, a drink. Ask the other people at the table if you can get them anything.

Many people make up their minds to buy because of your pleasant attitude, and the fact you haven't rushed by with your head down!

When you have time to make a second journey with the trolley, ask those who didn't order previously if you can get them anything this time. Offer another drink or something else to those who did order. Clearing empty cups, cans, bottles and the packaging from their table will usually be appreciated.

Protecting yourself and your stock

You want to sell your stock not report it stolen. Money left lying around is a particularly tempting target for the dishonest.

1 Never leave your trolley unattended.

2 Always be aware of the movement of people around you, especially if you have to turn your back on the trolley as you hand customers their order.

3 Watch for set-up accidents or other ploys to deliberately distract you. An accomplice may be hovering, ready to remove money or stock from the trolley.

At the end of service

As you unload the trolley, count the number of each product left.

Thoroughly clean down the trolley. Leave it dry, ready for restocking.

Sales and stock control

The formula for working out what you have sold (see example) is:

opening stock *plus* new stock *less* closing stock = number sold

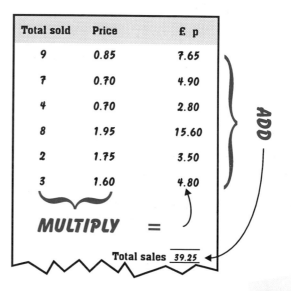

Item	Open stk	Stock in	Total	Close stk	Wast-age	Total sold
Pepsi	12	6	18	9	-	9
OJuice	5	10	15	8	-	7
Lem/ade	6	4	10	6	-	4
Lager	19	8	27	19	-	8
BLT	-	10	10	3	1	2
Ch&Tom	1	7	8	3	2	3

ADD =   **LESS** =

Total sold	Price	£ p
9	0.85	7.65
7	0.70	4.90
4	0.70	2.80
8	1.95	15.60
2	1.75	3.50
3	1.60	4.80

MULTIPLY =   **ADD**

Total sales 39.25

Assembling meals for distribution

This system of traying up meals is mostly used in hospital and airline catering. It is an assembly line, similar to those found in factories making computers, televisions, cars and countless other pieces of equipment. A conveyor belt moves the trays slowly past dispense points or stations. At each station a person places on the tray a particular dish, e.g. a bowl of soup, or adds something to what is already there, e.g. roast potatoes on the main course dish, alongside the roast meat.

Around six to eight trays can be completed per minute, loaded in trolleys and taken to the hospital wards or waiting aircraft. Systems for keeping the food chilled or hot include pre-heated bases on which the plate sits, insulated box-trays, and heated trolleys. With some systems all the food is trayed chilled, and re-heated in special ovens or trolleys, immediately before it is taken to the patient or airline passenger.

Dishes which are kept hot in a trolley, or reheated before service, have to be handled separately from cold dishes. The cold items, cutlery, napkins, etc. are put on the tray in advance. Hot dishes are kept in a separate section of the trolley, and put on the tray at the last moment.

Preparing the conveyor belt

Follow carefully the routine and rules of your work–place. Hygiene standards and production control have to be very strict because of the risks of bacteria multiplying during the time between cooking the food and delivering it to the customer.

There will be several people stationed on the assembly line once the traying up begins (see illustration on page 122, question 11, and photographs on page 123). The preparation and assembly tasks will be organised according to what has to be done and who is available. There may be a rota system, so that everyone gets to do each task over several days.

General preparation tasks

1 Check the conveyor belt is clean and working efficiently.

2 Turn on equipment which needs to get hot, e.g. hot cupboards and bain-maries for storing food, platewarmers (filled with plates).

3 Line up the trolleys ready for loading and despatch. Check they have been properly cleaned.

4 Collect supplies of trays, tray cloths, cutlery, plate covers, lids, napkins, sachets of salt, pepper, sugar, and any sauces to accompany the dishes on the menu. If you are wearing disposable gloves, keep some spare pairs at your station.

5 Prepare each station with ladles, spoons, serving tongs, fish slices and any other equipment to handle and portion the food.

6 Collect the patients' meal orders (if it is a hospital), and arrange them in the order of assembly.

7 Collect cold drinks and food.

8 At the last moment, collect hot food.

Menu specifications

In airline catering, all meals of one type are produced at the same time. Take as an example, dinner for the economy class passengers on the overnight flight to Harare. All 200 or so trays are made up with the same starter and sweet, a bread roll, cheese biscuits, cheese, butter, pack of cutlery (with salt and pepper already enclosed).

Hot main courses (where passengers usually have a choice of two) are made up on a separate assembly line. So are dishes for special diets.

Hospital patients have more choice, and can state when they want small portions. Some are on strict diets for medical or religious reasons. But as meals are assembled on a ward by ward basis, you do not know what choice each patient has made until the tray (with the marked-up menu card on it) reaches your station.

The kitchen have already processed the marked-up menu cards, probably by computer, so the chefs know how many portions of each dish to prepare and when they are required for. Dishes which do not keep well, like fried fish, are cooked in batches, so there is minimum delay before they reach the patient.

Assembling the trays

Your manager or supervisor works out the order in which the items go on to the trays so that the assembly runs smoothly.

There are three main stages, so for example you may find yourself:

- at the beginning of the run, placing the trays on the conveyor belt or the patients' menu cards, or the cutlery and condiments

- mid-way down, portioning and serving one of the day's dishes, or the vegetables for the main course (one person might do two different vegetables)

- at the end, covering the food or checking each tray, or removing the tray from the conveyor and placing it in the trolley.

When you are at a food station:

- look at the menu card first, e.g. to see if the patient wants custard with the apple pie

- do not allow yourself to be distracted – the conveyor belt is moving all the time

- work quickly but also take care to present the food attractively – gravy should not be dribbled over the rim of the dish, or the vegetables heaped on top of each other

- measure portions accurately – if a full ladle of soup is the standard portion, fill the ladle to the top each time

- keep a watchful eye on your stocks of food – warn the assembly supervisor in good time that you need more of your dish.

It causes great problems if a station runs out of food. The conveyor will have to be stopped. Trays on it may have to be rejected. If the delay is a long one, all the food in the trolley may be wasted.

Closing down

When all the trays have been completed, return any remaining food to the kitchen or dispose of as instructed.

Collect the spoons and other serving equipment you have been using and take them to the wash-up.

Leave your station tidy, ready for whoever does the cleaning.

Food production

After meal ideas have been discussed with the airline, the agreed presentation (shown in photographs, see foot of page 123 for an example) and portion sizes form the final specification. This must be strictly followed.

Laying-out of meals

Production must be organised so that hot dishes are blast chilled down to 2°C within 90 minutes of completion of cooking and held at this temperature. No food should be out of chilled conditions for longer than 30 minutes.

All food must be chilled to the same temperature and the containers used for traying-up must be cold. This avoids the formation of condensation (which would be ideal for bacteria growth).

Presentation

Dishes must not be packed with too much liquid. There is a risk that this will spill out of the container when the aircraft is climbing steeply, spoiling the presentation. For hot dishes which are in the aircraft galley being reheated, spillage can lead to a fire in the oven.

Meals placed in polystyrene boxes for delivery to the aircraft hot, must be checked for cracks, broken lids or pieces broken off the box – which all lead to heat loss. Tape should be used to seal gaps in lids. The metal canisters which hold the polystyrene boxes must be fully loaded to minimise heat loss.

Food safety and hygiene

Before being taken into designated clean areas:

- vegetables must be washed
- all items must be transferred to sanitised containers.

Items should be purchased in plastic (not glass) jars. Where this is not possible, the contents must be transferred into plastic containers.

Personal hygiene

Everyone should be aware of the dangers of cross contamination, and the bacteria which can be passed on by not washing and sanitising hands. Bacteria may also be passed on from coughs, sneezes, fingering ears, smoothing the hair and touching door handles.

During traying-up of meals, there should be no reason for any member of the team to leave the designated clean area. Hands must be washed and sanitised before starting production and re-washed before going to other production areas.

Jewellery (including watches) may not be worn in food handling areas (wedding rings are allowed, but must be covered with a blue plaster). Hair must be covered with a hat or helmet.

All staff must wear disposable plastic aprons (white in the cold kitchen area, red when handling raw meat), sleeve protectors and, when instructed, face masks. When leaving the production area, aprons and masks must be disposed of in the receptacle at the exit. (Plastic aprons are not to be worn in the hot kitchen area.) Body warmers are available on request for staff working in chilled areas.

Records

It must be possible to trace every item: when delivered, when cooked, when chilled, when compiled as a meal, when despatched, to which airline, time and aircraft.

These records must include the temperature when items are placed in the blast chiller, time taken to chill and temperature at completion of chilling.

Preparing and providing a tray service, Providing a trolley service
Assembling meals for distribution

1 What can you prepare in advance on trays for a) Continental breakfast, b) English breakfast, c) dinner?

2 How can you make sure the food arrives on time, at the right temperature?

3 Describe the procedure for delivering the tray to a hotel guest. What could go wrong, and what would you do?

4 What could have caused these problems, and how might they be prevented?

Room 232, where's my breakfast?

On the phone I specifically asked for ice with my wine

Room 13

These trays in the corridor must be dangerous, what if there's a fire?

I asked for tea and that is clearly a coffee pot!

Bill Office here, this room service check for room 45 you have just sent, they settled their bill hours ago

5 How can you display the items on your trolley to increase sales?

TROLLEY sales graph

6 What would you say to the person in charge of this trolley?

Fancy anything from my trolley?

evryfink cheep   lastout clearance

7 Give examples of what you can say to customers to persuade them to buy more?

Would you like a [croissant] with your [coffee]

I've got some [strawberries] as well

The [mushrooms] are our speciality

8 How do you make sure your trolley is not a safety risk to you or others?

not obstructing   watch out   always out
!
well maintained

9 What stock has been sold on this trolley? Comment on the way this form has been completed.

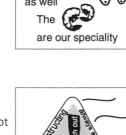

ITEM	OPEN STOCK	CLOSE STOCK
COKE	30	22
O. JUICE	20	11
ROLLS	25	4 OK / 2 WASTE
F. CAKE	5	2 / 1 TORN

10 What are your workplace rules for minimum temperature of hot and cold food for service? Why?

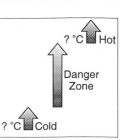

? °C Hot
Danger Zone
? °C Cold

11 What might happen if one of these stations runs out of food?

soup
veg 1
salads
rolls butter
trays

veg 2
main course
cold sweet
cutlery

12 For four dishes, state how portion sizes are measured.

13 Why is it important that the menu choice of hospital patients is followed accurately when traying up?

Delancey Hospital Diet Codes

LF	low fat
GF	gluten free
NS	no salt
K	kosher
V	vegetarian

14 What points should you look for when checking the completed tray? What would cause a tray to be rejected?

OTHER QUESTIONS FOR TRAY SERVICE ON PAGES 64 AND 66

Photographs of trays with thanks to LSG-Sky Chefs (question 12) and European Air Catering Services Ltd (question 14)

Temperatures of food must be regularly checked and recorded.

Good team work is essential to trouble-free production.

So is the preparation of everything you will need.

Trays should be complete and on their way to the wards without delay.

Here the trays are transported to wards in large heated trolleys.

An Inflight Catering Services cold lunch / dinner tray for a short haul flight, checked for cleanliness and layout to the airline's standard.

Element 1

Prepare catering trolley for service

Get trolley ready for use, clean, free from damage ☐ PC1

Prepare service equipment and sufficient stock for use ☐ PC2

▲ Service equipment: cash box, hot and cold beverage dispensers, refrigerated units, credit card printer, service cutlery, napkins & cutlery (disposable/non-disposable), crockery
Stock items: food and drink products, confectionery

Record stock levels prior to service ☐ PC3

Get refuse and waste food containers clean and ready for use ☐ PC4

Display food and drink products to effectively promote sales ☐ PC5

Deal with unexpected situations effectively & inform appropriate people ☐ PC6

Do your work in an organised, efficient and safe manner ☐ PC7

Element 2

Serve products from the catering trolley

Greet and deal with customers in a helpful, polite manner ☐ PC1

Give accurate information to customers and promote products ☐ PC2

Serve stock with clean, undamaged equipment ☐ PC3

Accurately calculate and record exact quantity of stock sold ☐ PC4

Clean trolley after service ☐ PC5

Deal with unexpected situations effectively & inform appropriate people ☐ PC6

Do your work in an organised, efficient and safe manner ☐ PC7

CHECKLISTS for UNITS 1NC1 and 1NC2 on pages 65 and 67.

Element 1

Prepare conveyor belt ready for run

Ensure conveyor belt is clean, free from damage, ready for use ☐ PC1

Locate service equipment ready for use ☐ PC2

▲ Bain-marie, trolleys, service utensils, trays; disposable/non-disposable crockery, cutlery, napkins

Assemble and store stocks ready for belt run ☐ PC3

▲ Food items, drink items, condiments, accompaniments

Select correct menu specifications ☐ PC4

Deal with unexpected situations effectively & inform appropriate people ☐ PC5

Do your work in an organised, efficient and safe manner ☐ PC6

Element 2

Assemble tray sets on the conveyor belt

Place correct service equipment and condiments on tray ☐ PC1

Ensure trays meet menu specifications ☐ PC2

Present food on the plates/food containers ☐ PC3

Anticipate shortfalls in stock and service equipment, and replenish ☐ PC4

Respond speedily to food production requirements ☐ PC5

Reject trays which do not meet menu specifications and report ☐ PC6

Assemble trays correctly in trolley for distribution ☐ PC7

Safely transport trolleys to area for distribution ☐ PC8

Store surplus stock ☐ PC9

Deal with unexpected situations effectively & inform appropriate people ☐ PC10

Do your work in an organised, efficient and safe manner ☐ PC11

Index